Interventions and Strategies in Counseling and Psychotherapy

Interventions and Strategies in Counseling and Psychotherapy

edited by
RICHARD E. WATTS, Ph.D.
and
JON CARLSON, Psy.D., Ed.D.,
ABPP

USA	Publishing Office:	ACCELERATED DEVELOPMENT *A member of the Taylor & Francis Group* 325 Chestnut Street Philadelphia, PA 19106 Tel: (215) 625-8900 Fax: (215) 625-2940
	Distribution Center:	ACCELERATED DEVELOPMENT *A member of the Taylor & Francis Group* 47 Runway Road, Suite G Levittown, PA 19057-4700 Tel: (215) 269-0400 Fax: (215) 269-0363
UK		ACCELERATED DEVELOPMENT *A member of the Taylor & Francis Group* 1 Gunpowder Square London EC4A 3DE Tel: +44 171 583 0490 Fax: +44 171 583 0581

Interventions and Strategies in Counseling and Psychotherapy

1 2 3 4 5 6 7 8 9 0

Printed by Edwards Brothers, Ann Arbor, MI, 1999.

A CIP catalog record for this book is available from the British Library.

∞ The paper in this publication meets the requirements of the ANSI Standard Z39.48-1984 (Permanence of Paper).

Library of Congress Cataloging-in-Publication Data
Interventions and strategies in counseling and psychotherapy / [edited by] Richard E. Watts, Jon Carlson

    p.   cm.
Includes bibliographical references and index.
ISBN 1-56032-690-5 (alk. paper)
  1. Counseling.   2. Psychotherapy.   3. Adlerian psychology.   4. Adler, Alfred, 1870-1937.   I. Watts, Richard E.   II. Carlson, Jon.
BF637.C6I533   1999
158'.3—dc21
                               98-49909
                                  CIP

ISBN: 1-56032-690-5

Contents

Preface

A major trend in counseling and psychotherapy is the move toward integration of various theoretical systems and/or approaches to therapy. The Adlerian theoretical position is both timely and valuable because it is clearly an integrative one. As noted in Chapter 1, contemporary Adlerian theory is an integration of cognitive, psychodynamic, and systemic perspectives, and remarkably resembles many of the "cutting edge" constructive approaches to therapy. In addition, it is a technically eclectic approach that readily adapts to the unique needs of clients.

The present volume contains creative and innovative applications of this integrative approach to counseling and psychotherapy. The contributing authors were selected because of the unique contributions they have made in the areas addressed in their respective chapters. Readers will discover that the views of the contributing authors do not always form a consensus, thus indicating that Adlerian theory is not—and should not be—a static and inflexible one; it continues to evolve and develop.

Because Adlerian therapy is both an integrative and technically eclectic approach, the ideas presented in this book can empower and enrich the work of all counselors and psychotherapists. Regardless of a practitioner's primary theoretical orientation, he or she may glean useful and valuable insights from the discussion of the specific applications, the case studies that accompany the applications, and the ancillary information contained in this volume.

Acknowledgments

We would like to express our sincere appreciation to each of the contributing authors for both their individual and their collective contributions to this volume. We would also like to express our gratitude to Dr. Joe Hollis for his guidance, support, and friendship. Finally, we are grateful to the excellent folks at Taylor and Francis for their assistance in bringing this project to fruition.

Contributors

Mark S. Carich, Ph.D.
Illinois Department of Corrections
Big Muddy River Correctional Center
Ina, IL 62846

Jon Carlson, Psy.D., Ed.D., ABPP
Department of Psychology & Counseling
Governors State University
University Park, IL 60466

Don Dinkmeyer, Sr., Ph.D.
Communication & Motivation Training Institute
Coral Springs, FL 33065

Timothy D. Evans, Ph.D.
Counseling Program
University of South Florida
Tampa, FL 33620

Charles A. Guarnaccia, Ph.D.
Department of Psychology
The University of North Texas
Denton, TX 76203

Terry Kottman, Ph.D.
Department of Educational Leadership,
   Counseling, & Postsecondary Education
The University of Northern Iowa
Cedar Falls, IA 50614

Amy Lew, Ph.D.
Connexions
Newton Centre, MA 02159

Michael P. Maniacci, Psy.D.
Adler School of Professional Psychology
Chicago, IL 60601

Carole Metzger, M.S.W.
Illinois Department of Corrections
Big Muddy River Correctional Center
Ina, IL 62846

Alan P. Milliren, Ed.D.
Counseling Program
University of Texas, Permian Basin
Odessa, TX 79762

William G. Nicoll, Ph.D.
Department of Counselor Education
Florida Atlantic University
Boca Raton, FL 33431

Michael Nystul, Ph.D.
Department of Counseling and Educational Psychology
New Mexico State University
Las Cruces, NM 88003

Robert Sherman, Ed.D., Professor Emeritus
Queens College, New York
12 Berkshire Drive
Cranbury, NJ 08512

Len Sperry, M.D., Ph.D.
Medical College of Wisconsin
Milwaukee, WI 53226

C. Edward Watkins, Jr., Ph.D.
Department of Psychology
University of North Texas
Denton, TX 76203

Richard E. Watts, Ph.D.
ACHVE Department
Kent State University
Kent, OH 44242

CHAPTER 1

Richard E. Watts

The Vision of Adler: An Introduction

According to Albert Ellis (1970), "Alfred Adler, more than even Freud, is probably the true father of modern psychotherapy" (p. 11). This quote is indicative of the remarkable vision and influence of Alfred Adler regarding contemporary approaches to counseling and psychotherapy. Adlerians and selected non-Adlerians have noted for some time the apparent influence of Alfred Adler's work on many theories of counseling and psychotherapy developed subsequent to the era of the so-called "three pillars"—Freud, Adler, and Jung. Despite the identification of many apparent lines of influence from Adler to modern theories, these individuals have documented a widespread lack of understanding of Adlerian contributions to mainstream counseling and psychotherapy (e.g., Allen, 1971a; Ansbacher & Ansbacher, 1956; 1979; Corey, 1996, Ellenberger, 1970; Freeman, 1993; Mosak, 1979; Sherman & Dinkmeyer, 1987; Singer & Salovey, 1993; Sweeney, 1989; Watts & Critelli, 1997). Ansbacher (1979) noted that after Adler's death in 1937, his name vanished for quite some time, except among the small groups of Adlerians. However, Adler's ideas were not antiquated. In fact, many were simply ahead of their time and have subsequently *reappeared* in contemporary approaches to counseling and psychotherapy, albeit with different nomenclature and without reference to Adler.

The purpose of this chapter is to introduce the reader to some of the fundamental tenets of Adlerian counseling and psychotherapy, and then to briefly discuss Adler's remarkable vision in regard to contemporary constructivist approaches to counseling and psychotherapy.

☐ A Brief Introduction to Adlerian Theory

Adlerian theory is an integration of cognitive, psychodynamic, and systems perspectives (Sperry, 1993). H. L. Ansbacher, a noted Adlerian scholar, described Individual Psychology as a

> holistic, phenomenological, teleological, field-theoretical, and socially-oriented approach to psychology and related fields. This approach is based upon the assumption of the uniqueness, self consistency, activity, and creativity of the human individual (style of life); an open dynamic system of motivation (striving for a subjectively conceived goal of success); and an innate potentiality for social life (social interest). (Manaster & Corsini, 1982, p. 2)

Philosophical Underpinnings of Adlerian Theory

The philosophical roots of Adlerian theory are largely found in the critical philosophy of Immanuel Kant and the "as if" philosophy of Hans Vaihinger (Ansbacher & Ansbacher, 1956; Ellenberger, 1970; Shulman, 1985). Both Kant and Vaihinger emphasized the proactive, form-giving, and fictional character of human cognition and its role in constructing the "realities" we know and respond to. Adlerian theory assumes that the organism has an inborn program (a Kantian, rather than Lockean perspective), and assumes that humans construct ways of viewing and experiencing the world and then take these fictions for truth (Ellenberger, 1970; Master, 1991; Shulman & Watts, 1997).

An Adlerian View on Human Agency

The Adlerian view of human agency stems chiefly from its aforementioned philosophical underpinnings. Thus, Adlerian theory espouses a proactive—versus reactive and representational—view of human cognition and organism; expressed in the construct known as the *creative power of the self* or *the creative self*. In discussing the creative self, Adler stated,

> Do not forget the most important fact that not heredity and not environment are determining factors. Both are giving only the frame and the influences which are answered by the individual in regard to his styled creative power (p. xxiv). . . . The individual is both the picture and the artist. He is the artist of his own personality. (Ansbacher & Ansbacher, 1956, p. 177)

Because of this creative power, people function like actors writing their own scripts, directing their own actions, and constructing their own personalties (Shulman, 1985; Shulman & Watts, 1997). Humans co-create the "realities" to which they respond.

An Adlerian View on Personality

An Overview of Lifestyle.   From the beginning, Adler cultivated a concept of a "psychological superstructure" that organized and guided the mental life of the individual (Stepansky, 1983). This "psychological superstructure" is a master plan or cognitive blueprint for coping with the tasks and challenges of life and is called the *lifestyle*, the Adlerian nomenclature for personality. The lifestyle, unique to each individual, is in Kelly's (1955) language a *personal construct system*, containing *core constructs*. It is uniquely created by the person, begins as a prototype for action in the world, and becomes progressively refined throughout life. Shulman (1973) and Shulman and Mosak (1988) describe the functions of the lifestyle: It organizes and simplifies coping with the world by assigning rules and values; it selects, predicts, anticipates; its perceptions are guided by its own "private logic"; it selects what information it allows to enter, what it will attend to, what affects will be aroused and what its response will be. According to Shulman (1985), the lifestyle contains certain key elements. These include core convictions or constructs about self and the world, and the interrelationship between the two; a construct about what the relationship should be; an image of one's ideal self; and a plan of action. All of these elements are attitudes, values, and meanings that the individual has creatively constructed in relation to his or her socially embedded context.

This is not to say, however, that the individual is readily aware of the convictions that guide his or her life. Mosak (1979) stated that although the lifestyle is the blueprint or map for coping with experience, it nevertheless remains largely out of one's awareness, Adler's process understanding of unconscious. Thus, both the construction of the individual's unique lifestyle and the goals and core constructs contained therein are also essentially unconscious (Allen, 1971b; Mosak, 1979; Shulman, 1985; Shulman & Watts, 1997).

According to Adlerian theory, the lifestyle is a *unity*, an organized and integrated whole (Forgus & Shulman, 1979). The lifestyle organizes and maintains the whole perceptual system of the individual, resulting in selective perceptual processing of all incoming information. Exhibiting a confirmatory bias, the organism looks for information confirming the core convictions of the lifestyle, selectively attending to information from experience that confirms what is already believes (Shulman, 1985; Shulman & Watts, 1997). This organismic penchant for perceptual selectivity thus greatly impacts the majority of cognitive functions; memory, learning, expectancy, fantasy, symbol creation.

Lifestyle and the Social Embeddedness of Humans.   Adler noted that humans are socially embedded and cannot be understood apart from their social context. In fact, the Adlerian perspective on the tasks of life—love, society, work, spirituality, self—is a strongly relational one. These tasks of life address intimate love relationships, relationships with friends and fellow beings in society, our relationships at work, our relationship with God or the universe, and our relationship with self (Manaster & Corsini, 1982; Mosak, 1979).

The lifestyle emerges from a young child embedded in a social context creating a sense of self in the relational world in which he or she interacts. This social context of children includes both the cultural values of children's culture of origin and their experiences within their *family constellation*, Adler's phrase for the operative influences of the family structure, values, and dynamics. Children, therefore, see others and the world as generally paralleling their first social environment, their family, and eventually frame the larger experience of life—and interpersonal relationships—on the basis of these initial relationships and perceptions (Manaster & Corsini, 1982).

The cardinal tenet of Adler's theory, *social interest*, is obviously a social–contextual one. According to Shulman (1985), Adler considered the tendency of human beings to form attachments (social feelings) to be a fact of life. Human striving is always in some way connected with relationships and human bonding. Social interest is the measure by which a person's movement through life, and thus the person's lifestyle, is assessed as either socially useful or socially useless. Persons who strive toward life goals in ways that promote the welfare and well-being of fellow humans evidence social interest, and their movement is described as socially useful. Those who strive toward life goals with no regard for humankind evidence diminished social interest, and their movement is described as socially useless. Thus, social interest is Adler's criteria for mental health (Mosak, 1979).

Aspects of Adlerian Therapy

Assessment.   Adlerians take a process view of individuals. Consequently, they do not view assessment as an event that categorizes the client with a static diagnostic label. Assessment is a continual process. Adlerians typically employ a variety of assessment techniques that tend to be more qualitative and idiographic than quantitative and nomothetic; for example, Adlerian's use of Life Style Analysis and similar forms of assessment (Allen, 1971a; Baruth & Eckstein, 1981; Eckstein, Baruth, & Mahrer, 1982; Gushurst, 1971; Powers & Griffith, 1987; Shulman & Mosak, 1988). This is not to say, however, that Adlerians do not make use of "standardized" assessment instruments and procedures. Whatever means Adlerians use in assessment, the purposes are typically more idiographically informed and are not used to place a static diagnostic label on a unique client or family for purposes of treatment.

Client–Therapist Relationship.   Adlerian therapy is commonly viewed as consisting of four stages. The first and, for most Adlerians, most important stage is entitled *relationship*. Because counseling and psychotherapy occurs in a relational context, Adlerians focus on the development of a respectful, collaborative, and egalitarian therapeutic alliance with clients (e.g., Ansbacher & Ansbacher, 1956, 1979; Dinkmeyer, Dinkmeyer, & Sperry, 1987; Manaster & Corsini, 1982; Mosak, 1979; Sweeney, 1989; Watts, 1998a). Therapeutic efficacy in the other stages of Adlerian therapy—analysis, insight, reorientation—is predicated upon the development and continuation of a strong therapeutic relationship.

Goal of Adlerian Therapy.   The basic goal of Adlerian therapy is to facilitate clients in experiencing new information that is discrepant with existing cognitive structures or lifestyle. Thus, clients have opportunity to create perceptual alternatives and modify or replace growth-inhibiting life themes or "scripts" with ones that are growth-enhancing. The ultimate goal for Adlerians is the development–enhancement of the client's social interest. Congruent with Adlerian personality theory, the goals of Adlerian therapy also have a relational orientation.

Techniques.   Adlerians are *technical eclectics*. That is, they use a variety of cognitive, behavioral, and experiential techniques. Selected techniques originally attributed to Adlerian therapy include acting "as if," catching oneself, confrontation, the magic wand technique, prescribing the symptom (paradoxical intention), pushbutton, spitting in the soup, the question, task-setting, and the tentative hypothesis–interpretation (Dinkmeyer, Dinkmeyer, & Sperry, 1987; Manaster & Corsini, 1982; Mosak, 1979; Sweeney, 1989). Additional sources for examining Adlerian techniques include Carlson and Slavik (1997) and Mosak and Maniacci (1998).

☐ The Vision of Adler

Corey (1996) stated that he believed that one of Adler's most important contributions to the field of counseling and psychotherapy was his influence on other systems. Adler's influence has been acknowledged by—or his vision traced to—the neo-Freudians (e.g., Ansbacher & Ansbacher, 1979; Ellenberger, 1970), existential therapists (e.g., Frankl, 1963, 1970; May, 1970, 1989), person-centered therapy (e.g., Ansbacher, 1990; Watts, 1998a), rational-emotive therapy (e.g., Dryden & Ellis, 1987; Ellis, 1970, 1973, 1989), cognitive therapy (e.g., Beck, 1976, Beck & Weishaar, 1989; Dowd & Kelly, 1980; Freeman, 1981, 1993; Freeman & Urschel, 1997; Raimy, 1975), reality therapy (e.g., Glasser, 1984; Wubbolding, 1993; Whitehouse, 1984), and family systems approaches (e.g., Broderick & Schrader, 1991; Carich & Willingham, 1987; Kern, Hawes, & Christensen, 1989; Nichols & Schwartz, 1995; Sherman & Dinkmeyer, 1987).

The vision or influence of Adler has been readily acknowledged by some, briefly acknowledged by some, and apparently ignored by others. Mosak (1979) noted that Adler was more concerned that his theoretical ideas survive than that he receive credit for the ideas. In some cases, as Mosak concludes, he got his wish.

The question naturally arises, why has Adler not been more widely recognized by theorists and practitioners? As noted earlier, Adler's theory of personality and therapy was simply ahead of its time. The psychological mindset of Adler's time (early 20th century) was materialistic, mechanistic, and deterministic. Adler's development of a phenomenological, nondeterministic theory was considered unscientific and unworthy of note by Freudians and behaviorists, who dominated the field for most of the 20th century. Thus, many of the creators of subsequent approaches to counseling and psychotherapy may not have attended to the pioneering work of Adler (Watts & Critelli, 1997).

Recently, however, the psychological *zeitgeist* has changed. There has been an epistemological shift in psychology toward a phenomenological, constructivistic perspective. It is not surprising, therefore, to find that many ideas originally presented in Adler's theory have "reappeared" in contemporary therapeutic approaches, although couched in different language and without acknowledgment of Adler (Watts & Critelli, 1997). This appears to be particularly true in regard to contemporary constructive approaches. Rather than rehashing in detail the influence of Adler on the aforementioned therapeutic approaches, the remainder of the chapter will address the vision of Adler as seen in the constructive therapies.

The name *constructive therapies* or *constructivism* has been used interchangeably by both constructivists and social constructionists. The constructivist approaches apparently evolved from cognitive-behaviorism (Guidano & Liotti, 1983; Mahoney, 1991, 1995), whereas the social constructivist approaches apparently evolved from family therapy and Ericksonian paradigms (Gilligan & Price, 1993; Hoyt, 1994a, b; Matthews & Edgette, 1997; Nichols & Schwartz, 1995; Watzlawick, 1984, 1990).

Adlerian theory's integration of cognitive, psychodynamic, and systems perspectives looks remarkably similar to constructivist approaches (Jones & Lyddon, 1997; Shulman & Watts, 1997; Watts, 1998b; Watts & Critelli, 1997). The Adlerian journal *Individual Psychology* has contained at least three papers since 1991 addressing the similarity between Adlerian and Constructivist approaches; two by Adlerians (Master, 1991; Scott, Kelly, & Tolbert, 1995) and one by a constructivist (Jones, 1995). The *Journal of*

Cognitive Psychotherapy has published two similar papers; one by Adlerians (Shulman & Watts, 1997) and one by constructivists (Jones & Lyddon, 1997). In addition, Michael Mahoney (April 1998, personal communication) and Robert Neimeyer (April 1998, personal communication), both well-known constructivists, have acknowledged Adler as a *protoconstructivist* theory. Apart from the articles and comments above, however, there apparently has been no substantive discussion addressing the similarity between Adler's visionary theory and contemporary constructive approaches. In reviewing a wide range of works by theorists and practitioners espousing a constructive position, very little mention of Adler's pioneering theory is found in the constructivist literature and even less is found in the writings of social constructionists (Bannister, 1977; Cade & O'Hanlon, 1993; DeJong & Berg, 1998; de Shazer, 1985, 1988, 1991, 1994; Efran, Lukens, & Lukens, 1990; Freedman & Combs, 1996; Friedman, 1997; Furman & Ahola, 1992; Gergen, 1991, 1994; Gilligan & Price, 1993; Goldberg, 1998; Goncalves, 1995; Guidano, 1991, 1995a, 1995b; Guidano & Liotti, 1983; Hoyt, 1994b, 1996a, 1996b; Joyce-Moniz, 1985; Kelly, 1955; Liotti, 1987, 1993; Littrell, 1998; Lyddon, 1995a, 1995b; Mahoney, 1985, 1988a, 1988b, 1989, 1991, 1995; Matthews & Edgette, 1997; Miller, Hubble, & Duncan, 1996; Neimeyer, 1987, 1993; 1995a, 1995b; Neimeyer & Mahoney, 1995; O'Hanlon & Weiner-Davis, 1989; Parry & Doan, 1994; Riikonen & Smith, 1997; Sechrest, 1983; Walter & Peller, 1992; Watzlawick, 1984, 1990; Weiner-Davis, 1992, 1995; White & Epston, 1990; Zimmerman & Dickerson, 1996).

Adlerian and Constructivist Similarities

Neimeyer (1995a) states that various constructive approaches share the following theoretical characteristics: They have a common or similar epistemology, and they have common or similar assumptions regarding the socially embedded nature of human knowledge. Hoyt (1994a) noted that, although the constructive approaches certainly have their differences, they share the following clinical–practical characteristics: They place strong emphasis on the developing a respectful therapeutic relationship, they emphasize strengths and resources, and they are optimistic and future oriented.

Using the theoretical and clinical characteristics listed by Neimeyer (1995a) and Hoyt (1994a) as an initial outline, the reminder of this chapter briefly discusses the common ground between the vision of Adler and the constructive approaches.

Knowledge Structures and Social Embeddedness.   Adlerian and constructivist theories share common epistemological roots in the critical philosophy of Immanuel Kant and the "as-if" philosophy of Hans Vaihinger. Both Adlerian and constructivist theories espouse epistemological positions asserting that humans construct, manufacture, or narratize ways of looking and experiencing the world and then take these *fictions* for truth (Ansbacher & Ansbacher, 1956; Ellenberger, 1970; Efran, Lukens, & Lukens, 1990; Goncalves, 1995; Greenberg & Pascual-Leone, 1995; Jones, 1995; Jones & Lyddon, 1997; Mahoney, 1991; Shulman & Watts, 1997; Meichenbaum, 1995; Parry & Doan, 1994; Watzlawick, 1990).

In discussing current neurobiological evidence for development of knowledge structures, narrative psychologists Parry and Doan (1994) state that one of the brain's primary functions is to create a "model" of the world, an internal blueprint or road map. This model is established early in life and becomes "reality"; it serves as a guide for subsequent life experiences, and selectively attends to—through modification or rejection—only that incoming data that fits with its "program." Interestingly, this is almost a verbatim description of the Adlerian perspective of the development of knowledge structures (see discussion of lifestyle above).

Adlerians and constructivists both affirm that humans are undeniably social beings and share a socially embedded view of personal knowledge. Both agree knowledge of oneself and the world is predicated upon and relative to knowledge of others. Adler noted that the tasks of life—love, society, work, spirituality, self—are fundamentally relationship-oriented. Both perspectives affirm, therefore, that one cannot understand human beings apart from their social contexts and the relationships therein (Ansbacher & Ansbacher, 1956, 1979; Gergen, 1991, 1994; Goncalves, 1995; Guidano, 1995a; Hoyt, 1996a; Jones & Lyddon, 1997; Lyddon, 1995a; Manaster & Corsini, 1982; Mosak, 1979; Neimeyer, 1995a; Shulman & Watts, 1997; Watts, 1998b).

With the current strong emphasis on multiculturalism, many mental health professionals have been drawn to constructive approaches because of their strong emphasis on the social embeddedness of humans and, consequently, human knowledge. Adlerian theory has long held this emphasis on social embeddedness. Furthermore, Adler and Dreikurs campaigned for the social equality of women and other minority groups as early as the 1920s and 1930s (Ansbacher & Ansbacher, 1978; Dreikurs, 1971; Hoffman, 1994). Thus, Adlerians and Adlerian theory addressed social equality issues and the sociocultural context of human understanding long before multiculturalism became chic in counseling and psychotherapy.

Clinical–Practical Characteristics.   As stated earlier, Hoyt (1994a) identified three clinical–practical characteristics that constructive approaches share. These characteristics essentially mirror what Adler and Dreikurs—and subsequent Adlerians—call *encouragement*, or the therapeutic modeling of social interest. For Adlerians, encouragement is both an attitude and a process of therapeutic intervention.

Adlerians typically do not view clients as "sick" and in need of a cure. Rather, clients are discouraged and thus great emphasis is placed on encouraging, restoring faith in the client's potentials and abilities to manage and overcome the problems of life.

The process of therapeutic encouragement includes: empathic listening, nonjudgmental acceptance, conveying respect for clients, and developing egalitarian relationships; having faith in clients and conveying that faith and confidence to them; viewing clients as decision makers; collaborative goal setting; focusing on strengths, assets, and resources clients already possess; identifying discouraging beliefs and facilitating perceptual alternatives; and focusing on efforts and incremental accomplishments rather than a "finished product." Adler and Dreikurs both firmly believed that encouragement was essential to all relationships, therapeutic and otherwise (Ansbacher & Ansbacher, 1956, 1979; Dinkmeyer & Dreikurs, 1963; Dinkmeyer & Losoncy, 1980; Dreikurs, 1967, 1971; Grunwald & McAbee, 1985; Mosak, 1979; Watts, 1998a, 1998b).

Selected Additional Similarities.   There are numerous other similarities between Adlerian and constructive approaches. A brief summary of a few selected similarities includes the following.

1. The Adlerian use of Life Style Analysis, including the use of early recollections helps to, in constructivist nomenclature, uncover the "hidden text" in the client's

life story (Parry & Doan, 1994). This hidden text is reminiscent of core constructs or lifestyle themes, in what Adler (1958) called the client's "story of my life."

2. Gergen's (in Hoyt, 1996a) discussion of the self finding its "moral identity" in relational context sounds very similar to the Adlerian notion of evaluating motivation and behavior as either socially useful or socially useless. In addition, Gergen states that an individual's "good moral reasons" necessarily stem from the repository of cultural wisdom. This sounds like Adler's description—borrowed from Kant—of societal "common sense" versus its antonym, "private logic."

3. Constructive descriptions of motivation for therapy (e.g., Littrell, 1998; Parry & Doan, 1994; Rosen, 1996) parallel the Adlerian position (e.g., Adler, 1956; Dreikurs, 1967; Manaster & Corsini, 1982). Both constructivists and Adlerians eschew the "medical model" perspective and take a nonpathological approach. They agree that clients are not "sick" and thus are not identified or "labeled" by their diagnoses. Rather, clients present for counseling because they are "demoralized" or "discouraged." According to Littrell (1988), clients "lack hope . . . One of our tasks as counselors is to assist in the process of restoring patterns of hope" (p. 63). Dreikurs (1967) noted that presenting problems are "based on discouragement" and without "encouragement, without having faith in himself restored, (the client) cannot see the possibility of doing or functioning better" (p. 62).

4. Constructivists emphasize a time-limited or brief approach to therapy. Stuart (1980) noted that Adler recommended time-limited therapy in the 1930s. Adler suggested limiting couple therapy to 8 to 10 sessions, but the idea was ignored by the therapeutic community.

5. Finally, several techniques originating with Adlerian therapy remarkably resemble ones used in constructive approaches. These include acting "as if," creating perceptual alternatives, early recollections, the magic wand technique, paradoxical intention (Adler called it "prescribing the symptom), the question, task-setting, and the tentative hypothesis–interpretation.

☐ Conclusion

The vision and influence of Adler was and is remarkable. Adler died in 1937 having created a personality theory and approach to therapy so far ahead of his time that contemporary "cutting-edge" theories and therapies are only now "discovering" many of Adler's fundamental conclusions, typically without reference to or acknowledgement of Adler.

Adler's vision and influence has been clearly acknowledged by some contemporary theorists and practitioners, but it has not been recognized by many mainstream professionals in counseling and psychotherapy. Adler's ideas were out of step with the dominant metaphors of his time, and, consequently, his theory was discounted, even though many of his ideas have been assimilated into subsequent theoretical positions.

This is not to claim Adler as the only viable forerunner of contemporary theories of counseling and psychotherapy or deny that later and contemporary theorists made their own unique contributions to the field. In fact, there is much of value for theoretical integration and clinical use in most contemporary therapeutic approaches. However, with the emergence of a phenomenological, constructivist perspective in the helping professions that looks so similar to the position Adler postulated, it may be time to "go back to the future"; that is, it may be time to take a new look at the past. To paraphrase a wise adage, "Of what use are giants if we refuse to stand on their shoulders?"

☐ References

Adler, A. (1958). *What life should mean to you*. New York: Capricorn.

Allen, T. W. (1971a). The individual psychology of Alfred Adler: An item of history and a promise of a revolution. *The Counseling Psychologist, 3*, 3–24.

Allen, T. W. (1971b). A lifestyle. *The Counseling Psychologist, 3*, 25–29.

Ansbacher, H. L. (1979). Introduction. In H.L. Ansbacher & R.R. Ansbacher (Eds.), *Superiority and social interest: A collection of Adler's later writings* (3rd ed; pp. 1–20). New York: Norton.

Ansbacher, H. L. (1990). Alfred Adler's influence on the three leading cofounders of humanistic psychology. *Journal of Humanistic Psychology, 30*, 45–53.

Ansbacher, H. L., & Ansbacher, R. R. (Eds.) (1956). *The Individual Psychology of Alfred Adler: A systematic presentation in selections from his writings*. New York: Harper Torchbooks.

Ansbacher, H. L., & Ansbacher, R. R. (Eds.) (1978). *Cooperation between the sexes: Writings on women, love, and marriage*. New York: Anchor.

Ansbacher, H. L., & Ansbacher, R. R. (Eds.) (1979). *Superiority and social interest: A collection of Adler's later writings* (3rd ed). New York: Norton.

Bannister, D. (Ed.) (1977). *New perspectives in personal construct theory*. New York: Academic Press.

Baruth, L., & Eckstein, D. (1981). *Lifestyle: Theory, practice, and research* (2nd ed.). Dubuque, IA: Kendall/Hunt.

Beck, A. T. (1976). *Cognitive therapy and the emotional disorders*. New York: Meridian.

Beck, A. T., & Weishaar, M. E. (1989). Cognitive therapy. In R. J. Corsini & D. Wedding (Eds.), *Current psychotherapies* (4th ed.; pp. 285–322). Itasca, IL: F.E. Peacock.

Broderick, C. B., & Schrader, S. S. (1991). The history of professional marriage and family therapy. In A. S. Gurman & D. P. Kniskern (Eds.), *Handbook of family therapy: Vol. II* (pp. 3–40). New York: Brunner/Mazel.

Cade, B., & O'Hanlon, W. H. (1993). *A brief guide to brief therapy*. New York: Norton.

Carich, M. S., & Willingham, W. (1987). The roots of family systems theory in Individual Psychology. *Individual Psychology, 43*, 71–78.

Carlson, J., & Slavik, S. (Eds.) (1997). *Techniques in Adlerian psychology*. Washington, DC: Accelerated Development.

Corey, G. (1996). *Theory and practice of counseling and psychotherapy* (5th ed.). Pacific Grove, CA: Brooks/Cole.

DeJong, P., & Berg, I. K. (1998). *Interviewing for solutions*. Pacific Grove, CA: Brooks/Cole.

de Shazer, S. (1985). *Keys to solution in brief therapy*. New York: Norton.

de Shazer, S. (1988). *Clues: Investigating solutions in brief therapy*. New York: Norton.

de Shazer, S. (1991). *Putting differences to work*. New York: Norton.

de Shazer, S. (1994). *Words were originally magic*. New York: Norton.

Dinkmeyer, D. C., Dinkmeyer, D. C., Jr., & Sperry, L. (1987). *Adlerian counseling and psychotherapy* (2nd ed.). Columbus, OH: Merrill.

Dinkmeyer, D., & Dreikurs, R. (1963). *Encouraging children to learn*. Englewood Cliffs, NJ: Prentice–Hall.

Dinkmeyer, D., & Losoncy, L. E. (1980). *The encouragement book*. Englewood Cliffs, NJ: Prentice–Hall.

Dowd, E. T., & Kelly, F. D. (1980). Adlerian psychology and cognitive–behavior therapy: Convergences. *Journal of Individual Psychology, 36*, 119–135.

Dreikurs, R. (1967). *Psychodynamics, psychotherapy, and counseling*. Chicago: Alfred Adler Institute of Chicago.

Dreikurs, R. (1971). *Social equality: The challenge of today*. Chicago: Adler School of Professional Psychology.

Dryden, W. & Ellis, A. (1987). Rational-emotive therapy. In W. Dryden & W. Golden (Eds.), *Cognitive–behavioral approaches to psychotherapy* (pp. 128–168). New York: Hemisphere.

Eckstein, D., Baruth, L., & Mahrer, D. (1982). *Lifestyle: What it is and how to do it* (2nd ed.). Dubuque, IA: Kendall/Hunt.

Efran, J. S., Lukens, M. D., & Lukens, R. J. (1990). *Language, structure, and change: Frameworks of meaning in psychotherapy*. New York: Norton.

Ellis, A. (1970). Humanism, values, rationality. *Journal of Individual Psychology, 26,* 11.

Ellis, A. (1973). *Humanistic psychotherapy*. New York: McGraw–Hill.

Ellis, A. (1989). Rational-emotive therapy. In R. J. Corsini & D. Wedding (Eds.), *Current psychotherapies* (4th ed.; pp. 197–238). Itasca, IL: F.E. Peacock.

Ellenberger, H. F. (1970). *The discovery of the unconscious*. New York: Basic Books.

Forgus, R., & Shulman, B. H. (1979). *Personality: A cognitive view*. Englewood Cliffs, NJ: Prentice–Hall.

Frankl, V. E. (1963). *Man's search for meaning*. New York: Washington Square Press.

Frankl, V. E. (1970). Fore–runner of existential psychiatry. *Journal of Individual Psychology, 26,* 38.

Freedman, J., & Combs, G. (1996). *Narrative therapy: The social construction of preferred realities*. New York: Norton.

Freeman, A. (1981). Dreams and images in cognitive therapy. In G. Emery & R. C. Bedrosian (Eds.), *New directions in cognitive therapy: A casebook* (pp. 224–238). New York: Guilford.

Freeman, A. (1993). Foreword. In L. Sperry & J. Carlson (Eds.), *Psychopathology and psychotherapy* (pp. iii–vi). Muncie, IN: Accelerated Development.

Freeman, A., & Urschel, J. (1997). Individual psychology and cognitive behavior therapy: A cognitive therapy perspective. *Journal of Cognitive Psychotherapy, 11,* 165–179.

Friedman, S. (1997). *Time–effective psychotherapy*. Boston: Allyn & Bacon.

Furman, B., & Ahola, T. (1992). *Solution talk: Hosting therapeutic conversations*. New York: Norton.

Gergen, K. J. (1991). *The saturated self: Dilemmas of identity in contemporary life*. New York: Basic Books.

Gergan, K. J. (1994). *Realities and relationships: Soundings in social construction*. Cambridge, MA: Harvard University Press.

Gilligan, S., & Price, R. (Eds.) (1993). *Therapeutic conversations*. New York: Norton.

Glasser, W. (1984). Reality therapy. In R. J. Corsini (Ed.), *Current psychotherapies* (3rd ed., pp. 320–353). Itasca, IL: F. E. Peacock.

Goldberg, M. C. (1998). *The art of the question: A guide to short-term question-centered therapy*. New York: Wiley.

Goncalves, O. F. (1995). Cognitive narrative therapy: The hermeneutic construction of alternative meanings. In M. J. Mahoney (Ed.), *Cognitive and constructive psychotherapies: Theory, research, and practice* (pp. 139–162). New York: Springer.

Greenberg, L., & Pascual-Leone, J. (1995). A dialectical constructivist approach to experiential change. In R. A. Neimeyer & M. J. Mahoney (Eds.), *Constructivism in psychotherapy* (pp. 169–194). Washington, DC: American Psychological Association.

Grunwald, B. B., & McAbee, H. V. (1985). *Guiding the family*. Muncie, IN: Accelerated Development.

Guidano, V. F. (1991). *The self in process: Toward a post–rationalist cognitive therapy*. New York: Guilford.

Guidano, V. F. (1995a). A constructivist outline of human knowing processes. In M. J. Mahoney (Ed.), *Cognitive and constructive psychotherapies: Theory, research, and practice* (pp. 89–102). New York: Springer.

Guidano, V. F. (1995b). Constructivist psychotherapy: A theoretical framework. In R. A. Neimeyer & M. J. Mahoney (Eds.), *Constructivism in psychotherapy* (pp. 93–110). Washington, DC: American Psychological Association.

Guidano, V. F., & Liotti, G. (1983). *Cognitive process and emotional disorders*. New York: Guilford.

Gushurst, R. S. (1971). The technique, utility, and validity of lifestyle analysis. *The Counseling Psychologist, 3,* 30–39.

Hoffman, E. (1994). *The drive for self: Alfred Adler and the founding of Individual Psychology*. Reading, MS: Addison-Wesley

Hoyt, M. F. (1994a). Competency-based future-oriented therapy. In M. F. Hoyt (Ed.), *Constructive therapies* (pp. 1–10). New York: Guilford

Hoyt, M. F. (Ed.) (1994b). *Constructive therapies*. New York: Guilford.

Hoyt, M. F. (1996a). Postmodernism, the relational self, constructive therapies, and beyond: A conversation with Kenneth Gergen. In M. F. Hoyt (Ed.), *Constructive therapies: Vol. 2* (pp. 347–368). New York: Guilford.

Hoyt, M. F. (Ed.) (1996b). *Constructive therapies: Vol. 2*. New York: Guilford.

Jones, J. V., Jr. (1995). Constructivism and individual psychology: Common ground for dialogue. *Individual Psychology, 51*, 231–243.

Jones, J. V., Jr., & Lyddon, W. J. (1997). Adlerian and constructivist psychotherapies: An constructivist perspective. *Journal of Cognitive Psychotherapy, 11*, 195–210.

Joyce-Moniz, L. (1985). Epistemological therapy and constructivism. In M. J. Mahoney and A. Freeman (Eds.), *Cognition and psychotherapy* (pp. 143–179). New York: Plenum.

Kelly, G. (1955). *The psychology of personal constructs* (2 vols.). New York: Norton.

Kern, R. M., Hawes, E. C., & Christensen, O. C. (1989). *Couples therapy: An Adlerian perspective*. Minneapolis: Educational Media Corporation.

Liotti, G. (1987). Structural cognitive therapy. In W. Dryden & W. Golden (Eds.), *Cognitive-behavioral approaches to psychotherapy* (pp. 92–128). New York: Hemisphere.

Liotti, G. (1993). Disorganized attachment and dissociative experiences: An illustration of the developmental-ethological approach to cognitive therapy. In K. T. Kuehlwein & H. Rosen (Eds.), *Cognitive therapies in action: Evolving innovative practice* (pp. 213–239). San Francisco: Jossey–Bass.

Littrell, J. M (1998). *Brief counseling in action*. New York: Norton.

Lyddon, W. J. (1995a). Cognitive therapy and theories of knowing: A social constructionist view. *Journal of Counseling and Development, 73*, 579–585.

Lyddon, W. J. (1995b). Forms and facets of constructivist psychology. In R. A. Neimeyer & M. J. Mahoney (Eds.), *Constructivism in psychotherapy* (pp. 69–92). Washington, DC: American Psychological Association.

Mahoney, M. J. (1985). Psychotherapy and human change processes. In M. J. Mahoney & A. Freeman (Eds.), *Cognition and psychotherapy* (pp. 3–48). New York: Plenum.

Mahoney, M. J. (1988a). Constructive metatheory: I. Basic features and historical foundations. *International Journal of Personal Construct Psychology, 1*, 1–35.

Mahoney, M. J. (1988b). Constructive metatheory: II. Implications for psychotherapy. *International Journal of Personal Construct Psychology, 1*, 299–315.

Mahoney, M. J. (1989). Participatory epistemology and psychology of science. In B. Gholson, W. R. Shadish, R. A. Neimeyer, & A. C. Houts (Eds.), *Psychology of science: Contributions to Metascience* (pp. 138–164). New York: Cambridge.

Mahoney, M. J. (1991). *Human change processes: The scientific foundations of psychotherapy*. New York: Basic Books.

Mahoney, M. J. (Ed.) (1995). *Cognitive and constructive psychotherapies: Theory, research, and practice*. New York: Springer.

Manaster, G. J., & Corsini, R. J. (1982). *Individual psychology: Theory and practice*. Itasca, IL: F. E. Peacock.

Master, S. B. (1991). Constructivism and the creative power of the self. *Individual Psychology, 47*, 447–455.

Matthews, W. J., & Edgette, J. H. (Eds.) (1997). *Current thinking and research in brief therapy: Solutions, strategies, & narratives*. New York: Brunner/Mazel.

May, R. (1970). Myth and guiding fiction. *Journal of Individual Psychology, 26*, 39.

May, R. (1989). *The art of counseling* (rev. ed.). New York: Gardner.

Meichenbaum, D. (1995). Changing conceptions of cognitive behavior modification: Retrospect and prospect. In M. J. Mahoney (Ed.), *Cognitive and constructive psychotherapies: Theory, research, and practice* (pp. 20–26). New York: Springer.

Miller, S. D., Hubble, M. A., & Duncan, B. L. (1996). *Handbook of solution-focused brief therapy*. San Francisco: Jossey–Bass.

Mosak, H. H. (1979). Adlerian psychotherapy. In R.J. Corsini (Ed.), *Current psychotherapies* (2nd ed., pp. 44–94). Itasca, IL: Peacock.

Mosak, H. H., & Maniacci, M. (1998). *Tactics in counseling and psychotherapy*. Itasca, IL: Peacock.

Neimeyer, R. A. (1987). Personal construct therapy. In W. Dryden & W. Golden (Eds.), *Cognitive-behavioral approaches to psychotherapy* (pp. 224–260). New York: Hemisphere.

Neimeyer, R. A. (1993). Constructivistic psychotherapy. In K. T. Kuehlwein & H. Rosen (Ed.), *Cognitive therapies in action: Evolving innovative practice* (pp. 268–300). San Francisco: Jossey-Bass.

Neimeyer, R. A. (1995a). An invitation to constructivist psychotherapies. In R. A. Neimeyer & M. J. Mahoney (Eds.), *Constructivism in psychotherapy* (pp. 1–10). Washington, DC: American Psychological Association.

Neimeyer, R. A. (1995b). Constructivist psychotherapies: Features, foundations, and future directions. In R. A. Neimeyer & M. J. Mahoney (Eds.), *Constructivism in psychotherapy* (pp. 11–38). Washington, DC: American Psychological Association.

Neimeyer, R. A., & Mahoney, M. J. (Eds.) (1995). *Constructivism in psychotherapy*. Washington, DC: American Psychological Association.

Nichols, M. P., & Schwartz, R. C. (1995). *Family therapy: Concepts and methods* (3rd ed.). Boston: Allyn & Bacon.

O'Hanlon, W. H., & Weiner–Davis, M. (1989). *In search of solutions: A new direction in psychotherapy*. New York: Norton.

Parry, A., & Doan, R. E. (1994). *Story revisions: Narrative therapy in a postmodern world*. New York: Guilford.

Powers, R. L., & Griffith, J. (1987). *Understanding life-style: The psycho–clarity process*. Chicago: The Americas Institute of Adlerian Studies.

Raimy, V. (1975). *Misunderstandings of the self*. New York: Jossey-Bass.

Riikonen, E., & Smith, G. M. (1997). *Re-imagining therapy: Living conversations and relational knowing*. London: Sage.

Rosen, H. (1996). Meaning-making narratives: Foundations for constructivist and social constructionist psychotherapies. In H. Rosen & K. T. Kuehlwein (Eds.), *Constructing realities: Meaning-making perspectives for psychotherapists* (pp. 3–54). San Francisco: Jossey-Bass.

Scott, C. N., Kelly, F. D., & Tolbert, B. L. (1995). Realism, constructivism, and the Individual Psychology of Alfred Adler. *Individual Psychology, 51*, 4–20.

Sechrest, L. (1983). Personal constructs theory. In R. J. Corsini & A. J. Marsella (Eds.), *Personality theories, research & assessment* (pp. 229–285). Itasca, IL: F.E. Peacock.

Sherman, R., & Dinkmeyer, D. (1987). *Systems of family therapy: An Adlerian integration*. New York: Brunner/Mazel.

Shulman, B. H. (1973). *Contributions to individual psychology*. Chicago: The Alfred Adler Institute.

Shulman, B. H. (1985). Cognitive therapy and the individual psychology of Alfred Adler. In M. J. Mahoney & A. Freeman (Eds.), *Cognition and psychotherapy* (pp. 243–258). New York: Plenum.

Shulman, B. H., & Mosak, H. H. (1988). *Manual for life style assessment*. Muncie, IN: Accelerated Development.

Shulman, B. H., & Watts, R. E. (1997). Adlerian and constructivist psychotherapies: An Adlerian perspective. *Journal of Cognitive Psychotherapy, 11*, 181–193.

Singer, J. A., & Salovey, P. (1993). *The remembered self: Emotion and memory in personality*. New York: Free Press.

Sperry, L. (1993). Psychopathology and the diagnostic and treatment process. In L. Sperry & J. Carlson (Eds.), *Psychopathology and psychotherapy* (pp. 3–18). Muncie, IN: Accelerated Development.

Stepansky, P. E. (1983). *In Freud's shadow: Adler in context*. London: The Analytic Press.

Stuart, R. B. (1980). *Helping couples change: A social learning approach to marital therapy*. New York: Guilford.

Sweeney, T. J. (1989). *Adlerian counseling* (3rd ed.). Muncie, IN: Accelerated Development.

Walter, J., & Peller, J. (1992). *Becoming solution–focused in brief therapy.* New York: Brunner/Mazel.

Watts, R. E. (1998a). The remarkable similarity between Rogers's core conditions and Adler's social interest. *Journal of Individual Psychology, 54,* 4–9.

Watts, R. E. (1998b). *Echos of Adlerian theory/therapy in contemporary constructivist approaches.* Unpublished Manuscript.

Watts, R. E., & Critelli, J. W. (1997). Roots of contemporary cognitive theories in the Individual Psychology of Alfred Adler. *Journal of Cognitive Psychotherapy, 11,* 147–156.

Watzlawick, P. (Ed.) (1984). *The invented reality: How do we know what we believe we know?* New York: Norton.

Watzlawick, P. (1990). *Munchhausen's pigtail.* New York: Norton.

Weiner–Davis, M. (1992). *Divorce–busting: A revolutionary rapid program for staying together.* New York: Simon & Schuster.

Weiner–Davis, M. (1995). *Change your life and everyone in it.* New York: Simon & Schuster.

White, M., & Epston, D. (1990). *Narrative means to therapeutic ends.* New York: Norton.

Whitehouse, D. (1984). Adlerian antecedents to reality therapy and control theory. *Journal of Reality Therapy, 3,* 10–14.

Wubbolding, R. E. (1993). Reality therapy with children. In T. R. Kratochwill & R. J. Morris (Eds.), *Handbook of psychotherapy with children and adolescents* (pp. 288–219). Boston: Allyn & Bacon.

Zimmerman, J. L., & Dickerson, V. C. (1996). *If problems talked: Narrative therapy in action.* New York: Guilford.

2

CHAPTER

William G. Nicoll

Brief Therapy Strategies and Techniques

Over the past few decades, the movement toward more focused, directive, and change-oriented models of counseling—the brief therapies—has continued to develop rapidly. At this point, it is probably safe to say that brief therapy constitutes the state of the art regarding actual practice within the greater mental health field. Some counselors have embraced the new brief therapy paradigms and others have expressed a sense of validation as brief therapy more directly reflects the realities of their work settings. Still other counselors and therapists have fought and argued against the brief, time-limited approaches. However, no matter what a counselor's position regarding brief therapy, it seems irrefutable that the movement to time-limited, directive, change-focused models is a reality in the delivery of today's mental health services.

This movement toward brief therapy may be viewed as the logical result of a combination of factors affecting the mental health delivery system. Four factors appear particularly relevant. First, outcome research on the effectiveness of therapy has consistently shown brief therapy approaches to be at least equally effective as the long-term, time-unlimited therapies (Butcher & Koss, 1978; Koss & Shiang, 1994; Steenbarger, 1992). Reviews of the outcome research literature by Johnson and Gelso (1980) and Gelso and Johnson (1983) add an interesting dimension to the outcomes discussion. Their findings suggest that when therapy effectiveness is measured by therapist ratings, the bias is toward favoring long-term therapies. However, when effectiveness is measured by more objective measures—such as third-party observers, standardized measures, or even client self-ratings—the time-limited, brief therapies appear as effective as long-term models. With outcomes being comparable for the client, additional benefits realized by the economy of time and costs for the client would argue for using of a brief therapy approach.

Research on the process of change in counseling and therapy has also supported the move to the brief therapies. The research evidence to date has suggested that the greatest gains in treatment typically occur early in therapy (Howard, Kopta, Krause, &

Orlinsky, 1986). Garfield (1989), for example, found that most change appears to occur in the first eight sessions. Such evidence appears to support the use of brief, intermittent therapy. The counselor or therapist works with the client for relatively short durations of time and then interrupts, rather than terminating, treatment. This allows the client time to integrate changes into his or her life. Therapy may then be resumed later to work on other issues in a similar focused, time-limited manner.

Budman and Gurman's study (1988) added a further interesting dimension to the research support for brief therapy. Their meta-analytic review of therapy effectiveness found that the studied treatments ranged from 7 to 17 sessions per client. The outcome research in counseling and psychotherapy may therefore be regarded as consisting of comparisons between time–limited brief therapy and time–unlimited brief therapy.

A second factor driving the movement toward brief therapy paradigms stems from the research on client expectations of counseling and therapy. Research findings have increasingly suggested that clients come expecting an active, directive counselor who will structure the sessions and move them toward problem resolution (Budman & Gurman, 1988; Garfield, 1986; Shapiro & Budman, 1973). Despite therapist intent, it appears that most clients come to therapy for relatively few sessions. Phillips (1985) found the average number of therapeutic treatment sessions to be four, with a median of one session. Garfield's research indicated that up to 50% of clients do not return for the second session. This strongly suggests the need for therapists to structure even the initial session as if it were a one-session intervention. Haley (1990) suggested that this may reflect the changing nature of clients seeking counseling assistance. In the earlier years of counseling and psychotherapy (when most traditional, long-term, "depth" models were developed), clients largely elected to come for therapy voluntarily. Increasingly, however, clients today are being "sent" to counseling by a third party such as a parent, school staff, judge, and so forth. Mental health services are also more widely accepted and therefore sought by the general population. Many "higher functioning" clients come to counseling seeking help with a particular life situation, crisis, or problem area and are not inclined toward long-term analysis or therapeutic processes.

Thus, it appears that the movement to the brief therapies is an aligning of what the client seeks from counseling with the treatment the counselor is prepared to provide. From this perspective, brief therapy becomes a true "client-centered" approach in that the counselor provides the treatment sought by the client (i.e., direct and problem resolution focused) rather than the treatment advocated by a particular theory of counseling and therapy.

A third factor involved in the move to the brief therapy models is the problem of increased counseling caseloads without increases in funding to increase counseling staff to serve those caseloads. This is particularly true for many counselors working within educational and community agency settings. For example, school counselors are often expected to serve all the counseling and guidance needs for a caseload of 500 to 800, or more, students. Further compounding the problem is the reality that the school counselor's job description includes far more than only providing individual and group counseling, parent–family counseling, and teacher consultation services for these students. The nature of the position mandates that school counselors receive training in the more time-efficient models of brief counseling. Community agency counselors also commonly report large caseload problems. Such agencies frequently experience increasing demands for services without adequate financial support from funding sources. The problem of growing agency caseloads, combined with insufficient staffing, requires moving to more time- and cost-efficient treatment paradigms.

Finally, the fourth factor involved in the rapid movement to the briefer therapy models is the influence and policies of third-party insurance providers and the managed-care health provider industry. Such cost-conscious businesses often pay the counseling service fees and thus have the power to dictate what services they will cover. Increasingly, such providers have limited reimbursement for both outpatient and inpatient mental health treatment. In effect, such policies are tantamount to mandating time-limited, brief therapeutic interventions.

Some have attempted to argue that managed-care policies are the sole or primary reason for the move to brief therapy. This is simply not true. The issues of large caseloads, the research data as to what clients actually seek from counseling, and the outcome research literature are all much more compelling reasons for the move to brief, time-limited therapies. There are many legitimate problems with the third-party provider and managed-care approach to providing mental health services. Regarding the move to brief therapies, however, managed care has perhaps served as a catalyst forcing counselors to acknowledge the growing "cultural transition" within the field. The transition from time-unlimited, traditional therapies to the time-limited, directive, change-oriented treatment paradigms has been long evolving and is, perhaps, overdue in the field.

The move to more short-term, directive counseling models may be understood as the culmination of a long-evolving movement within the counseling and psychotherapy field. Its origins can be traced back at least some 80 years to the very origins of modern psychotherapeutic methods. The work of the Viennese psychiatrist Alfred Adler, in particular, can be viewed as seminal to the current brief therapy models. Adler's work stood in contrast to the intrapsychic-focused, "depth," or analytical models of Freud and Jung. Adler first advocated for a therapeutic paradigm focused not on intrapsychic conflicts but on how the individual attaches meaning to, and chooses to deal with, the social environment. Adler focused attention on how individuals interpret and interact with their social environment. He suggested that therapy must focus on assisting clients to alter mistaken or flawed assumptions about life and relationships and changing counterproductive interactions with the social environment.

Adler first suggested the emphasis in therapy turn more toward understanding the interpersonal nature of behavior and the facilitating of change processes rather than on analyzing intrapsychic processes. This alternate approach to psychotherapy eventually contributed to the famous split between Adler and Freud and the resultant two "camps" for psychotherapy: the long-term, analytical model of Freud's Psychoanalytic Society and the more directive, social context–oriented approach of Adler's Free Psychoanalytic Society. Over the course of the century, alternate paradigms focusing more on facilitating change through direct, brief, and resolution-oriented processes have served as perhaps the subplot in the history of psychology.

The more directive, briefer approach has been further advanced and developed by the work of Albert Ellis, William Glasser, Milton Erickson, Jay Haley, Gregory Bateson, and Michael White, to name but a few. Only during the past two decades, however, has this alternate, brief therapy paradigm finally emerged from the background and into the accepted mainstream of mental health services. Consequently, we have seen in recent years the emergence of many "new" models of counseling and psychotherapy advocating a shorter, more direct, empowering, and change-oriented approach. Most notable among these new brief therapy models would be the strategic, solution-focused, and narrative therapy models. The remaining sections of this chapter delineate an integrative framework based in Adlerian psychology and systems theory that enables counselors and therapists to use the strategies and techniques of all the brief therapies within a unified conceptual framework.

☐ Characteristics of Brief Therapy

Five essential characteristics form the basis for an integrative framework for brief therapy: time limitation, focus, counselor directiveness, symptoms as solutions, and the assignment of behavioral tasks. For the most part, these essential characteristics are reflected in most models of brief therapy. Particular models may differ about which of the characteristics they most emphasize, but explicitly or implicitly they are, for the most part, integral aspects of effective brief therapy.

First, as in all brief therapy approaches, the counselor and client work within a time-limited context. Therapist and client essentially establish a contract during the first session regarding the number, frequency, and duration of therapy sessions. This therapeutic contract is subject to review and modification as therapy progresses. However, the beginning time limit on treatment serves two essential functions for therapy. First, it conveys an optimistic expectation that change, progress, and growth are possible, and in a brief amount of time. Second, the establishment of time limitations appears to serve the function of motivating both client and counselor to work more quickly and directly than when time is considered unlimited.

The issue of time limitations to therapy is often misunderstood. Although a time limit is set for therapy, it does not mean the counselor–client relationship ends at the final session. The counselor–client relationship is more analogous to that of the family practitioner in medicine. The counselor and client essentially agree to work intensively for a specific length of time around the current, presenting issue or symptoms. Then, once progress or growth is realized, active work in therapy ceases for an indefinite time period. Therapy is more interrupted than terminated at this point. In the future, the client may choose to return to therapy to work on further or new issues in his or her life. The client is thus provided with time to integrate and consolidate changes into his or her life before moving on to other areas of concern.

Brief therapy also allows the counselor to be flexible in using time. Counseling sessions do not need to be of the traditional 50-minute, once-per-week format. A longer initial session or two might be scheduled, followed by shorter (e.g., 30 minutes) follow-up sessions. Sessions may be scheduled weekly or semiweekly at first and then every other week or monthly depending on the issues and needs of the client.

The second primary characteristic of the brief therapies is that of focusing. Counselor and client agree to focus their work on a single, key area or issue of current concern in the client's interpersonal life. The idea of focusing therapy on a single issue of current concern is perhaps more important than time limitations in defining brief therapy. As noted by Wells and Phelps (1990), the key to successful brief therapy is therapeutic "focusing." Brief therapy is more about focus than it is about time. The counselor must strive to keep therapy focused to create change in a current area of concern in the client's life. Brief therapy does not address ancillary issues at this time. If explored at all, they are examined only in terms of how they relate to or affect the current focus issue. Therapeutic focusing involves the identification of one, central issue or concern to the client that will serve as the target of counseling intervention.

The third characteristic of the brief therapies involves the counselor–client relationship. Counselors take a direct and active role in therapy by structuring the session and working with clients as partners in understanding the dynamics of issues and creating change. The counselor further assumes an optimistic, empowering attitude regarding the client's capacity to change. Through a focus on the capabilities and strengths of the client, the counselor empowers the client by aligning with his or her competence rather than by taking the position of focusing on problems, weaknesses, and inadequacies. Such practice serves largely a function of further discouraging the client and reinforcing defense mechanisms. Being pathology-focused may actually prolong treatment by increasing resistance.

A fourth characteristic of the brief therapies involves how the counselor views the client's presenting symptoms or problematic behaviors. The emphasis is placed on finding ways to resolve life concerns, not on trying to diagnose the etiological factors leading to the presenting symptoms. Brief therapy is about resolving, not identifying causes for, client concerns. Furthermore, presenting behavioral patterns of the client are understood not as problems per se, but instead as limited or counterproductive solutions to some underlying focus issue. The client's presenting behaviors are not the problem. These behaviors are viewed as solutions the client uses in an attempt to deal with an issue in his or her life. In essence, the client is seen as "stuck" using the same behavioral patterns to solve a problem without realizing that these patterns often serve to maintain the problem, avoid the problem, or, in many cases, exacerbate the problem.

Viewing presenting behavioral patterns not as problems but as the client's solution to the true problem is similar to the way in which medicine views presenting symptoms. Medical symptoms are the body's solutions to infection or disease processes. For example, coughing is not a problem but merely the body's way of solving the problem of an obstructed trachea. Similarly, a high fever is the solution used by the body to fight a bacterial or viral infection. So, too, in brief therapy we see presenting symptomatic behaviors of the clients as the methods they are currently using to address another underlying issue or concern.

Finally, the fifth characteristic of the brief therapies is that clients are assigned behavioral tasks to do outside therapeutic sessions. Thus, activity and behavioral change, not passive suffering or emoting, is clearly established as the expectation for the client in therapy. Change takes place between counseling sessions, not within counseling sessions. The counselor and client use the sessions to gain a fuller understanding of the underlying issue and how it is manifested in the client's behavioral patterns. From there, they work toward seeking alternate behavioral solutions that will create growth and change rather than problem maintenance.

☐ A Conceptual Framework for Brief Therapy

Every therapeutic approach has, at its foundation, some implicit or explicit assumptions about behavior that serve to guide the counselor in assessment and intervention. The integrative approach delineated in this chapter is primarily an integration of Adlerian psychology and systems theory. The model provides the counselor or therapist with a schema for understanding both client behavior and the process of brief therapy.

Behavior is understood as occurring on a three-tiered basis (see Figure 2.1). This three-tier model is applicable to understanding all systems, be they an individual, a family, a couple, a culture, or a business or organization. Brief therapists initially strive to understand their client's presenting concerns at all three levels.

The first level of assessment is that of identifying the client's precise actions and emotions and the social context in which they occur. This level of behavior assessment focuses on what the client does and how he or she feels as he or she engages in that behavior. The counselor works with the client to decide exactly in what situations or

Level 1: How? (I/we do . . . and feel . . .)

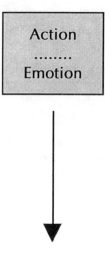

Level 2: What for? (In order to . . .)

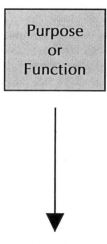

Level 3: Why? (Because . . .)

Figure 2.1. The Three Levels of System Behavior

circumstances the presenting issue occurs (and does not occur) and how the client is acting and feeling in relation to the presenting issue. Verbs that imply possession such as *to be* and *to have* are avoided in brief therapy. Such verbs serve the function of labeling clients and implicitly communicate to the client that he or she possesses some form of pathology, disease, or character flaw. Although such verbs are commonly used in the mental health diagnostic–assessment process, the implied message to the client is considered counterproductive for facilitating change and growth in brief therapy.

After determining the "how" of the client's behavior, the counselor probes deeper by addressing the second level of behavior; the function served by the client's actions. That is, to assess the "what-for" question of the presenting behavior. Consistent with Adler's pioneering work, causation (determinism) is rejected. Symptoms are assumed to serve a purpose or function for the client in some capacity. This purpose can often be discovered by placing the behavioral patterns in their social context and following the interaction patterns between the client and involved significant others or between the client and life expectations (career, marriage, social, etc.). As the sequence of interactions is followed, the function of the behavior is slowly revealed.

For example, a 10-year-old boy was referred for defiant, acting-out behaviors in his reading class. In the brief therapy process, it emerged that he used such behaviors to get out of his classroom. Through such defiant behavior he could leave with an image of power and strength among his peers. The alternative, from this boy's perspective, was to stay in the room and be exposed as a nonreader and face certain humiliation. His behavioral symptoms were his solution to a social threat created by his reading problem. Similarly, a female client used her depressing behaviors of withdrawal, inactivity, and sadness to mobilize first her parents—and then, later in life, her husband—to provide greater attention, assistance, and service. It is important to remember, however, that the client is not often consciously aware of the purpose or function of his or her behavior.

The third and deepest level of understanding behavior involves investigating the client's idiosyncratic rules of interaction. This level answers the third and final question of why the client handles life in this manner. *Why* refers here to the rationale or logic system underlying the presenting behavior patterns and not to causal factors. This concept, taken from general systems theory, refers to the idea that all systems function on the basis of a relatively small, yet highly salient set of systemic rules (or metarules) that govern all operations of the system.

With the individual, various theoretical models of counseling and therapy have referred to this idea using terms such as the client's basic assumptions, apperceptions, phenomenological perspective, private logic, belief systems, and so forth. The essential component driving all behavior is the client's idiosyncratic cognitive schema, a cognitive framework whereby he or she attaches meaning to life experiences and, therefore, chooses, consciously or unconsciously, behaviors. The rules-of-interaction concept is consistent with the theoretical principles of many leading cognitive therapies from Adler's individual psychology to constructivism.

The rules-of-interaction concept also holds in couples counseling where we strive to understand the couples' unique, unwritten "contract of expectations" (Hawes, 1989). All couples relate to one another based on a set of assumptions and expectations regarding their relationship, one another's roles, and the normative expectations for fulfilling those roles. So, too, in family counseling, most all approaches recognize the need to address the "family rule system" (Nichols & Schwartz, 1995), that is, the unique metarule system that organizes family interaction patterns and structures. The importance of these rules of interaction is even seen at the macrosystemic level when working with organizations, businesses, and cultures. The focus is always on understanding the preconscious set of rules by which meaning is attached to events and on which behaviors are selected whether one chooses to call them organizational culture, business culture, or shared worldview. At the root of all human behavior (individual, familial, organizational, or cultural) lies this key concept of the rules of interaction.

Once these rules are recognized and understood, then all behavioral patterns become understandable and, to some extent, predictable. If one starts with an assumption (i.e., rule of interaction) that he or she is incapable of doing anything well or "well enough," then it is quite likely that he or she will seek to avoid tasks and responsibilities (purpose) that would predictably end in failure. Avoiding failure may be accomplished in a variety of ways. These include the demonstration of one's incompetence to others so that they will expect less or the charming of others into helping and doing things for oneself (including making decisions) or by developing symptoms (e.g., phobias) that excuse one from those aspects of life where one feels most susceptible to failure.

The key to brief therapy lies in obtaining an understanding of the client's behavior at all three levels and then focusing intervention at the third level—rules of interaction. Unless the client is helped to view or understand life from a different perspective, real change will not occur. Without a shift in perspective, one may observe short-term changes (more to please the counselor–therapist) or first-order behavioral changes (i.e., change without change) that are merely new ways of doing the same old thing.

These three interrelated levels of behavior might be viewed as analogous to the children's bop-bag or punching-bag toy. The first level, behavioral actions and emotions, would be the head of the toy. The second level, purpose or function of behavior, would be the body. The rules of interaction would then constitute the weighted bag at the bottom of the bop-bag. Thus, although one might temporarily move the location of the head (symptomatic behaviors) and even the body to some degree (function) through forceful intervention aimed at the head (symptom), eventually the bop-bag will return to its original position (i.e., homeostasis). Clients, like the bop-bag, will only maintain lasting change if intervention is focused on the third level, the rules of interaction (i.e., weighted base). Just as one must move the weighted base of the bop-bag if the head is to remain permanently in a new location, so too must counseling focus on shifting the client's rules of interaction for lasting behavioral change to occur.

☐ Four Stages in Brief Therapy

The three levels of behavior can be translated into a four-stage schema for the brief therapy process. The four stages are identified with the acronym BURP: Behavioral description of the presenting problem, Underlying rules of interaction assessment, Reorientation of the client's rules of interaction, and Prescribing new behavioral rituals. This four-stage process is not necessarily followed in a simple, mechanistic manner. Instead, the brief therapist proceeds through each session following this general four-stage process more in terms of a structured flow than in a lock-stepped manner. Variations in the model are often necessary given the particular client and presenting issue. This four-stage process model merely provides the brief therapist with a structure for each session and to keep the client focused on moving toward change and growth.

Behavioral Assessment

In obtaining a description of the presenting issue, the therapist seeks a detailed behavioral description of how the problematic situation manifests in the client's daily life. At the beginning of brief therapy, the counselor must strive to have the client describe the presenting issue of concern in behavioral (i.e., actions and emotions) terminology. This requires the client to use action verbs (i.e., verbs ending in *ing*) when discussing the focus issue. The therapist gently directs the client away from using possession verbs such as *to be* and *to have*. Such verbs (e.g., *I am, I have,* or *I suffer from*), although commonly used by clients to describe the reason for coming to counseling, carry the implicit message that the client is somehow afflicted with a personality flaw, disorder, or disease that he or she has little or no power to change. Using terminology that implies the possession of pathology places the client in a double-bind situation. The therapist is left asking clients to change something over which they have no control or responsibility. For example, rather than allow a statement such as "I am depressed," the counselor might ask the client to describe specific times and situations in which he or she felt sad and depressed. Questioning at the assessment stage would focus on such things as "What did you do the last time this occurred?" "Who else was affected?" "What did they do?" and "How did you respond?"

Through such questioning, the counselor not only obtains a complete understanding of the presenting issue but simultaneously begins the reorientation process through a change in the language of therapy. The language of brief therapy avoids the implication of passive suffering by, or victimization of, the client due to processes beyond his or her control. Action-oriented terminology involves something similar to a hypnotic suggestion process through the implied message that one chooses to use certain behaviors and therefore always has the capacity to choose different ones. Without directly stating so, the therapist begins to shift the client's perspective from "What I suffer from" to "How I deal with"—in other words, a shift from an external locus of control to an internal locus of control.

Other useful phrases for the brief therapist to use in moving the client away from a passive, suffering perspective and toward an active, problem-resolution perspective include, "Tell me about the last time this occurred." Or "What happens when you are anxious (depressed, out of control, etc.)?" By attending to the client's responses, a therapist can begin to identify how the client acts and feels, under what situations the symptoms are most likely to occur, and what purpose may be served by such actions (symptoms).

The latter question, regarding under what situations the symptoms are most likely to occur, begins to move the therapist's understanding to the second level of behavior, the purpose or function of the symptoms. By identifying whom in the client's social environment is affected by or involved in the symptomatic behavior and the specific social situations where the problems occur, hypotheses can be developed as to the possible conscious or unconscious purpose of the client's symptoms. It is important, however, to recognize that although the client may be consciously aware of what he or she does, he or she is often less aware of his or her actual emotional responses. Furthermore, the purpose of the behavior (Level 2) and the rules of interaction underlying the behavior (Level 3) are usually outside the client's conscious awareness. It is the task of the brief therapist to discover the second and third levels of behavior in order to obtain a complete understanding of the dynamics behind the presenting issue.

Underlying Rules of Interaction

Careful attending to how the client describes the presenting issue, the situations where it occurs, and the behavioral sequences involved will provide the brief therapist with clues as to the possible purpose served (or intended to be served) by the client's problematic behaviors. It may also be helpful for the brief therapist to begin forming hypotheses as to possible underlying rules of interaction whereby the client perceives, attaches meaning to, and chooses behaviors in his or her life. The client, although not consciously aware of his or her underlying rules of interaction, will often act "as if" his or her perceptions were the correct and only possible perspective.

By placing oneself in the client's position and seeing the presenting situation from the client's perspective (i.e., rules of interaction), the client's behaviors (or symptoms) become completely understandable and logical to the therapist. This enables the brief therapist to strategically take the therapeutic position of aligning with (through understanding) the client's symptoms and thus to become an ally rather than an adversary. In this manner, resistance in therapy can be avoided or minimized. Only when the client first feels understood and accepted, rather than criticized and attacked, is he or she likely to be receptive to working with the counselor toward change.

There are numerous counseling techniques that can be used by a counselor to quickly gain an accurate understanding of the rules of interaction supporting and maintaining the presenting problem. It is not within the scope of this chapter to discuss these techniques in detail. However, a few techniques might be mentioned that are described more fully elsewhere. Early childhood recollections have been found useful when understood as metaphors for the client's current rules of interaction rather than as historical events (Mosak, 1972). Family stories and family genograms can help reveal rules of interaction derived from the client's family system (Nicoll & Hawes, 1984). The "magical question" ("How would your life change, be different if you did not suffer from these symptoms?") described by Dreikurs (1954) and later by proponents of solution-focused brief therapy can be useful for detecting possible rules that support the use of the symptom to avoid a perceived greater problem for the client (e.g., "if only I did not suffer from this depression, I could be successful in a job and live successfully on my own rather than be dependent on my mother for support").

I will illustrate the first two steps in the brief therapy process, the assessment stage, by identifying the dynamics of a presenting issue at all three levels for understanding behavior.

A 21-year-old man came to counseling because of recent problems he had experienced with panic attacks. These attacks suddenly began shortly after returning to campus for his third year of study. The problem had escalated to the point that he was initially hospitalized and then sent home for treatment. Since returning home, the attacks had significantly decreased, but he was concerned over possible recurrence of the anxiety problems.

When asked to describe one of his most recent panic attacks, the young man stated that they typically occurred in the evenings at his dormitory. He would awaken feeling very agitated, frightened, and sweating profusely to the point where he had difficulty breathing. His roommate had to call for emergency assistance from the campus medical center. Such attacks had never occurred in his first two years of study. However, during those years, his older brother had been a graduate student at the same school, graduating the previous spring semester. This was the client's first semester "out in the world" alone.

Further investigation into his underlying rules of interaction revealed a view of life as very dangerous and unpredictable and a view of himself as naive and vulnerable. For example, his early recollection focused on an incident at the age of 8 when he was in the kitchen with his alcoholic father.

> My father and I were laughing and joking about something when suddenly he turned around toward me and hit me in the mouth with his fist as hard as he could . . . . I bounced off the wall and fell to the floor. Never could figure out what I had said or what happened to cause him to hurt me like that.

Further, as the youngest of three boys with an explosive, alcoholic father, he had aligned closely with his oldest brother and his mother. "I was the type of kid always clinging to Mom's apron strings or tagging along with my older brother."

In this case, we see how the three levels of behavior can be quickly observed during the first two stages of brief therapy. Rather than viewing the client as "suffering from" panic attacks (a position of powerlessness and victimization), he could be seen as someone who, owing to early life experiences, has come to perceive the world as very dangerous and unpredictable, a place where one could be easily hurt (rule of interaction). Consequently, this young man had developed an approach to life whereby he sought safety and security by aligning with individuals he viewed as stronger, more capable, and protective of him (purpose). When placed in a situation without such supports, he resorted to unconsciously reminding himself of how dangerous his situation could be, and thus experienced panic attacks. Interestingly, the result was hospitalization and returning to live at home under the safety and protection of his mother. Thus, he had found safety and protection through the anxiety disorder symptoms. His presenting symptoms, anxiety, served as his "solution" to an unpredictable and dangerous world. They returned him to the protection of a safe environment.

Reorientation Process

Through careful exploration of the behavioral–emotional dimension of the presenting issue—including placing such behavior within a social context (i.e., where does it occur, who else is involved, and how do others respond?)—and exploring the client's underlying rules of interaction, a more precise picture can be obtained of the dynamics of the client's behavior. Now, the brief therapy process can be directed to the issue of facilitating change. However, it cannot be stated too strongly that the key to brief therapy—to initiating change processes—lies in careful attention to the assessment stages and accurately identifying the three levels of the client's behavior. The great paradox of brief therapy is that the key to successful brief interventions is to proceed slowly through the assessment stages.

The dynamics of change begin with the process of reorientation, that is, helping the client to view his or her behavior from a different perspective. Albert Einstein is credited with saying that one cannot solve a problem with the same thinking that created it. This is very much the essence of brief therapy. The therapist must assist the client in obtaining a new perspective, insight, or understanding of the presenting issue. Once the client changes his or her perspective, new behavioral options will be sought that are consistent with this new position.

For example, if the client's rules of interaction consist of themes that he or she is inept, incapable, and likely to fail at anything attempted, then he or she is highly unlikely to engage in any challenging task alone. Such an individual may instead develop a myriad of behaviors (symptoms) that all serve the function of protecting him or her from failure. Behaviors such as avoidance, procrastination, displays of incompetence, forgetfulness, excessive anxiety, and so forth may all be used as excuses for poor performance or to solicit others to step in and provide assistance. Without an alteration in this perspective, the client will engage in first-order change processes, at best. That is, he or she will create new ways of doing the same thing, avoiding the perceived certain failure. Tasks may be attempted halfheartedly or successes minimized or explained away in some way (e.g., "I was lucky," "The task was easy, anyone could do it").

True change involves second-order change processes—a fundamental or morphogenic shift in how the existing situation is understood and addressed. This is the challenge to the therapist in facilitating change through brief therapy. The process of reorientating the client's perspective takes place subtly throughout the session but quite directly at the third stage. Many techniques may be used in the reorientation process. Reframing, relabeling, humor, confrontation, metaphors, and language changes are just a few of the commonly used therapeutic intervention techniques that serve the purpose of reorienting the client's current perceptions.

The reorientation process can be illustrated in the example provided earlier regarding the young man suffering from panic attacks. Initially, reorientation is begun with the language change in the process of brief therapy. Rather than speaking of how he suffers from these sudden, unpredictable panic attacks, the language of therapy focuses on where he is when the attacks occur, what he does, and who steps in to assist. The language suggests an active, not passive, role for the client and further carries an implication or hypnotic suggestion that he could choose to act differently. Later, more direct reorientation strategies might involve reframing the issue from the medical model ("I suffer from this disorder") to a relationship model ("I scare myself to such a point that I am then placed in a safer, protected environment"). This latter position enables the client to start seeking alternate ways of handling his self-doubts and dealing with situations he finds potentially threatening. The reorientation involves a move away from looking at how the client passively suffers to seeing how he actively seeks safety. This constitutes a more empowering position for enabling change and growth by emphasizing competence and capability rather than pathology and incapability.

Prescribing New Behavioral Rituals

The final stage in the brief therapy process involves prescribing new behavioral rituals. Such rituals consist of new behavioral tasks for the client to perform outside therapy. Brief therapy, as stated previously, is based on the assumption that change occurs not within the therapy session but between therapy sessions. The client is not allowed to assume the role of passive sufferer but is instead expected to actively engage in the change process outside therapy.

Rituals can be defined as regular, repeated actions that serve the purpose, or function, within a system of reaffirming or maintaining underlying rules of interaction. Religious rituals, for example, are used to reaffirm a church's belief system. Ritual activities in the workplace usually reinforce the corporate culture and define and reaffirm what is deemed important or valued in the organization. Weekly posting of the top salesperson, for example, is a ritual that serves the purpose of reminding all employees that competition for sales volume is what is most valued and rewarded.

Similarly, a client's symptoms might be viewed as ritualistic behaviors that serve the function of reaffirming for the client his or her underlying rules of interaction. As such, they often develop into self-fulfilling prophecies. Experiencing a panic attack, for example, might serve the function of avoiding a feared situation while simultaneously reaffirming the client's underlying rule of interaction that he or she is somehow flawed and incapable of coping with certain life situations effectively. Consequently, when the client is helped to view his or her symptoms and situation differently (i.e., through a reorientation process), he or she will need to learn new behavioral options (rituals) that will help deal with the presenting situation more effectively and reaffirm the new, healthier perspective regarding oneself, others, and life.

Rituals involve actions. This last step in the brief therapy process involves the prescribing of new behavioral patterns for the client to use when dealing with the presenting concern from the new perspective. Many types of rituals can be used depending on the client's needs. For example, new interaction steps might be introduced into a repetitive sequence between husband and wife for handling conflict (changing the choreography rituals). In addition, an individual might be taken out of, or placed into, an ongoing problem interaction to change the sequence (changing the actor's rituals). Other commonly prescribed rituals include restoring positive rituals, connecting rituals, desensitization rituals, and boundary-making rituals (Christensen, Bitter, Hawes, & Nicoll, 1997).

The prescribing of new behavioral rituals involves the client in actively making changes in his or her life outside the therapy session. However, it cannot be emphasized enough that the success of these prescriptions is based entirely on the extent to which the therapist can successfully create a shift, change, or reorientation in the client's original rules of interaction. The reorientation process is the key to change. It is the shifting of the bop-bag's base. Only when the client can view his or her symptoms from a new perspective will he or she be prepared to seek and then use alternate behavioral strategies. New behavioral rituals are directives given to the client for handling the presenting situation differently that will simultaneously serve the function of reaffirming this new perspective. The following case example illustrates the change process delineated by this integrative brief therapy framework.

☐ Case Example

A 45-year-old male client came to counseling due to feelings of distress and depression related to his second divorce that had occurred some 10 months earlier. He related lingering doubts about whether the divorce was a good decision, adding that he had a history of making bad decisions. Consequently, he now spent most of his time alone brooding over his situation, criticizing himself, and avoiding any situations outside his work setting that might lead to forming new social relationships.

After initially reframing by normalizing his "lingering doubts" regarding the wisdom of the divorce as normative in the first year postdivorce, the client was invited to explore the nature of his previous marital relationships. This was suggested as a way to gain a better understanding of how his relationships had failed so that he might avoid such problems in the future. He offered the explanation (rule of interaction) that he was a nice, gentle man who seemed to always end up with very demanding and irrational women. This, he believed, resulted in inevitable problems as he was unable to tolerate their unpredictable and irrational complaints and demands. His typical manner of coping with these "irrational" complaints and demands in both marriages had been to stay longer at work, move out of the house for a week or more, or engage himself in another task and thus avoid these "unproductive confrontations." He reported often feeling "uptight and anxious" about going home or would get angry whenever a "trivial matter" was raised as a concern by his wife (i.e., Level 1, specific behaviors and emotions identified).

This initial investigation suggested that the client found confrontation and conflict particularly threatening and difficult and therefore sought always to avoid or distance himself from conflicts (Level 2, purpose of behavior). The early childhood recollections technique (Mosak, 1972) proved effective in obtaining a clearer understanding of the client's rules of interaction. He recalled a situation at about age 7 when he awoke late at night to the sound of his parents fighting and arguing loudly downstairs. After initially trying to block out the frightening sounds by hiding under his bed with a pillow over his ears, he climbed out the bedroom window and walked up to the top of a small hill across the road. There, he reported finding peace and tranquillity sitting under a tree, a full moon overhead. He could see his mother and father on the lawn but could no longer hear the troublesome sounds of their conflict. In this early childhood recollection, we observe a theme (rule of interaction) that conflict is uncontrollable, threatening, and to be avoided at all costs. His method for coping in life was to avoid or escape from any conflict or potential conflict situation. This strategy, however, only served to exacerbate the situation as problems remained unresolved in his marriages, further frustrating his spouses.

The therapist could now fully understand the client's symptoms based on the three levels of behavior. Viewing conflict as threatening and uncontrollable, he sought to avoid or distance himself from any conflict situation. Long work hours, moving out of the home for short periods, or engaging himself in other tasks and thus being "too busy" to discuss the matter were behaviors used for conflict avoidance. His current symptoms of depression, brooding, and self-criticism also served the function of avoiding further social relationships and thereby the potential for experiencing similar interpersonal conflicts. The therapist could now align with the client's symptoms as useful conflict avoidant strategies. At the same time, the therapist could reframe the client's symptoms and presenting issues not as suffering from mild depression and poor decision-making skills but rather as methods he used to avoid conflict. It could also be pointed out that the price he pays for avoiding conflict is that the conflict is never resolved, but further escalated, and true intimacy in a relationship is never realized.

As this client explored his relationships from this new perspective, he came to view himself not as a passive victim of his own inadequacies and the complaints of irrational wives, but instead as someone who tended to overimpress himself with the potential problems of conflicts. As such, he had perfected the fine art of conflict avoidance (i.e., reframing with a focus on competence rather than pathology). Consequently, the client was helped through role-playing exercises to learn new behavioral strategies for disclosing his difficulties with conflict situations and to ask for assistance from those close to him as he learned to use new strategies for resolving conflicts. Eventually, this led to the client choosing to reunite with his ex-spouse and working on the issues of their relationship directly.

This case study example illustrates the application of the integrative framework for brief therapy. Different clients and different presenting issues will require the use of alternate strategies and techniques. However, the process of all brief therapy interventions follows a similar pattern of first identifying specific behaviors and emotions used by the client in relation to the presenting problematic life situation. Then the brief therapist uses appropriate techniques to obtain a better understanding of the client's underlying rules of interaction (i.e., the idiosyncratic cognitive schema the client uses to assign meaning to life situations). On the basis of this understanding, the therapist helps the client toward considering the presenting symptoms or issue from a new perspective (reorientation) and then assists the client in identifying new behavioral strategies (i.e., rituals) for resolving the presenting concern.

☐ References

Budman, S. H., & Gurman, A. S. (1988). *Theory and practice of brief therapy.* New York: Guilford.

Butcher, J. N. & Koss, M. P. (1978). Research on brief and crisis-oriented psychotherapies. In S. L. Garfield & A. E. Bergin (Eds.), *Handbook of psychotherapy and behavior change* (2nd ed.; pp. 725–768). New York: Wiley.

Christensen, O., Bitter, J., Hawes, C., & Nicoll, W. G. (1997). *Strategies & techniques in brief therapy: Individuals, couples and families.* (Training manual available from the Adlerian Training Institute, P.O. Box 276358, Boca Raton, Fl. 33427).

Dreikurs, R. (1954). The psychological interview in medicine. *American Journal of Individual Psychology, 10,* 98–122.

Garfield, S. (1986). Research on client variables in psychotherapy. In S. Garfield & A. Bergin (Eds.), *Handbook of psychotherapy and behavior change* (3rd ed.; pp. 213–256). New York: Wiley.

Garfield, S. L. (1989). *The practice of brief psychotherapy.* New York: Pergamon.

Gelso, C. J., & Johnson, D. H. (1983). *Explorations in time-limited counseling and psychotherapy.* New York: Teachers College Press.

Haley, J. (Speaker). (1990). *The first therapy session: How to interview clients and identify problems successfully* (cassette recording). San Francisco: Jossey-Bass Audio Programs.

Hawes, E. C. (1989). Therapeutic interventions in the marital relationship. In R. M. Kern, E. C. Hawes, & O. C. Christensen (Eds.), *Couples therapy: An Adlerian perspective* (pp. 77–114). Minneapolis, MN: Educational Media Corp.

Howard, K. I., Kopta, S. M., Krause, M. J., & Orlinsky, D. E. (1986). The dose-effect relationship in psychotherapy. *American Psychologist, 41,* 159–164.

Johnson, D. H., & Gelso, C. J. (1980). The effectiveness of time limits in counseling and psychotherapy: A critical review. *Counseling Psychologist, 9,* 70–83.

Koss, M. P., & Shiang, J. (1994). Research on brief psychotherapy. In A. E. Bergin & S. L. Garfield (Eds.), *Handbook of psychotherapy and behavior change* (4th ed.; pp. 664–700) New York: Wiley.

Mosak, H. H. (1972). *Early recollections as a projective technique.* Chicago: Alfred Adler Institute.

Nichols, M. P., & Schwartz, R. C. (1995). *Family therapy: Concepts and methods* (3rd ed.). Boston: Allyn & Bacon.

Nicoll, W. G., & Hawes, E. C. (1984). Family lifestyle assessment: The role of family myths and values in the client's presenting issues. *Individual Psychology, 41,* 147–160.

Phillips, E. (1985). *Psychotherapy revised: New frontiers in research and practice.* Hillsdale, NJ: Erlbaum.

Shapiro, R., & Budman, S. (1973). Defection, termination, and continuation in family and individual therapy. *Family Process, 12,* 55–67.

Steenbarger, B. N. (1992). Toward science-practice integration in brief counseling and therapy. *The Counseling Psychologist, 20,* 403–450.

Wells, R. A., & Phelps, P. A. (1990). The brief psychotherapies: A selective overview. In R. A. Wells & V. J. Giannetti (Eds.), *Handbook of the brief psychotherapies* (pp. 3–26). New York: Plenum Press.

CHAPTER

3

Michael Nystul

Problem-Solving Counseling: Integrating Adler's and Glasser's Theories

The four-step problem-solving model presented in this chapter represents an integration of the approaches of Alfred Adler and William Glasser. It is a procedure that can be used with children and adults and can be adapted to the unique facets of clients in terms of diversity. The approach can be integrated into most counseling approaches and has particular use as an adjunct to brief counseling. Although the problem-solving model can be used in as few as one session, it can provide an in-depth analysis of unconscious processes associated with resistance in counseling. In addition, it has a built-in mechanism to enhance the motivation for engaging in positive change. The chapter begins by describing how the problem-solving model represents a new dimension to Adlerian psychotherapy. It then provides a detailed description of the model and how it can be used in the counseling process. The chapter ends with a case example illustrating the use of the problem-solving method in counseling.

☐ New Dimensions to Adlerian Psychotherapy

The problem-solving approach described in this chapter evolved out of the spirit of the special issue of *Individual Psychology* titled "On Beyond Adler" (Carlson, 1991). This special issue encouraged the development of new directions for Adlerian psychology so it can continue to be a leading force in contemporary psychology.

The problem-solving model has several unique characteristics that enable it to go beyond Adler. These include avoiding problems associated with the concept of basic mistakes; addressing thoughts, feelings, and behaviors; fostering client motivation and minimizing resistance; and integrating aspects of Adler's and Glasser's theories. A brief overview of these new dimensions to Adlerian counseling and psychotherapy follows.

Avoiding Problems Associated with the Concept of Basic Mistakes

Nystul (1994a) contended that Adlerian counseling and psychotherapy tends to over-emphasize cognition by focusing on reorienting clients from their basic mistakes. Mosak (1989) noted that basic mistakes are faulty views toward oneself or others involving such processes as overgeneralizations ("people can't be trusted") and minimization or denial of one's worth ("I'm dumb").

Nystul (1994a) identified several reasons why the concept of basic mistakes is in direct conflict with Adlerian theory. First, it is discouraging to point out clients' basic mistakes (they will become aware of another thing wrong with them). Basic mistakes emphasize what is wrong with a client—not what is right—and contribute to a patho-logical focus versus a strengths perspective. Second, the concept of basic mistakes con-flicts with the Adlerian construct *private logic*. Nystul described the relationship be-tween basic mistakes and private logic as follows.

> Dreikurs (1973) defined private logic as "the unconscious ideas, concepts, intentions, and goals which the individual acts . . . and the hidden reasons which justify a person's actions, needs, and thoughts" (pp. 1–32). As the private logic evolves, it creates biased appercep-tions as a means of justifying mistaken behavior (Dreikurs, 1950). From the perspective of people's biased apperceptions, everything people think, feel, or do serves a purpose or use and that is to move toward goals. Therefore, all thoughts (including what others might consider to be basic mistakes) will be perceived by individuals as useful concepts to help them better understand their situation and move from a perceived minus to a perceived plus. Providing clients with the "insight" that they have basic mistakes may foster resis-tance in the counseling process. This type of "insight" may not communicate an under-standing of the client's private logic in the psychology of use associated with the client's thoughts. The "insight" that a client has a basic mistake may therefore be resisted because it is not consistent with the client's apperceptual field.
>
> Dinkmeyer and Dreikurs (1963) suggested that a phenomenological perspective could be used to gain an understanding of the client's biased apperceptions. This approach would communicate respect for the client's private logic as the counselor attempts to understand the psychology of use associated with the client's thoughts, feelings, and behaviors. (Nystul, 1994a, pp. 272–273)

Thoughts, Feelings, and Behaviors

Adlerian counseling and psychotherapy has focused on reorienting clients from their basic mistakes (faulty cognitions; Nystul, 1994a). It has therefore to a large degree been a cognitive psychology stressing the role of cognition in emotional distress (Forman & Crandall, 1991; Nystul, 1994a). Adlerian counseling and psychotherapy is similar to Ellis's (1989) rational–emotive therapy in that the therapist directs "a substantial effort to rectifying mistaken beliefs and misconceptions" (Forman & Crandall, 1991, p. 141).

Nystul (1994a) suggested that a more holistic approach to counseling and psy-chotherapy would be directed at helping clients learn the necessary thoughts, feelings, and behaviors associated with efficient approaches to life. An efficient approach is characterized by learning how to meet one's needs without the costs associated with inter-fering with the rights of others. Inefficient approaches have numerous costs that impede movement toward need gratification and tend to interfere with the rights of others.

Fostering Client's Motivation and Minimizing Resistance

The problem-solving model has a built-in mechanism to foster clients' motivation and minimize clients' resistance and relapse. It enhances clients' motivation by making them aware of the costs of their inefficient approaches. Self-efficacy is enhanced, because clients can learn to use the problem-solving method on their own as they become their own self-therapists. The approach also reduces resistance and relapse, because clients discover that their new approach would be more efficient and cost-effective than their old approach (i.e., it can meet their needs without the costs).

Integrating Adler's and Glasser's Theories

The problem-solving method provides an example of how Adlerian psychology can be integrated with current psychotherapies. This should not be surprising as Corey (1996) suggested that Adlerian psychology contributed to the theoretical foundations of most contemporary psychotherapeutic approaches. In addition, Adler's (1969) and Glasser's (1965, 1986) theories have complementary theoretical constructs that make them par-ticularly well suited for integration (Gamble & Watkins, 1983, Whitehouse, 1984). For example, Corey (1996) noted that both theories view behavior from a teleological (pur-poseful, goal directed)–phenomenological perspective. Also, Adler's concept of encour-agement and discouragement is similar to Glasser's concept of success–failure identi-ties (Corey, 1996). In addition, Gamble and Watkins provided a practical illustration of the integration of Adler's and Glasser's theories in terms of disciplining children.

☐ The Problem-Solving Approach

Dixon and Glover (1984) suggested that all counseling, to a large degree, is problem solving (i.e., people attempting to resolve problems or issues of concern). A number of problem-solving methods have been developed for counseling representing various theoretical orientations (e.g., behavioral; Kanfer & Busemeyer, 1982) and special topics (e.g., learning; Anderson, 1993). McClam and Woodside (1994) identified several com-mon characteristics that problem-solving approaches tend to share. For example, they provide a clear structure for the counseling process that delineates the role and func-tion of the counselor and client. Problem-solving approaches also use discreet steps that can be taught to clients and used to prevent future problems. In addition, problem-solving methods are well suited for short-term, time-limited counseling because they are problem centered and solution focused.

The following problem-solving method can be used at any point in the counseling process but would be particularly useful as a type of intervention that could be used after the counseling goal has been determined (e.g., overcoming problems with anxiety, depression, or anger). In addition, the problem-solving method can be used to gain an understanding of the counseling process in terms of how problems are formulated, why they continue, and what can be done to resolve them. This aspect of the problem-solving method can be useful regardless if the counselor and client use the four-step method as an intervention tool.

When using the problem-solving method, the counselor is encouraged to be sensitive to issues of diversity and to adjust the approach to the unique and emerging needs of clients. An overview of the four steps of the problem-solving method is now provided.

Step 1: Identifying the Inefficient Approach

The process of identifying the inefficient approach parallels that of Glasser's (1965) reality therapy and its focus on the client's current behavior ("What are you doing? Is it working for you?"). Together counselors and clients identify the most salient issues that appear to interfere with their counseling goals. For example, if the long-term counseling goal is to have more meaning in life and the person is doing a great amount of self-doubting, depression could be the most salient issue blocking movement toward enhanced meaning in life. The next step is to add the suffix *ing* to the short-term goal (i.e., *depressing*) to help clients realize the control they have over their behavior (i.e., they can choose to engage in depressing and must accept responsibility for that choice).

Step 2 : Exploring the Psychology of Use

Step 2 uses Adlerian concepts and procedures and is the most important part of the problem-solving method. It attempts to explore the purposes and goals to determine the psychology of use of the client's inefficient approach.

From the perspective of the psychology of use, all behavior—including problematic behavior—has a purpose or use. Nystul (1995) explored the origins of problematic behavior as follows.

> Nystul (1994a) noted that many problem behaviors (such as angering) originate in childhood as a means of meeting one's basic needs. Unfortunately, what works in childhood may not work in adolescence or adulthood. Nystul suggested that the concept of private logic can be used to understand why it is so difficult for people to change. Private logic consists of thoughts that originate in childhood and continue into adulthood and serve to justify the behavior associated with meeting basic needs (Dreikurs, 1973). Unfortunately, the private logic may trick people into believing that the thoughts and behaviors that were useful to meet basic needs as children are required to meet basic needs as adolescents and adults. (Nystul, 1995, p. 298)

Counselors can explore the psychology of use and private logic by exploring their clients' early memories. This can involve saying to clients, "I'm sure the depressing [or whatever] must have met some of your needs once, or you wouldn't be doing it. I wonder when it all began, when you first remember engaging in depressing?" As the counselor and client explore these early memories together, they can attempt to identify what needs were met. Maslow's (1968) hierarchy of needs can be used to facilitate this process.

The process of exploring the psychology of use promotes several positive outcomes in counseling. First, it is encouraging and communicates respect to clients in terms of identifying the payoffs associated with inefficient approaches. This is in contrast to other counseling methods that point out clients' basic mistakes (Adlerian) or irrational ideas (rational–emotive therapy). When clients' inefficient approaches are categorized in such negative terms as these, clients can feel discouraged and may develop resistance to the counseling process. The psychology of use perspective is more positive in nature in that it seeks to enhance the counseling relationship.

Another advantage of exploring the psychology of use is that it promotes normalizing versus pathologicalizing in the counseling process. Mosak (1991) noted that contemporary psychology focuses too much on what is wrong and not enough on what is right with people. From the perspective of the psychology of use and private logic, it is predictable and normal to expect clients to behave in ways they believe meet their needs. Normalizing has a positive effect in counseling in that it promotes a strengths perspective and avoids tendencies toward self-criticism, catastrophicizing, and other negative tendencies (Nystul, 1994b).

Step 3: Enhancing the Client's Motivation

Clients typically desire change and seek out counseling to facilitate growth and development. Unfortunately, there can be many obstacles to the change process undermining the client's resolve and motivation. Some of the obstacles to change and potential solutions are as follows.

The Client Is Discouraged.   A discouraged client often lacks the necessary energy and enthusiasm to follow through and work toward goal resolution. One of the most powerful tools counselors can use is the Adlerian process of encouragement (Dinkmeyer, Dinkmeyer, & Sperry, 1987). Encouragement helps clients believe in themselves and develop self-efficacy and the "can-do" spirit. Encouragement creates a positive self-fulfilling prophecy that may provide the necessary momentum to move a client toward goal resolution. Counselors can be encouraging in a number of ways such as the use of encouraging statements (e.g., "You can do it"). Perhaps the most important facet of encouragement lies in the overall communication of optimism and belief in the human potential that all people have. A counselor who communicates these messages to a client conveys hope that motivates a client to keep trying and persevering (Nystul, 1985).

The Private Logic Resists Change.   Motivation modification is an Adlerian concept that attempts to explore underlying thoughts that motivate movement toward inefficient approaches to life (Nystul, 1985, 1995). Central to this process is the role that private logic plays in generating one's inefficient approach. The private logic is to a large degree formulated during early childhood and remains fairly stable throughout life (Nystul, 1995). It therefore can be tricked into thinking that what worked as a child must work as an adult.

Unfortunately, the primitive interpersonal tools that children tend to rely on to meet their needs often have a paradoxical effect on need gratification in adulthood. When clients become aware of the paradoxical effect of their inefficient approaches, they may be more willing to let go of that approach. This in turn will tend to maximize motivation and minimize resistance to the counseling process.

Cost–Gain Analysis.   Homans' (1962) social exchange theory evolved from social psychology and is an attempt to understand human motivation. This theory suggests that people will be motivated to change if they perceive they will gain more from the change than they will lose or if it will cost them more if they do not change. The field of addiction counseling will attest to the significance of this logic in that people tend to be motivated to give up drinking (or whatever) when they believe it is costing them more than they are getting from it.

Step 3 of the problem-solving approach suggests that a cost–gain analysis can be useful in helping clients understand how much their inefficient approach is costing them and what they can gain with giving it up. As counselors conduct a cost–gain analysis, they will often identify one very significant cost that is referred to as the *paradoxical point*. The paradoxical point is the point in a person's life when an efficient approach becomes an inefficient one (or, as Glasser (1965) would say, a behavior that is no longer working for them). For example, depressing as a child can work by getting attention and fostering love and belonging needs. As an adult, depressing will tend to have the opposite (or paradoxical effect) on meeting basic needs (e.g., depressing can isolate a person from his or her family). Once clients become aware of the paradoxical effect of their inefficient approach, they will tend to be very motivated to give up that approach.

Step 4: Developing a More Efficient Approach

Step 4 involves helping clients develop a new approach that meets the needs identified in Step 2 without the cost associated with their inefficient approach. Step 4 is sensitive to the reality that change is a very difficult process for people and that interventions must attempt to minimize inherent tendencies to resist change. Several factors that are associated with resistance to change should be considered.

Change Is Maximized When It Is Consistent with the Self-Concept.   Hamachek (1990) noted that the self-concept tends to remain consistent over a person's life span, and people tend to behave in a manner that is consistent with their self-image. Change may therefore be resisted when it is perceived as a threat to one's self-image and maximized when it is not a threat to the self-image. Thus, interventions and associated change processes should complement the client's self-image as much as possible. Glasser's (1976) concept of positive addiction reflects this type of process. For example, a person with an addictive personality who abuses drugs can substitute marathon running for drug abuse. At times it may also be necessary to enhance the self-concept, such as when a person has low self-esteem. Encouragement can play a major role in helping a client have a more positive self-concept and sense of self-efficacy.

Appropriate Goal Recognition Is Necessary for Lasting Change.   It is important to work on goals that clients are committed to and that are developmentally appropriate. In addition, interventions should be directed at both accomplishing counseling goals and addressing the underlying problem etiology associated with the goals. This will foster an in-depth, comprehensive change process and will minimize tendencies toward symptom substitution and relapse. Exploring the psychology of use and private logic are examples of in-depth approaches to psychotherapy, as they involve exploring unconscious processes that can be associated with resistance to counseling and relapse.

Change Is Enhanced When It Is Perceived to Be Consistent with Need Gratification.   As mentioned earlier, the private logic tends to be tricked into thinking that what worked as a child is required for need gratification as an adult. Asking clients to give up or change what worked as a child (e.g., depressing) may be resisted, because it is perceived to conflict with need gratification. To overcome this tendency toward resistance, efficient approaches must meet the needs that were satisfied by the inefficient approach without the costs.

Change Is Facilitated by a Sense of Control.   Glasser (1986) stressed the role of control in psychological functioning. According to his theory, feeling a sense of control is positively correlated with mental health and productivity. Glasser's technique of adding *ing* to the new approach can be used (as was done in Step 1) to help clients become aware of the choices they have in exercising their new approach. For example, if a new approach is to be more optimistic, the client can think in terms of engaging in his or her optimizing approach.

Selecting a New Approach

The actual process of selecting a new approach involves picking something the client feels comfortable doing that can modify or replace the inefficient approach. For example, a client can replace depressing with optimizing. The counselor can then help the client learn the thoughts, feelings, and behaviors necessary to be successful in the new approach. It is also important (when possible) to develop an approach that is consistent with the client's self-concept in order to minimize resistance. For example, if a client wants to be perceived as outgoing, then the new approach should incorporate outgoing characteristics.

Adler's techniques of acting "as if" and catching oneself (see Mosak, 1989) can be used to facilitate Step 4. Acting "as if" can involve having clients waking up in the morning and telling themselves they will spend the day acting as if they are an optimizing person. This technique helps promote a self-fulfilling prophecy regarding the use of their new approach. Catching oneself involves identifying signals associated with one's problematic behavior (such as feelings of sadness when one is depressing) and catching oneself before one goes too far with depressing and develops a full-fledged "case of the blues."

☐ Case Example

The following is a case example illustrating the four-step problem-solving method. John was a 45-year-old Anglo who was self-referred to a community mental health clinic. He had a PhD in mathematics and was a professor at a major university. It was his third university position; he had been fired from the previous two positions for angry outbursts with his department heads over trivial issues like not getting enough travel money for conferences.

John's presenting issue during the first counseling session was that he was unhappy in his work and worried that his wife was going to leave him because of "his immature temper tantrums." John's tantrums involved yelling and screaming and on one occasion throwing dishes and breaking them on the kitchen wall while his children were in the kitchen. John said "the flying-dish episode" had pushed his wife to the brink of a separation or divorce because now she was worried about the children's safety.

John stated he was worried about losing his current job and his marriage. He was aware that his tantrums were immature and self-defeating. He had tried to stop, but said his anger came out in uncontrollable rages. He did not know what to do and turned to counseling as a last-ditch effort to get his life together. John seemed mildly depressed during our initial interview but did not appear to have a recognized mental disorder according to the *Diagnostic and Statistical Manual of Mental Disorders* (4th ed.; American Psychiatric Association, 1994). At the end of the first session, John and I agreed to have improved interpersonal relations as his long-term counseling goal and anger management and communication skills as short-term counseling goals. During the second session, the four-step problem-solving method was selected as an intervention strategy to work on anger management. I began by orientating the client to the approach by giving him a brief overview of the four steps that were outlined in a handout that I gave him. I also suggested that in time he could learn to use the four-step method to become his own self-therapist to resolve problems as they emerged. The client seemed quite delighted that he could learn how to use a tool to put himself in control of his mental health. We then proceeded to work through the four-step model over a period of two months for one session per week.

Step 1: Identifying the Inefficient Approach

It was quite obvious that angering was the inefficient approach that seemed to play a central role in John's interpersonal relations problems. He was intrigued by the idea of adding *ing* to *anger*, because it suggested that he could have some control over his anger (i.e., it was something he was choosing to do and he needed to be aware of his choices). John wanted to believe he had control over his anger versus holding on to his previous contention that anger was part of some uncontrollable rage.

Step 2: Exploring the Psychology of Use

Step 2 involved exploring the psychology of use associated with John's angering problem. This was accomplished by telling him, "I'm sure that your angering has a purpose or use or you would not be doing it. I wonder when it all began, when you first remember engaging in angering." As he shared several early memories, we began to gain insight into the etiology of John's angering.

John's early memories (EMs) were as follows.

EM 1. I was a second-grade student in a new school. I had no friends. One day I got in a fight during recess. I hit the other guy on the nose and blood went everywhere. A bunch of children started to circle around us and began saying "Wow! That guy sure is tough." I finally felt like I was somebody. The next day several kids wanted to be my friend.

EM 2. I was around 5 years old. I remember playing soldiers with a friend who came over to the house. We traded some army men, and he tried to gyp me. I got mad and started yelling at him and he left my house, and I got my way with the trade.

EM 3. It was my birthday. I was 11. Some idiot shoved my girlfriend, Ann, into the rose bushes. She cried, and I went berserk beating the heck out of that fool. Ann gave me a big kiss for my gallantry. I felt 10 feet tall.

A review of John's early memories showed him using his angering to meet his basic needs of love and belonging and self-esteem. I explained to John that it was not surprising that he used angering during his formative years to solve his problems. I noted that children do not tend to have sophisticated tools to deal with conflict situations. They rely on more basic primitive methods such as "If you have my toy, then I'm going to take it back." This insight normalized John's angering, and he became less defensive about it.

Step 3: Enhancing the Client's Motivation

Throughout my counseling with John, I tried to be encouraging and convey hope and a belief in his ability to be successful in his reaching his goal of improved interpersonal relations. That positive energy seemed to create momentum to help us move toward goal resolution.

I also helped John understand the role private logic plays in creating resistance to change. The concept of private logic helped John understand why adults hold on to such immature methods of handling things. He began to see how impressionistic events such as those reflected in his early memories could have a lasting effect on his private logic and trick him into thinking he must engage in angering to meet his basic needs. John's insight into his private logic had an encouraging and normalizing effect on him. He began to understand why he continued to act so immaturely even though he knew it was childlike to throw tantrums. He was also encouraged because he believed that awareness of these unconscious processes was one step toward overcoming them.

We went on to conduct a cost–gain analysis. This involved reviewing what his angering was costing him and what he would gain by giving it up. Costs included health problems, such as increased problems with high blood pressure and tendency toward strokes, impaired interpersonal relations (especially in relation to family and work), and depression. A major cost (paradoxical point) was that angering was undermining his need gratification associated with love and belonging and self-esteem. This was exemplified by his wife's threatening to leave him "if he didn't grow up and control his anger." Gains associated with developing a more efficient approach included meeting his needs without identified costs, enhanced self-control and self-efficacy, and learning a problem-solving approach he could use to become his own self-therapist to deal with future problems. John seemed especially motivated to give up his angering when he realized it was having a paradoxical effect on his need gratification.

Step 4: Developing a More Efficient Approach

Step 4 involved helping John identify a new approach that could meet his love, belonging, and self-esteem needs without the costs identified in Step 2. It was decided that being more assertive would be the new approach. We added the *ing* suffix (*asserting*) to help him feel more in control of his new approach.

We also did several things to minimize resistance to change. First, we discussed his asserting approach within the context of his self-concept. John had a need to be perceived as a "nice guy" so that had to be factored in to his assertiveness training. It was decided that he would be politely assertive.

Second, we used Glasser's (1976) concept of positive addiction by using what was positive in his old approach (angering) to formulate his new approach (asserting). It was determined that angering was a very focused activity that got attention from others. These positive characteristics were incorporated into his asserting (i.e., it also would be a focused, attention-getting activity).

I then helped John develop the thoughts, feelings, and behaviors necessary to be successful in his new approach. This approach involved several techniques and procedures from gestalt therapy, cognitive behavior therapy, and the Adlerian techniques of acting "as if" and catching oneself. Standard procedures in assertion training were also used.

By the sixth session, John was using his new approach on a regular basis—starting each day with his acting "as if" exercise to get him mentally focused for success. John had some minor setbacks with his angering over the next couple of weeks. By the 8th week into counseling, John felt he had sufficient control over his problem and was able to catch himself before he went too far with his angering. In addition, John was able to begin using his four-step problem-solving method to address other problems such as dealing with perfectionism.

☐ Summary and Conclusion

This chapter provided an overview of a four-step problem-solving model that integrated Adler's and Glasser's theories. It has the advantage of being both a time-limited, solution-focused method and an approach that generates an in-depth analysis of unconscious processes (e.g., private logic and psychology of use). Other advantages include a built-in mechanism to foster client motivation and minimize tendencies toward resistance to change and relapse. The approach can be used with individuals as young as 6 years old to help with such problems as stalling in the classroom or fighting on the playground. It can also be used informally to provide another dimension to conceptualizing the counseling process without actually going into the four steps with a client. For example, the counselor could enhance relationship building and assessment by communicating respect and normalizing through an accurate understanding of the client's private logic and psychology of use.

As in all approaches, the problem-solving method must be used within the context of a multicultural society sensitive to environmental forces that can have an impact on human growth and development. The problem-solving method should therefore be used in conjunction with other procedures to address the unique and emerging needs of clients.

☐ References

Adler, A. (1969). *The practice and theory of individual psychology*. Paterson, NJ: Littlefield-Adams.
American Psychiatric Association. (1994). *Diagnostic and statistical manual of mental disorders* (4th ed.). Washington, DC: Author.
Anderson, J. R. (1993). Problem solving and learning. *American Psychologist, 48*, 35–44.
Carlson, J. (1991). On beyond Adler. *Individual Psychology, 47*, 2.
Corey, G. (1996). *Theory and practice of counseling and psychotherapy* (5th ed.). Pacific Grove, CA: Brooks/Cole.
Dinkmeyer, D., Dinkmeyer, D, Jr., & Sperry, L. (1987). *Adlerian counseling and psychotherapy*. Columbus, OH: Merrill.
Dinkmeyer, D., & Dreikurs, R. (1963). *Encouraging children to learn*. Englewood Cliffs, NJ: Prentice Hall.
Dixon, D. N. & Glover, J. A. (1984). *Counseling: A problem solving approach*. New York: Wiley.
Dreikurs, R. (1950). *Fundamentals of Adlerian psychology*. Chicago: Alfred Adler Institute.
Dreikurs, R. (1973). The private logic. In H. H. Mosak (Ed.), *Alfred Adler: His influence on psychology today* (pp. 19–32). Park Ridge, NJ: Noyes Press.
Ellis, A. (1989). Rational emotive therapy. In R. J. Corsini & D. Wedding (Eds.), *Current psychotherapies* (4th ed., pp. 197–240). Itasca, IL: F. E. Peacock.
Forman, B. D., & Crandall, J. E. (1991). Social interest, irrational beliefs, and identity. *Individual Psychology, 47*, 141–149.
Gamble, C. W., & Watkins, C. E. (1983). Combining the child discipline approaches of Alfred Adler and William Glasser: A case study. *Individual Psychology, 39*, 156–164.
Glasser, W. (1965). *Reality theory*. New York: Harper & Row.
Glasser, W. (1976). *Positive addiction*. New York: Harper & Row.
Glasser, W. (1986). *The control therapy—reality therapy workbook*. Canoga Park, CA: Institute for Reality Therapy.
Hamachek, D. (1990). *Psychology in teaching, learning, and growth* (4th ed.). Boston: Allyn & Bacon.
Homans, G. C. (1962). *Sentiments and activities*. New York: Free Press of Glencoe.
Kanfer, F. H., & Busemeyer, J. R. (1982) The use of problem solving and decision making in behavior therapy. *Clinical Psychology Review, 2*, 239–266.
Maslow, A. H. (1968). *Toward a psychology of being* (2nd ed.). New York: Van Nostrand Reinhold.
McClam, T., & Woodside, M. (1994). *Problem solving in the helping professions*. Pacific Grove, CA: Brooks/Cole.
Mosak, H. H. (1989). Adlerian psychotherapy. In R. J. Corsini & D. Wedding (Eds.), *Current psychotherapies* (4th ed., pp. 65–118). Itasca, IL: F. E. Peacock.

Mosak, H. H. (1991). Where have all the normal people gone? *Individual Psychology, 47,* 437–446.

Nystul, M. S. (1985). The use of motivation modification techniques in Adlerian psychotherapy. *Individual Psychology, 41,* 489–495.

Nystul, M. S. (1994a). Increasing the positive orientation to Adlerian psychotherapy: Redefining the concept of "basic mistakes." *Individual Psychology, 50,* 271–278.

Nystul, M. S. (1994b). Normalizing and structuring approaches in the counseling process. *Counseling and Human Development, 26*(8), 11–12.

Nystul, M. S. (1995). A problem solving approach to counseling: Integrating Adler's and Glasser's theories. *Elementary School Guidance and Counseling, 29,* 297–302.

Whitehouse, D. G. (1984). Adlerian antecedents to reality therapy and control theory. *Journal of Reality Therapy, 3,* 10–14.

CHAPTER

Mark S. Carich
Carole Metzger

Hypnotherapy

Hypnosis and hypnotherapy have always been controversial subjects within Adlerian circles. Adler (1935) and Dreikurs (1963) maintained that hypnosis, hypnotherapy, or trance work were "taboo" practices. This was primarily based on the issues of power, control, and interpersonal manipulation, along with mystical connotations of hypnosis. This can be quite understandable given the last half of the 19th century and first half of the 20th century. However, the knowledge base since then has grown. In the modern era, thanks to the pioneering work of Milton H. Erickson, David Cheek, William Kroger, Ernest Hilgard, and others, the mystical aspects of hypnosis have been thoroughly explored and demystified. Excellent resources on hypnotic behavior and trance work include the American Society of Clinical Hypnosis (ASCH; 1973), Crasilneck and Hall (1975), Edgette and Edgette (1995), Hammond (1988, 1990), Kroger (1977), Rossi (1993), Wester and Smith (1984), Yapko (1984), and Zilbergeld, Edelstein, and Araoz (1986). This modern work has lead to new and different understandings about hypnosis and the hypnotic relationships between the subject and operator. Thus, hypnosis and hypnotherapy are no longer viewed as magical behaviors facilitated by deviant manipulation.

Hypnosis has been regarded as a very useful tool in psychotherapy and Adlerian therapy (Carich, 1990a, 1990b). This chapter presents a neo-Adlerian approach to hypnotherapy. The case study demonstrating the approach is an unusual one. The case study involves the use of hypnotic approaches with a sex offender. This is unusual because hypnosis is not commonly used with sex offenders. Even though most sex offenders are very dissociative in nature and can be very good hypnotic subjects, mainstream sex-offender treatment professionals do not recognize the value of hypnosis.

Hypnotic interventions are usually not the entire treatment but are used within a treatment regimen. There is a large body of literature supporting hypnotic-oriented brief therapy based on Ericksonian approaches (Haley, 1973; Havens, 1985). Typically, for Adlerians, hypnotherapy consists of techniques integrated into the treatment process.

☐ An Overview of Hypnosis

To gain a basic understanding of hypnotherapy, a brief overview of hypnosis is provided.

Definition

Hypnosis has been defined a number of ways over the years by many experts in the field (ASCH, 1973; Carich, 1990a, 1990b; Edgette & Edgette, 1995; Hammond, 1988, 1990; Yapko, 1984). For the purposes of this chapter, hypnosis is defined as a dissociated state or an altered state of awareness. The altered state is based on the subject's fixated attention. More specifically, the "hypnotic subject" is totally engrossed and highly focused on specific stimuli to the point of being oblivious to immediate surroundings. The stimuli may be either overt or covert. This is recognized by most leading authorities in hypnosis as requiring an altered state of awareness using unconscious processes.

The unconscious levels of awareness are best viewed as a process (Carich, 1990a, 1990b, 1994b). The consciousness continuum can be arbitrarily divided into at least three levels: immediate conscious awareness, subconscious or preconscious (memory processes outside of current awareness but available to conscious awareness), and unconscious processes (out of awareness or hidden processes). It is a hypothetical construct used to describe a dynamic set of processes flowing in a stream of awareness ranging from immediate awareness to away from the center of immediate awareness. Consciousness and unconsciousness form a holistic, complementary relationship between left- and right-brain hemispheric functioning. The unconscious processes involve the state-dependent memory learning and behavioral system (referred to as SDML & B; Rossi, 1993). Rossi postulated these processes as fundamental aspects of encoding, decoding, perceiving, and interpreting of information. The SDML & B system and/or the unconscious involves both dissociative and/or hypnotic behaviors described below. This view stems from the work of Adler, Erickson, Rossi, and Jung.

Hypnotic behaviors essentially stem from unconscious right-brain hemispheric functioning. A range of hypnotic behaviors include the following: daydreaming; fantasy; becoming absorbed, totally focused, and concentrated on selected stimuli to the point of being oblivious to immediate surroundings (i.e., getting lost in a book, TV program, song on the radio, movie); catalepsy (or immobilized rigid muscular behaviors, suspended limbs); heightened suggestibility; state of relaxation; and regressing back in time (e.g., pondering memories; ASCH, 1973; Carich, 1990a, 1990b; Edgette & Edgette, 1995; Erickson, Rossi, & Rossi, 1976; Hammond, 1988, 1990; Kroger, 1977; Lankton & Lankton, 1983). Hypnotic behaviors are natural states of behavior that occur in everyday life. Rossi (1993) has connected the concept of the SDLM & B system located in the hypothalamic limbic system of the brain as the central processing areas of dissociation and trance states.

There are a number of myths concerning hypnosis. Several key myths are summarized below:

- Hypnosis is unnatural and evil (fact: Hypnosis is natural, useful, and healthy)
- Subject loses all control in the trance (fact: Subject is in full control)

- Subject will do anything in trance (fact: Subjects will not violate their value system)
- Subjects are weak and gullible (fact: Subjects are not weak or gullible, as they are in full control)
- Subjects are prone to divulge secrets (fact: Subjects will only divulge what they are comfortable with sharing)
- Only a certain kind of person can be hypnotized (fact: Most, if not all, people experience trance throughout the day)
- Trance is a sleep state (fact: Trance states have their own distinct physiological characteristics)
- Trance equals therapy (fact: Trance is a set of interventions used in the therapeutic process; Carich, 1990a; Hammond, 1988, 1990; Yapko, 1984)

☐ Adlerian Connections to Hypnotherapy

There are a number of Adlerian connections to hypnotherapy. The mere fact of using hypnotic techniques goes beyond Adler. However, Adlerian tactics and concepts are connected to hypnotherapy. These connections include reframing, metaphors imagery, early recollections, guiding fictional goals, the "as if" technique, and encouragement (Carich, 1990b).

Adler's original tactics intervene at various levels of awareness. Hypnotic interventions enhance the above tactics by directly accessing unconscious processing. However, it is important to note that the Adlerian techniques often create spontaneous trance states with clients. Thus, these interventions—without the formal trance protocol—use unconscious processes and create a hypnotic effect. Each Adlerian connection is briefly discussed below.

Reframing is commonly used in many psychotherapies. Adler called it *prosocial redefinition*. Reframing is the changing of one's perceptual view or frame of reference from a dysfunctional one to a functional frame (Mozdzierz, Maechitelli, & Lisiecki, 1976; Watzlawick, Weakland, & Fisch, 1974). Successful reframing involves changing the client's perception at an emotional and unconscious level. Thus, reframing without formal trance usually involves some spontaneous-level trance state. Used in hypnotherapy, it can be very powerful.

Likewise, imagery uses and accesses right hemispheric unconscious processes. Imagery is the covert process of what we refer to as mentally envisioning a scene, event, person, place, thing, scenario, stimulus, or response. The most effective imagery uses all sensory modalities (Aroaz, 1982). This method goes beyond Adler's original conception. Imagery is one of the central processes of most hypnotherapy. It is considered a direct link or access modality to unconscious processes (Lankton & Lankton, 1983; Rossi, 1993).

Another related tactic is the use of metaphors. Adler first described using metaphors in therapy years ago (Ansbacher & Ansbacher, 1956; Carich, 1989b; Mosak, 1989). The definition and use of metaphors has been tremendously expanded since Adler's original use (Erickson, Rossi, & Rossi, 1976; Haley, 1973; Hammond, 1988, 1990; Havens, 1985; Lankton & Lankton, 1983; Yapko, 1984).

Metaphors are symbolic representations of the meaning of one element to another. There are many different forms, such as word plays, stories, puns, jokes, and images. Metaphors are easy methods or ways to communicate therapeutic messages at both conscious and unconscious levels. Quite often, metaphors bypass defensive structures and therapeutically affect the client. This involves the direct and indirect use of unconscious processes. Metaphors create and use spontaneous trance states and hypnotic effect.

The techniques of collecting early recollections (ERs) described by Olson (1979), Mosak (1989), and others are another link to unconscious processes. This was initially designed to access or collect the client's earliest memories. Age regression is the unconscious version of collecting ERs and is based on accessing memories and memory states by recalling specific events while in a trance state (Carich, 1990b; Rossi, 1993; Rossi & Cheek, 1988). As the client relieves the situation, these memories can be fully or partially reexperienced. The fully reexperienced type of age regression is called revivification; the partially reexperienced type is called partial regression. Partial regression consists of the client dissociating self from the experience, as a hidden observer. This is an extension of Adler's use of ERs. The use of ERs quite often creates spontaneous trance states while the client recalls memories. In hypnotherapy, memories are recalled directly from unconscious processes.

The "as if" technique was based on the concepts of guiding fictions or fictional goals (Ansbacher & Ansbacher, 1956; Carich, 1989b, 1991). This technique was based on Adler's philosophical notions of a futuristically oriented psychology. This technique was expanded to include the hypnotic techniques of pseudo–time distortion and age progression (Carich, 1990b, 1991). Pseudo–time distortion is the deliberately induced distortion or confusion of time. Age progression consists of instructing the client to experience his or her future at specific ages. Applications include helping the client develop resources for future use by projecting the client into the future, behavioral rehearsal, and enhancing coping responses to specific events that may occur in the future. These techniques were originally developed by Milton Erickson (Havens, 1985).

A combination of these techniques are presented in the case study. The tactics listed above are used within a specific type of structure. The structure is presented below.

☐ Stages of Hypnotherapy

There are a number of ways to conduct hypnotherapy. For example, there are formal or direct approaches and informal or indirect ones. Direct approaches involve a formal hypnotic protocol or structured induction. Formal trance work is based on using a structured protocol to induce trance states and work on issues. Informal trance work involves a nonstructured (informal) trance induction. This unstructured approach involves indirectly facilitating trance states and/or using naturalistic trance states toward therapeutic goals. Informal trance work occurs throughout most psychotherapy sessions. We use a structure consisting of specific stages of a hypnotherapeutic session (Carich, 1990a). These six stages include the following: (a) developing treatment plans and trance preparation, (b) trance induction, (c) hypnotic depth, (d) problem exploration by means of subconscious questioning, (e) working or intervention stage, and (f) reorientation or exiting stage.

It is assumed that the clinician has developed a rapport with the client before trance work. Each stage is discussed below.

Trance Preparation

In traditional and formal trance work, it is important to prepare the client for the hypnotic experience and outcome. More specifically, the myths of hypnosis are discussed, along with different hypnotic phenomena. It is important to discuss fears of hypnosis, expectations, and to assess fear–phobic responses in general (i.e., fear of woods, beaches, water, flying, etc.) It is important to avoid using metaphors that evoke fear, unless the fear is targeted in treatment. In this stage, a deeper rapport can be established. Specific treatment plans and interventions are developed. This includes developing interventions and hypnotic scripts.

Trance Induction

Trance induction is the facilitation of a trance state or experience. As discussed earlier, there are two different basic forms of induction: direct and indirect. Direct inductions involve a formal protocol based on specific scripts. Indirect approaches involve using metaphors, spontaneous trance states and/or hypnotic behaviors, word plays, and so forth. We use formal inductions and also use spontaneous trance behavior. Hypnotic inductions have been discussed in the literature (e.g., ASCH, 1973; Edgette & Edgette, 1995; Hammond, 1988, 1990; Kroger, 1977; Zilbergeld et al., 1986).

Some basic principles of trance induction include the following: (a) use of a low, soothing, slow, monotone voice; (b) repetition of phrases; (c) voice inflection and emphasis on selected words; (d) use of flexibility in choices built into suggestions and messages (such as "and allow yourself," "you may"); (e) use of the client's and contextual behaviors to facilitate trance experiences; (f) narrowing the focus of the client's concentration and attention span to include specific internal and/or external stimuli; and (g) using naturalistic unconscious, hypnotic behaviors.

Hypnotic Depth

Hypnotic depth refers to the degree that the client achieves a complete level of relaxation or trance state. The necessity of achieving deep levels of hypnotic trance for hypnotherapy is a controversial one. The range extends from light trances to deep somnambulistic trances (ASCH, 1973). In somnambulistic trances, a variety of hypnotic behavior can be used (Edgette & Edgette, 1995). It appears that not everyone has the ability to reach somnambulistic levels. We believe that it is important to reach a sufficiently deep state of relaxation in order to bypass various defensive structures.

Problem Exploration

The fourth stage is problem exploration through subconscious questioning. More information concerning the client's problems can be ascertained in trance states. Questions exploring the client's problems are concretely and simply stated (unless the desired effect requires less clear and precise language). Typically, ideomotor or dynamic behaviors are used as a form of communication (Rossi, 1993; Rossi & Cheek, 1988; Wick, 1986). These are nonverbal, involuntary unconscious behaviors elicited from the client while in trance. The therapist establishes one set of responses for "yes" and a different set of responses for "no." Responses usually occur through micro finger movements. Clients may also verbalize responses. However, these responses tend to be slow and choppy in nature. There is not a specific time frame set for the problem-solving stage; a few minutes to entire sessions may be devoted to subconscious questioning.

Working Stage

The working stage consists of using selected interventions to address and resolve the client's presenting and secondary issues. Both hypnotic and posthypnotic suggestions are given. Posthypnotic suggestions are therapeutic prescriptions to do something in the future (after the session) or therapeutic messages enacted after the session. There are a variety of metaphors, interventions, scripts, directives, suggestions, and so forth (Crasilneck & Hall, 1975; Edgette & Edgette, 1995; Haley 1973; Hammond, 1988, 1990; Havens, 1985; Havens & Walter, 1989; Wester & Smith, 1984). The tactics previously discussed in this chapter are typically used in hypnotherapy. These tactics are packaged and integrated with direct and indirect suggestions, along with intersession hypnotic and posthypnotic suggestions.

Exiting Stage

The last stage is exiting the trance state. In this stage, the client is reoriented to the immediate surroundings, as the trance state is formally terminated. The outcome is monitored.

☐ Case Study and Analysis

This case study was selected because of its uniqueness. The case involves the use of hypnosis or trance work with a sex offender who was soon to leave an intensive institutional treatment program. The offender was released several weeks after this session. The session was taped and is fully transcribed below.

The uniqueness of this chapter and case study is the combination of hypnotherapy and contemporary sex-offender treatment. The vast majority of leading hypnotherapists do not treat sex offenders. The converse is also true; the leading sex-offender treatment authorities do not use hypnosis. Thus, the uniqueness of this case study is the hybrid of using hypnosis as one set of interventions in an intensive regiment of sex-offender treatment. This hybrid is rooted in neo-Adlerian approaches.

A brief preface to sex-offender treatment is provided below. The differences between treating sex offenders and traditional clients are highlighted.

Overview of Sex-Offender Treatment

Contemporary approaches to sex-offender treatment and therapy are discussed by Carich (1996); Carich and Adkerson (1995); Haavens, Little, and Petre-Miller (1990); Knopp (1984); Laws (1989); Marshall, Laws, and Barbaree (1990); Schwartz and Cellini (1988, 1995); and Salter (1988). These are some of the most widely respected professionals in the field.

The Dissociative Aspects of Offending: The Hypnotic Connection.
Dissociative behaviors are considered unconscious right hemispheric functioning involving a sense of detachment (Carich, 1990a, 1990b, 1994b; Rossi, 1993). Dissociation is the psychological basis of hypnosis and state-dependent memory learning and behavior. Most sex offenders are very dissociative at some level (Carich, 1994a). They can make excellent hypnotic subjects by accessing various dissociative behaviors. Some of these dissociative behaviors include a sense of detachment, possible age regressions, derealization, temporarily suspended disinhibitors, dream life, fantasies or fantasy life, splitting off or compartmentalizing to an extreme, the occurrence of psychological aspects of trance states, the presence of ego state behaviors, depersonalization, spacing out, psychopathic glibness, and being oblivious to immediate surroundings. Many of these behaviors occur during the offense, as evident when offenders describe their offending.

These behaviors are indicators of and accesses to hypnotic states. The only problems stem from the various antisocial, narcissistic, and schizoidal features of hard-core sex offenders (Carich, 1996). These offenders may not trust the clinician and are overly guarded and secretive. Thus, strong rapport needs to be in place before hypnotic treatment.

Sex-Offender Treatment.
The contemporary sex-offender therapy approach differs from traditional psychotherapies. In traditional psychotherapies, voluntary clients define and set goals. This traditional therapy is often insight oriented and less directive. A psychotherapist is more supportive, empathic, and for the most part trusting and shares the control of treatment in an effort to help the client to move toward relief of his or her emotional pain. Both sex-offender therapy and traditional psychotherapy can be technically eclectic in using a wide variety of interventions to enhance treatment. In sex-offender therapy, the client usually seeks treatment because of legal requirements and the goals are set by the community to have a safer society. Thus, the client's experience is feeling that he or she is having change demanded of him or her. The sex-offender clinician is typically less empathic in the beginning of the change process and remains skeptical as well as suspicious throughout the process. Especially in the initial stages of treatment, "pain" or discomfort is induced as the offender faces the psychosocial consequences of his or her behavior, therefore using anxiety for the change process. The field is changing, however, as the use of compassion in offender treatment has reemerged.

Sex-offender treatment has strongly emphasized that there is no cure and that recovery is a lifelong process. There are interventions for the sex offender to make the choice to stop offending. The offender must continuously work toward an offending-free lifestyle by learning to make appropriate choices to not reoffend. A sexually deviant offender may have multiple patterns of victim types, paraphilias, and offense types. The teleology (purposes of behavior) of an offender is that he or she derives immense pleasure from offending and is not merely seeking sexual gratification. The most popular type of sex-offender treatment is a confrontational, cognitive–behavioral approach. This treatment usually occurs in a group setting.

The goals of the sexual perpetrator in treatment involves the offender taking 100% responsibility and accountability for his or her behavior by full disclosure; honesty; experiencing social interest in the forms of victim empathy, remorse, and compassion for others; and facing victim impact issues. Another major goal is for the offender to change his or her dysfunctional lifestyle behaviors. These offending behaviors are rooted in cognitive distortions. Distortions have to be addressed and challenged in order to change ingrained maladaptive belief systems.

The "hard-core" sex offender—that person with extensive antisocial and narcissistic, borderline, or schizoidal characteristics or lifestyle behaviors (Carich & Adkerson, 1995)—is different from the typical client who seeks psychotherapy. The approach for sex-offender treatment requires change from the traditional psychotherapy approaches in setting the structure for the client and treatment milieu. The therapist must know the background of the client's deviant behavior. This knowledge may be obtained by using collateral information (police reports, clinical historical documents, current/past observations, interviews) as well as traditional social history and clinical interview information. The goal is to focus on the deviant problems along with contributing factors rather than helping the client to see his or her strengths, as is often done in traditional psychotherapies. The sexual perpetrator many times has "tuned out" his or her feelings. Therefore, the treatment goal is to connect thoughts and behaviors with the client's feelings.

The sex-offender treatment requires using repetition for the client to learn new ways of thinking, feeling, and behaving, which will create a new belief system and values in the client's life. The clinician assumes the role of a strict teacher rather than nurturer. The therapy approach for the sexual perpetrator has many key areas to be addressed, including, but not limited to, 100% responsibility, cognitive restructuring, reconditioning to enhance appropriate arousal, experiential processes, victim empathy, social skills, family work, relapse prevention skills, and management of deviant behavior as well as arousal, anger, and stress. It is of the utmost importance for the sex offender to change at all levels of awareness and to be integrated in a new lifestyle.

Sex-offender therapy is a young field and is open to change incorporating traditional approaches. The case study presented below shows a unique blending of techniques and therapies to achieve the high standard of treatment that is required to achieve the behavioral changes in a sex offender and, ultimately, to prevention relapse. The assault cycle is the offender's modality of carrying out his or her sexual deviant behavior. It is the perpetrator's patterns of perverted sexual behavior. The assault cycle includes the assault and relapse process. Cycle behaviors include enablers, defenses, distortions (i.e., denial, justify, secrets), other disowning behaviors, disinhibitors, cues and risk factors, and so forth. The cycle(s) may change over time. It is held that at certain points in the offender's life, he or she may not be in a cycle. A tool that can be used to prevent lapse is interrupting the cycle. The actual client is the safety of society along with the sex offender. The frequently used slogan in sex-offender therapy is "No More Victims!"

☐ Case Study

The client in this case study was a sex offender named John (not his real name). He had spent 10 years in an intensive sex-offender group therapy treatment program. This was his second incarceration for sexual offenses. John was in his late 30s, divorced, with a number of issues. Most of his core issues centered around acceptance; feeling stupid and inadequate; inferiority in general and surrounding sex, education, and so forth; poor self-worth; lack of self-confidence. John had multiple victim types, victims, and offense types. For example, he had raped adult women (several victims), flashed teenage and adult women, and molested several boys. He was a drug abuser and an alcoholic.

As a child, a friend of John's family attempted to molest him. In his family of origin, he was verbally and physically abused. In addition, he had learning disabilities and related problems.

As is often the case, hypnotherapy was not the entire treatment. In fact, this session was in support of intensive group therapy. The hypnotherapeutic interventions were introduced toward the very end of treatment. Because he requested the session, he was very motivated and receptive. The main thrust of this session was to wrap up 10 years of intensive group treatment by emphasizing the following therapeutic messages:

- Further instilling the recovery goal: No more victims!
- Further resolving past developmental and core issues at both conscious and unconscious levels of awareness
- Reinforcing that he was not stupid and that he could cope with his learning disabilities
- Future preparation, in terms of coping with high-risk factors
- Ego strengthening (encouragement)
- Instilling relaxation techniques
- Enhancing deviant arousal controls

The actual session was transcribed verbatim. Some wording may be fragmented and awkward, however, because hypnotic language is not geared to left hemispheric functioning.

Verbatim Hypnotic Session

Induction.   The chair can be comfortable, it's up to you to make it comfortable or not. Take a few deep breaths. Close your eyes, take some more deep breaths, real deep. Inhale, exhale, real deep. Allow yourself to relax. Notice that you are pushing out tension, with each exhale. Get more comfortably relaxed. Several more deep breaths. Listen to my voice. Notice that you can hear other voices, noises, maybe telephones, doors, people talking, footsteps, just ignore them and listen to my voice and if you decide to hear them you may deeply relax even more, drifting deeper and deeper into relaxation. Allow your muscles to relax, starting with your head muscles, simply push out any tension in your head, head muscles, the top of your head and the back of your head.

Just push tension out. Notice with each breath, you can relax even more and more, feeling even more relaxed. Allow your face to relax, your cheeks, push out any tension in your face, allow your neck to relax, pushing out any tension in your neck muscles. That's it, just simply relax. Allow your shoulders to relax, pushing out any tension in your shoulder muscles. Feel the warmth and relaxation flowing through your shoulders. Now allow your arms to relax, pushing out any tension from your shoulders to your elbows, elbows to your hands, through your fingers. Allow your wrists to relax, your hands and your fingers pushing out any tension, through your fingertips. Feel the relaxation, comfort, warmth, and relaxation. Allow your back muscles to relax, by pushing out any tension from your upper back, middle back, and lower back. Feel the warmth of relaxation, comfort. Allow your chest muscles to relax and your stomach muscles. Feel the relaxation, the comfort, push out any tension through your legs, leg muscles, from your thighs to your knees, knees to your calves. Let go any tension, just push it out. Allow your ankles to relax, and your feet to relax, pushing out any tension through out toes.

Deepening Depth. As I count from 1 to 5 allow yourself to more fully relax and drift deeper and deeper into relaxation with each count and on 5 feeling very, very relaxed and receptive. 1, drifting deeper, deeper, 2, 3, drifting, drifting, deeper, deeper, 4, drifting, drifting, 5, feeling so deeply relaxed and comfortable as I count from 1 to 7, drift even more deeper into relaxation and comfort. 1, drifting, 2, 3, drifting even deeper, deeper, 4, drifting, 5, drifting, 6, and 7. Feeling so deeply relaxed and comfortable. Just simply listen to my voice and drift deeper and deeper. That's it, drift even deeper, deeper.

Idea Motor Signaling. Notice that you can make a little movement in your finger for a yes signal in case I ask some questions, you can answer with a small movement in your finger, yes. Which finger will that be? Thank you. And for a no? Thank you.

Working Phase. Now allow yourself to remember your *commitment* and *motivation* to maintain *no more victims* and to remain victim free. Feel the intensity of that commitment. The burning desire to maintain recovery. Remember always, your commitment to recovery, during good times, bad times, tough times, stressful times and anytime that *you want no more victims*. To maintain victim free. Allow yourself to take a journey perhaps by getting on a train, to take a journey [using an ambivalent and age progression/pseudo–time distortion]. We'll call this journey a recovery journey. See yourself getting on a train, do you see yourself getting on a train? Thank you [ideomotor signal indicating yes]. Notice that you have come real far, far, and far on this journey. Notice that you will be able to experience a variety of things on this journey. One of the things is to further learn how to reduce your deviancy, notice that you can reduce your deviant arousal or urges, cravings, whatever you want to call it through imagery. One way is to simply put all of your deviancy into an ice ball. Pack it, pack it. That's it, keep packing it. Give me a signal as to when your ice ball is packed with deviancy. That's it [pause] that's it [pause] that's it. Now notice, John, that you can melt the ice ball with a welding torch. Just see yourself melting the ice ball, melting it, melting it, use the torch to melt it, watch it shrink smaller, smaller, melt, melt, shrink smaller, smaller, melting, melting, disappearing, disappearing, gone, vaporized into nothing.

Notice the relief, give me a little yes signal when that's complete [ideomotor signal]. Thank you. Notice that you can continuously melt the ice ball when necessary in your own mind. Now, John, picture a control dial in your mind and see the dial. It is a deviant control dial, or you may call it a deviant arousal control dial. With this dial you can shrink or make smaller, urges, smaller, smaller, by turning the intensity down, the intensity down. Picture the dial and turn it down lower, lower until the deviant urges are gone. Notice that you can use this dial at any time. Now on your journey, let's go back into time, on the train, the recovery train, back into time, visualize yourself experiencing the times you perceived that you were being told you were stupid and thought you were a failure and that you can tell yourself now that you're not stupid and not a failure. That *you are smart and successful* as obvious to everyone else and tell yourself over and over that you are not stupid and not a failure and that you are smart and successful. That it is OK to have a learning disability as a lot of people do and that you can learn successfully to cope with it using good coping skills instead of trying to cover it up. Just simply accept that you have a learning disability and that you can cope around it, with it as other people do. Now notice that you can take care of yourself by allowing big John hugging little John, especially in those times at school that were troubling and let me know when you see yourself hugging yourself. Yes, that's it. Notice how warm and comfortable, confident, secure that you feel. Feel the warmth, your own inner security and comfort and confidence, anytime that you have the image of yourself, hugging yourself, feel the warmth, comfort, confidence inner security, your strength, notice the strength that you have when you visualize and see an eagle, a tiger, and a bear. The strength that you have the inner security, confidence that you have when you see or visualize in your mind, a tiger, bear, in particular an eagle. Now going back into time again, notice that you need to further let go of any resentments and anger that you may place in a balloon with a basket. Just simply visualize a balloon with a basket and place all your anger, resentment, into that basket. Give me a yes signal when that is visualized. OK. Simply let go, notice that the balloon takes off goes, goes, goes, gets smaller, smaller, gone, and eventually burns up. Notice that you have the capability to forgive and let go of any resentments. Notice how good it feels to let go of past pain, hurts, and anger. Notice the burden lifted when you don't have to carry around a lot of hurt and anger, the paranoia of it all. Notice that you don't have to be paranoid. Perhaps alert and aware but not paranoid. Notice that you can take care of yourself. For example, giving yourself a hug and feeling the most inner confidence and security, comfort, and the warmth of your inner strength and allow yourself to get in touch with them. Notice that people are not perfect, that you are not perfect, people make mistakes, that's part of life. Now allow yourself to get back on the train and move forward, going to the present where you can still be confident and secure, comfortable especially any time you need to, hug yourself or visualize an eagle, tiger, or bear. Feel the warmth of the inner security confidence. Notice that you relate better with people in the present. As we go into the future, using the skills and knowledge that you have obtained in treatment and skills that you will obtain as life goes on. Now go into your future, see yourself dealing with your brothers and sisters, mother and father and significant others differently as you did in the past as adults. Notice that you can feel better about yourself in these relationships and relationships with others, whether it be supervisors in the future, parole agents, whoever. Notice that you can relax and deal with your anxieties as need be, that you can use good coping skills and function. Notice that you can use your relapse intervention skills to effectively cope with triggers, that you can become aware of triggers through cues and use interventions appropriately. Now take a moment, John, and feel better about yourself. As we go back to the present time and that you can get rid of your inferiorities and maintain your self-worth and that you don't need to victimize to maintain your worth and take a moment and reflect upon yourself.

Exit.   Now, John, as I count from 1 to 3, with each count you may feel even more secure, confident. And when I get to 3, you will open your eyes *feeling very aware, alert, relaxed, and comfortable.* With each count you will become more aware, alert, and relaxed. 1, feeling more aware, relaxed, secure and confident. 2, beginning to open your eyes. *and 3.*

Postcase Analysis

The induction was a basic relaxation protocol of pushing out tension (Carich, 1989a, 1990a). Ideomotor signaling was established to communicate directly with the client's unconscious processes.

The trance was packaged in an imagery metaphor referred to as the recovery train that goes forwards and backwards in time. The forward imagery journey train involves a combination of pseudo–time distortion hypnosis as-if and age progression techniques (Carich, 1990b, 1991). The journey backwards in time involves a partial age regression technique. With these tactics, the client was able to experience both past and future events. The past and future were tied together with new perceptions and behaviors, especially involving interactions between family members.

The most effective metaphors used were the images of an ice ball and a control dial. The control dial was discussed and described in detail by Carich (1990c). These metaphors were more ambiguously constructed, and the client was able to more fully use them. He, in fact, placed all kinds of deviancy, tension and anxiety, and negative thinking in the ice ball and melted it away. Likewise, he used the control dial tactics the same way.

In terms of the ego-strengthening or encouragement metaphors, animals were used. These animals represent strength for the client. Strength and confidence were paired or associated together. Thus, the client could visualize the selected animal and feel strong and confident. Likewise, straightforward ego-strengthening suggestions were provided.

The metaphor of placing anger and resentments in a balloon was used. The imagery of letting go of the balloon symbolically represented letting go of anger resentments. The self-nurturing imagery metaphor of "hugging self" was used to reinforce and enhance self-worth, security, independence, and so forth.

Outcome of the Session

There were several noticeable differences in the client subsequent to the hypnotherapy session. Clinical staff and program group members observed that the client was more confident and comfortable while he was presenting his assault cycle in a larger group setting. He was able to use the new skills acquired during the hypnotherapy of making choices to detach appropriately to the problematic core area of his learning disabilities.

He demonstrated this by reading a going-away card he received from the other program members. The card was presented to him during a therapeutic house meeting with 90 members and staff present, and he was not afraid to ask for help with some of the words he was having difficulty reading.

Another noticeable difference was that he stated he was more relaxed and said he was able to sleep for several nights before his release from incarceration. Before the hypnotherapy, the client was having extreme difficulty with anxiety and sleep disturbance due to his upcoming release. He also appeared and stated that he was less paranoid and yet remained conscious of his surroundings. The client held to his appropriate beliefs and values when experiencing constructive criticism or feedback without being hypervigilant and/or argumentative. He stated that he felt more secure and was able to work more quickly on intellectual matters and processes. In the past, he had demonstrated and had disclosed that he found intellectual matters cumbersome. This client perceived that he visualized internal processes, group interactions, and interpersonal relationships more clearly. He displayed an improved self-concept and high level of self-worth as a result of not being so disturbed by his learning disability and accepting his situation as being part of who he is as a whole human being.

Following his release from prison, he moved to a halfway house for aftercare treatment. He regularly corresponds with institutional staff to relate his past institutional experiences. In the most recent correspondence, his handwriting had improved considerably. The processes discussed throughout this section can be key indicators of the dynamics involved in the recovery processes.

☐ Conclusion

Adler's original concepts and theories were ground breaking at the time and are still useful. The original concepts, however, need to be adapted to contemporary theory and therapy. Even though Adler (1935) and Dreikurs (1963) disliked the use of hypnosis, Adlerian theoretical and therapeutic ideas—with some adaptation—form the basis of hypnotherapy. Thus, the material presented in this chapter on hypnotherapy builds on and adds to the pioneering work of Adler and subsequent Adlerians.

☐ References

Adler, A. (1935). Hypnosis and suggestion. *Current Psychology and Psychoanalysis, 4*(1), 25–26.

American Society of Clinical Hypnosis. (1973). *A syllabus on hypnosis and a handbook of therapeutic suggestions*. Des Plaines, IL: American Society of Clinical Hypnosis Education and Research Foundation.

Ansbacher, H., & Ansbacher, R. (Eds.). (1956). *The individual psychology of Alfred Adler*. New York: Basic Books.

Araoz, D. L. (1982). *Hypnosis and sex therapy*. New York: Brunner/Mazel.

Carich, M. S. (1989a). Push–release technique. *The American Society of Clinical Hypnosis Newsletter, 30*(3), 3.

Carich, M. S. (1989b). Variations of the "as if" technique. *Individual Psychology, 45*(4), 538–545.

Carich, M. S. (1990a). The basics of hypnosis and trance work. *Individual Psychology, 46*(4), 401–410.

Carich, M. S. (1990b). Hypnotic techniques and Adlerian constructs. *Individual Psychology, 46*(2), 165–177.

Carich, M. S. (1990c). Symbolic imagery: The dial box shrinking technique. In C. D. Hammond (Ed.), *Handbook of hypnotic suggestions and metaphors* (p. 400). New York: W. W. Norton.

Carich, M. S. (1991). The hypnotic as if technique an example of beyond Adler. *Individual Psychology, 47*(4), 509–519.

Carich, M. S. (1994a). Dissociative and hypnotic elements of the offending mode. *INMAS Newsletter, 7*(3), 10–11.

Carich, M. S. (1994b). Unconscious processes. In R. Corsini (Ed.), *Encyclopedia of psychology: Volume III* (2nd edition). New York: Wiley.

Carich, M. S. (1996). *Identifying risk behaviors of sex offenders*. Springfield, IL: Illinois Department of Corrections.

Carich, M. S., & Adkerson, D., (1995). *Adult sexual offender assessment packet*. Brandon, VT: Safer Society Press.

Crasilneck, H., & Hall, J. (1975). *Clinical hypnosis principles & applications*. New York: Grune & Stratton.

Dreikurs, R. (1963). The interpersonal relationships in hypnosis: Some fallacies in current thinking about hypnosis. *Psychiatry, 25,* 219–226.

Edgette, J. A., & Edgette, J. S. (1995). *The handbook of hypnotic phenomena in psychotherapy*. New York: Brunner/Mazel.

Erickson, M. H., Rossi, E. L., & Rossi, S. I. (1976). *Hypnotic realities: The induction of clinical hypnosis and forms of indirect suggestions*. New York: Irvington.

Haley, J. (1973). *Uncommon therapy: The psychiatric technique of Milton H. Erickson, M.D.* New York: W. W. Norton.

Hammond, C. D. (Ed.). (1988). *Hypnotic induction and suggestions: An introductory manual*. Des Plaines, IL: American Society of Clinical Hypnosis.

Hammond, C. D. (Ed.). (1990). *Handbook of hypnotic suggestions and metaphors*. New York: W. W. Norton.

Haavens, J., Little, R., & Petre-Miller, D. (1990). *Treating intellectually disturbed sex offenders: A model residential program*. Brandon, VT: Safer Society Press.

Havens, R. A. (1985). *The wisdom of Milton H. Erickson*. NY: Irvington.

Havens, R. A., & Walter, C. (1989). *Hypnotherapy scripts: A neo-Ericksonian approach to persuasive healing*. New York: Brunner/Mazel.

Knopp, F. H. (1984). *Retraining adult sex offenders: Methods & models*. Syracuse, NY: Safer Society Press.

Kroger, W. S. (1977). *Clinical and experimental hypnosis*. Philadelphia: J. B. Lippincott.

Lankton, S. R., & Lankton, C. H. (1983). *The answer within: A clinical framework of Ericksonian hypnotherapy*. New York: Brunner/Mazel.

Laws, D. R. (Ed.). (1989). *Relapse prevention with sex offenders*. New York: Guilford Press.

Marshall, W. L., Laws, D. R., & Barbaree, H. E. (Eds.). (1990). *Handbook of sexual assault*. New York: Plenum Press.

Mosak, H. (1989). Adlerian psychotherapy. In R. Corsini & D. Wedding (Eds.), *Current psychotherapies* (4th ed., pp. 51–94). Itasca, IL: F. E. Peacock.

Mozdzierz, G. J., Macchitelli, F. J., & Lisiecki, J. (1976). The paradox in psychotherapy: An Adlerian perspective. *Journal of Individual Psychology, 32,* 232–243.

Olson, H. (1979). The hypnotic retrieval of early recollections. In H. A. Olson (Ed.), *Early recollections: Their use in diagnosis and psychotherapy* (pp. 223–229). Springfield, IL: Charles C Thomas.

Rossi, E. L. (1993). *The psychobiology of mind-body healing: New concepts of therapeutic hypnosis* (rev. ed.). New York: W. W. Norton.

Rossi, E. L., & Cheek, D. B. (1988). *Mind-body therapy: Methods of ideodynamic healing in hypnosis*. New York: W. W. Norton.

Salter, A. C. (1988). *Treating child sex offenders & victims: A practical guide*. Beverly Hills, CA: Sage.

Schwartz, B. K., & Cellini, H. R. (Eds.). (1988). *A practitioner's guide to treating the incarcerated male sex offender*. Washington, DC: NIC.

Schwartz, B. K., & Cellini, H. R. (Eds.). (1995). *The sex offender: Corrections, treatment and legal practice*. Kingston, NJ: Civic Research Institute.

Watzlawick, P., Weakland, J., & Fisch, R. (1974). *Change: The principles of problem formation and problem resolution*. New York: Gardner Press.

Wester, W., & Smith, A. (Eds.). (1984). *Clinical hypnosis: A multidisciplinary approach*. St. Louis: Lippincott.

Wick, E. (1986). Ideomotor and verbal responses in hypnosis. In B. Zilbergeld, M. G. Edelstein, & D. L. Araoz (Eds.), *Hypnosis: Questions and answers*. New York: Brunner/Mazel.

Yapko, M. D. (1984). *Trance work: An introduction to clinical hypnosis and psychotherapy*. New York: Irvington.

Zilbergeld, B., Edelstein, G., & Araoz, D. L. (Eds.). (1986). *Hypnosis: Questions and answers*. New York: W. W. Norton.

CHAPTER

Michael P. Maniacci

Clinical Therapy

One of the growing movements in the practice and research of psychotherapy is integration (Norcross & Goldfried, 1992; Sperry, 1995). Attempts have been and are being made to move the multitude of different systems of psychotherapy toward more measurable, testable hypotheses and postulates. As videotape research allows clinicians the opportunity to explore not only the theory of psychotherapy but its actual practice and application, a more basic view of human change processes is beginning to emerge. Clinicians are beginning to observe and record what is actually said and done in sessions, instead of simply relying on memorial reconstructed accounts.

The origins of the psychotherapy movement can be traced to many sources, but it is fairly well accepted that the Wednesday Society meetings of the early psychoanalysts mark one of its crucial turning points (Ellenberger, 1970). Of the "big three," Adler, Freud, and Jung, Adler was the only one who not only wrote about what he did in therapy, but actually demonstrated it to groups of clinicians and interested observers (Adler, 1930/1982; Terner & Pew, 1978). Adler's public demonstrations were considered revolutionary by some and outlandish and unprofessional by others. Nonetheless, he demonstrated his clinical work with adults, children, and families.

Adler was not a gifted writer, nor did he write many works for the professional public, especially after World War I. By then, his works took on a more social-psychological emphasis, being directed mainly at the lay public for general consumption. Because of this and the fact that his base of interested colleagues was not primarily medically trained people but rather social workers, educators, and psychologists, Adler kept his language simple, his concepts (relatively) clear, and his style minimal (Hoffman, 1994). These factors, along with the aforementioned willingness to publicly demonstrate his approach, have created a curious phenomenon: Adler is constantly being "rediscovered." It is almost as if generation after generation of psychotherapists "move toward" the basic principles of Adlerian psychotherapy. Given the emphasis on videotape research, theoretical integration, and the proliferation of therapy training programs (therefore requiring more systematic and uniform teaching and not relying exclusively on mentorship), it is understandable that constructs are becoming more simple and tactics more "commonsensical."

Adler (1956) worked with a large variety of clients. Not only did he work with what were traditionally labeled "neurotic" clients in individually oriented therapy, he also worked with psychotic, "criminal," and institutionalized ones. Many of his clients had clear-cut organic pathology and somatic dysfunction as well. In addition, as noted above, Adler worked with children, adolescents, and families.

Clinical Therapy: An Overview

Adler was, in many ways, the first integrationist or, as he is sometimes referred to, the first technical eclectic. If one looks at his writings, one see that they can be broken into approximately four general categories:

- Adler's work as a physician, addressing himself to the medical, somatic aspects of individual functioning (Adler, 1907/1917, 1934/1964)
- Adler's work as a psychoanalyst, addressing himself to the issues of unconscious dynamics, dreams, childhood reconstructions, and clients' resistances (Adler, 1912/1983, 1978)
- Adler's work as a family therapist, addressing himself to systems concepts, family dynamics, and family transactions (Adler, 1930/1982)
- Adler's work as an educator and counselor, addressing himself to couples and parent education, school reform, and social change (Adler, 1931; Adler & Associates, 1930)

He apparently moved fairly easily from one role to the other, and frequently without specifying when and how such "switches" were to be accomplished. By report, he was considered a master clinician (Hoffman, 1994).

Clinical therapy, as conceptualized in this chapter, involves working with complex cases typically involving several components. Problem complexity is typically high, as is the degree of dysfunction and the number of people affected by it. In diagnostic language, there are quite often two or three Axis I conditions, at least one full Axis II disorder (with traits of others being prominent), and some kind of somatic, Axis III complication. The principle clinician in charge of the case must be well versed in diverse treatment modalities and strategies and well networked to other professionals who have the required expertise to assist in the treatment and management of the case.

Adlerian psychotherapy provides a solid base for integrating diverse treatment modalities and formats (Sherman & Dinkmeyer, 1987). As this chapter demonstrates, we are not necessarily moving "on beyond Adler" as much as we are trying to follow the path he laid out at the turn of the century (Huber, 1991).

☐ Adlerian Psychotherapy: The Basic Model

Dreikurs (1967) and other Adlerians have systematized Adler's work. The basic model is one involving four stages, or phases, of therapy. These can occur on a micro or macro level; that is, each of these stages can take place not only as discrete segments of the entire therapy, but within each session itself. Each phase is discussed according to two components: the principle task of the clinician, and the principle task of the patient.

Relationship

During this phase, clinicians work to establish rapport, build trust, and align treatment goals. Clients are asked to be willing, to some extent, to establish and maintain contact with the clinician, be honest, and be open to the possibility of change.

Investigation

Clinicians need to explore the problems as presented (including the problem's history, onset, and severity), examine the relevant dynamics of the person or persons who are presenting such problems, and listen attentively and earnestly. Clients are expected to be communicative, open to exploration, and willing and able to focus on some aspect of the problem long enough to allow some conceptualization to begin to take place.

Interpretation

Clinicians begin to formulate the problem into a coherent pattern (that may or may not be shared with the patient, either in its entirety or in selected parts), devise a methodology for remediation, obtain some kind of feedback regarding the appropriateness of the remediation plan, and move ahead with that plan. Patients are asked to provide feedback, offer corrective or confirming data to the plan, and engage in some sort of mutual problem-solving strategy designed to eliminate the problem.

Reorientation

The clinician facilitates the implementation of the plan, educates where needed, confronts where required, and encourages change. Clients demonstrate, to some degree, a willingness to change, an acceptance of help, and motivation to implement the remediation plan. Feedback is provided by them to the clinician regarding the plan's success or lack of success.

Dreikurs (1967, pp. 5–14) provided an outline for conducting an initial interview. First, the clients are encouraged to describe their situation in detail, in their own words. Dreikurs considered this the *subjective* condition. Next, they are interviewed to determine what he called the *objective* condition. Their functioning is assessed along three dimensions: work, sexuality, and friendship. Finally, the two conditions (i.e., subjective and objective) are linked by what Adlerians refer to as "the question": Clients are asked what would be different in their lives if the presenting problem was removed. Their answers, which are addressed in greater detail below, typically provide an indication of the functional purpose of the symptoms.

Dreikurs (1967) and other Adlerians (e.g., Powers & Griffith, 1987; Shulman & Mosak, 1988) have also systematized the investigation and interpretation phases. In what has become known as the Life Style Interview, typically conducted just after the initial interview, clients are asked to describe their childhood backgrounds regarding their sibling relationships, physical and sexual development, school adjustment, social adjustment, parental relationship, and neighborhood and community involvement, after which a summary of the material is provided, which Adlerians call the *summary of the family constellation*. Next, clients' early recollections are examined, interpreted projectively, and the projective dynamics summarized into what is called the *summary of the early recollections*. This latter summary serves as the basis on which a list of problematic convictions, attitudes, and behaviors are derived, as are a set of assets and strengths. These two lists are then linked to the presenting problem, typically demonstrating how the presenting problem is an outgrowth of clients' potentially mistaken notions about how they found their place in their family of origin.

☐ The Theory of Clinical Therapy

Following is the theoretical model on which the practice of clinical therapy is conducted. The model is Adlerian, but also integrative, and is based on a number of sources, the Adlerian ones in particular being Adler (1956), K. A. Adler (1972), Dreikurs (1967), Maniacci (1996a, 1996b, in press), Mosak (1977, 1995), Mosak and Maniacci (1993a, 1993b, 1995), Nikelly (1971), Powers and Griffith (1987), Shulman (1973), Shulman and Mosak (1988), Sicher (1991), Sperry (1995), Sperry and Carlson (1996), and Wexberg (1929/ 1970). Following Adler's original conceptualization, there are two principal parts (each with relevant subparts) and an additional part:

I.   The general diagnosis
   A.   The initial interview
   B.   *Diagnostic and Statistical Manual of Mental Disorders* (DSM; American Psychiatric Association, 1994) multiaxial diagnosis and Adlerian (biopsychosocial) case formulation
   C.   The treatment plan (five levels of intervention)

II. The special diagnosis
   A.   Investigation of the early childhood situation
   B.   Assessing–testing the current style
   C.   Summarizing the data and presenting it to the client–client system

III. The dynamic formulation
   A.   Relevance of above data to out-of-session tasks
   B.   Relevance of above data to in-session tasks

☐ The General Diagnosis

The Initial Interview

The general diagnosis requires a thorough initial clinical interview. After a survey of the Adlerian literature and a number of years under the supervision of Adlerian (and non-Adlerian) clinicians in diverse settings, I constructed the following initial interview guide. It has six key areas:

I.   Identifying information, addressing the question "Who are you?"
II. Presenting problem, addressing the question "What brings you here?"
III. Background data, addressing the question "How long has this problem been an issue for you?"
IV. Current functioning, addressing the question "How is this problem affecting you?"
V.   Treatment expectations, addressing the question "What would you like us to do about it?"
VI. Clinical summary, addressing the issue "Here is what seems to be going on. . . . What do you think of this plan?"

The interview is semistructured for a number of reasons. First, as stated in the introduction, the clients being addressed in this chapter have complicated presentations, histories, and dynamics. Communication with referral sources, colleagues, and agencies (including hospitals and medical staff) requires a sophisticated assessment orientation that assumes, first and foremost, that every client presentation may be multifaceted, involved, and multidetermined with regard to etiology. Until proven otherwise, the case is assumed to be complex. The interview follows this outline.

Initial Interview Questionnaire.

I.   Identifying information
     A. Name (first, last; maiden name)
         1.   Ethnicity
     B. Age and birthdate
     C. Marital status
         1.   Spouse's name (first, last; maiden name) and age
         2.   Previous marriages (for either)
     D. Children (list names and ages)
     E. Home address and telephone number (own/rent)
     F. Work address and telephone number
         1.   Occupation
     G. Emergency telephone number and contact person
         1.   Relationship to client
     H. Parents (names and ages; marital status)
     I. Siblings (names and ages; marital status)
     J. Education (including military service)

    K. Religion
       1. Current
       2. Family of origin
    L. Medical history
       1. Last physical examination
       2. General health
       3. Medications (including nonprescription)

II. Presenting problem
    A. What brings you in today? Why now? (*DSM* diagnostic interview data may be used here as needed)
    B. When did it start?
    C. What else was going on at that time?
    D. When is it worse? When is it better?
    E. What do you do about it? How?
    F. Who is most affected by it?
       1. Who is the first to know when it happens? Then who?
       2. Who doesn't know? Why not?

III. Background data
    A. Childhood
       1. How did you get along with kids?
       2. Who was your best friend? Why?
       3. How were your grades? What teachers did you like? Why? What teachers didn't you like? Why?
    B. Adolescence
       1. Peers
       2. Dating
       3. High school
    C. Early adulthood
       1. Relationships
       2. Early jobs
       3. College–military
    D. Previous therapy
       1. For how long and with whom (name and address)?
       2. What did you learn? Why did you stop?
       3. What worked in that therapy? What didn't?
       4. What did you like about the therapist's style? What didn't you like?

IV. Current functioning
    A. Work
       1. What do you do?
       2. How do you feel about it? Why?
       3. Relationship to authority, peers, subordinates
       4. What would you change?
    B. Social
       1. How often do you see your friends?
       2. What is your social life like?
       3. Who are your best friends? Who are you most intimate with? Why?
       4. What would you change?
    C. Sex
       1. Describe current relations

    2. Describe current difficulties

    3. What would you change?

  D. How does your presenting problem interfere with these tasks?

    1. Currently

    2. Past year (better or worse)

V. Treatment expectations

  A. The question: What would be different in your life if you didn't have this presenting problem?

  B. Why do you think this is happening? How do you explain it?

  C. What can I do for you? How can I be of assistance?

  D. How long will it take?

    1. How will we both know when we're done?

    2. Should anyone else be involved?

  E. Who is the most famous person of all time?

    1. Why that person?

VI. Clinical summary

  A. Is this a primarily a medical or psychological problem, or both?

    1. Referrals

    2. Consultations (supervision)

  B. What is the person's style of movement (toward, away, against, etc.)?

  C. Against whom is the complaint presented?

  D. What is the purpose of the symptom(s)?

  E. What modalities (e.g., individual, couple, family, group) should be considered and when?

  F. What therapeutic style (e.g., cognitive, behavioral, insight-oriented, nondirective) might be best initially? Later on?

This interview is merely a guideline and should be tailored to meet the needs of the particular situation and client. As experience is gained with it, clinicians report that it can be completed in 45 to 60 minutes (or, if being used for precise, *DSM* diagnoses, 60 to 120 minutes or longer, as needed). Should the need arise, the interview outline need not be followed at all; yet, at some point in time, the material asked for in this outline will need to be gathered for most problems.

Although a detailed examination of the significance of each of the sections and questions is beyond the scope of this chapter, a few points can be highlighted from some of the sections. For example, Section IG, "Emergency telephone number," can be a goldmine. Besides being useful for crisis situations, it can yield useful information to the clinician about the client's choice of a support system in times of emergency. Not only can Section IL, "Medical history," yield detailed information regarding possible somatic complications, but the data regarding medications and general health can offer some initial insights into the dynamics of treatment compliance. Does this client comply with his or her recommended care? Does the client know the side effects, dosages, and indications or contraindications of his or her medications? This section, in particular, can be the first indicator of the client's intended compliance with therapy.

In Section IIA, knowing why the client decided to seek help at this particular time can be illuminating. In IIF, knowing who is most affected by the problem can lead clinicians to see the social consequences of having such a problem (many clients will initially report themselves as most affected; in that case, clinicians should press on and ask, "Who else, after you, is most affected?").

Section IIIA, "Background data," is designed to provide clinicians with a glimpse of the client's overall style from early in the life span. The first three questions (IIIA, 1, 2, 3) are intended to be repeated for each developmental period, modifying the questions to the appropriate context. For instance, finding out who the client selected as a best friend during each development period, and why, can lead to insight regarding the type of person the client is likely to be open with. If a male client responds to question IIIA2, "Who was your best friend?" with "John, he could make me laugh no matter what," the clinician may want to be sensitive to the fact that a precondition for the client being open and revealing may be that the clinician uses humor at an appropriate time. Should such a pattern repeat itself throughout the rest of Section III and continue throughout Section IVB, "Current functioning, social," the chances of such a style being continued in the present time (and therefore probably required in the therapeutic relationship) are great. Along similar lines, IIID, "Previous therapy," can provide data useful in determining what to use in this current treatment and, significantly, what to avoid.

Section V, "Treatment expectations," is crucial but frequently overlooked. Eliciting the client's formulation for what bothers him or her and how long remediating it might take can do a great deal to help align goals and negotiate treatment strategies. Of particular interest from an Adlerian perspective are the first and last questions in this section, VA and VE. A bit of a longer look at each will demonstrate why.

"The question" (VA) is used to help provide differential diagnosis and the purpose of the symptom (Adler, 1956; Dreikurs, 1967). When the presenting problem involves a specific symptom, there are typically three responses clients give to the question. For example, a client presenting with vague, heretofore undiagnosed headaches, is asked, "What would be different in your life if you didn't have these headaches?"

Primarily somatic: "Nothing, my head wouldn't hurt."

Primarily psychosocial: "Well, I'd be able to go back to work"

Primarily a blend (i.e., a somatic problem being used for a psychosocial gain): "My head wouldn't hurt so much and I'd be able to work."

A good mental status examination, medical history, and referral to a competent physician is still required (Maniacci, 1996b), but the answer to the question can be quite illuminating.

Question VE, "Who is the most famous person of all time?" and the subsequent "Why that person?" can tap into the patient's perceptions of key values (Lombardi, 1973). The answer can provide a glimpse of the key organizing values in the patient's style. For example, a woman who responds, "Jesus Christ, because he gave his life for us," may have self-sacrifice as a key value in her life, whereas a man who responds, "Jesus Christ, because he is God and all powerful," probably has power issues organizing his style.

Giving just one instance of how the interview questionnaire can be used *in toto*, the answer to VE can be used to evaluate the answer to IIB and C. The response to the question about the most famous person taps into a key organizing value of the patient. By linking that answer to "When did it start" and "What else was going on at that time?" clinicians can assess an important point: Was that key organizing value challenged or severely disputed in the time around the onset of symptoms? If so, then the symptoms may serve the purpose of safeguarding the patient from dealing with the potential nullification of that value, or even be an attempt to maintain that value in the face of disconfirming feedback from the social network–environment. For example, if Jeff reports that the most famous person is "Michael Jordan, because everybody knows his name and admires him," a key organizing value for Jeff may be recognition and attention. It might not be surprising to find that what was happening around the time Jeff's symptoms emerged was the birth of his first child. A glance at Section II, "Identifying information, siblings," reveals that Jeff is the youngest born sibling. The birth of his first child may be eliciting a reaction Adler (1956) called *dethronement*. This can be further explored in the Life Style Assessment and in further interviews.

DSM Multiaxial Diagnoses and Adlerian (Biopsychosocial) Case Formulations

The relationship of Adlerian case formulations to the *DSM* has been discussed elsewhere by Sperry and Maniacci (1992) and is the focus of a separate chapter by Sperry in this book. A brief overview of that material is provided here.

Except for the clearly organic pathology listed in the *DSM*, most of the diagnoses are what Adler (1956) and Dreikurs (1967) would have considered a catalogue of inferiority complexes, that is, issues patients have that they believe are interfering with their meeting the tasks of life. The five-axis system is conceptualized by the proponents of the *DSM* (American Psychiatric Association, 1994) like this:

Axis I—Clinical syndromes, developmental disorders, and V codes

Axis II—Personality disorders (including traits) and mental retardation

Axis III—Somatic issues (relating to the management of Axis I and II disorders)

Axis IV—Psychosocial stressors

Axis V—Global Assessment of Functioning (GAF) Scale

Diagnosis proceeds along each axis. The Initial Interview Questionnaire is keyed to elicit a five-axis diagnosis. Axis I diagnoses are arrived at by checking Sections IIA and IIIA, "Presenting problems and background data." Axis II diagnoses are assessed by using the same sections. Axis III diagnoses are assessed by means of Section IL, "Medical history." Axis IV dynamics are derived from Section II B and C, "When did it start?" and "What else was going on at that time?" Axis V, the GAF, is determined by examining the functioning in life tasks, Section IV, "Current functioning." By using such a questionnaire, not only is Dreikurs' (1967) original conceptualization of the initial interview maintained (i.e., subjective and objective conditions followed by the question), clinicians can arrive at a five-axis diagnosis.

From an Adlerian perspective, the five-axis system can be conceptualized as follows (Sperry & Maniacci, 1992):

Axis I—The "neurotic arrangement"

Axis II—The lifestyle

Axis III—Organ inferiorities–organ jargon

Axis IV—Shock effects–exogenous factors

Axis V—Barometer of the life tasks

Briefly summarized, the formulation works this way. Clients move through life with a particular style of life, or pattern (Axis II). That style may have been formed (in part) by their particular organ inferiorities or expressed by means of organ jargon (Axis III). These clients meet a situation for which they are unprepared (Axis IV), given their particular way of construing life and their place in it (Axis II). They "arrange" their symptoms (Axis I) in order to evade the tasks (Axis V). The symptoms selected (Axis I) may in part be chosen because of their relationship to the preexisting style (Axis II), their preexisting biological make up (Axis III), and their current psychosocial environment or culture (Axis IV).

Once the multiaxial diagnosis is derived, and the case formulation is worked out, the treatment plan can be developed. An example of such a work-up is provided in the case example section below.

The Treatment Plan (Five Levels of Intervention)

The treatment plan is put in place after an initial workup. It is tentative and can be modified, with the client's collaboration, at any time. It guides the treatment decisions and serves as an index of treatment compliance that can help guide clinical interventions (see below). A model for organizing the treatment plan into a hierarchical structure is provided:

A. Crisis stabilization (typically directed at the acute, Axis I disorder)

B. Medical–somatic interventions (typically directed at the Axis I and III disorders)

C. Short-term goals (usually directed at the Axis IV situation for which the client lacks the requisite skills, given his or her style)

D. Long-term goals (mostly directed at the Axis II disorder or traits, typically requiring more intensive, multilevel interventions)

E. Ancillary services (those services that may be needed to facilitate the Axis V functioning, such as teaching skills or linking to agencies, that will help raise the level of adaptive functioning)

Classically, crisis intervention work is done for the first level of recommendations. In most cases, this can be managed in 1–3 sessions. Medical–somatic interventions and short-term goals can be established and completed usually in 5–15 weekly scheduled sessions; most short-term goals entail behavior modification or skill building, that is, keeping the existing lifestyle (personality) intact but simply working with patients to modify its use. Long-term goals, such as lifestyle (personality) modification, can be expected to take anywhere from 1 to 2 years worth of work (or more), if attainable and advisable at all.

☐ The Special Diagnosis

Investigation of the Early Childhood Situation

Most clinicians believe the assessment process is completed with the five-axis diagnosis and the case formulation. Adlerians have long advocated tailoring the treatment to the particulars of the case. Whereas the general diagnosis provides nomothetic concepts to the case (i.e., provides guidelines for the typical, general management of the case), the special diagnosis asks clinicians to strive for idiographic specificity (i.e., understand the case in its particulars, according to this particular patient in this situation at this point in time). The nomothetic level can be quite useful as a guideline for typical treatments for typical types of cases, and it can facilitate research into general dynamics involving large clusters of data, such as diagnostic categories, psychosocial stressors, and overall clinical presentations. The idiographic level, however, is not as much concerned with research and the accumulation of facts and data as it is with treatment and clinical work per se. Except for case studies, the primary use of idiographic material is for tailoring treatment to the specifics of the case.

The early childhood situation of the client can be explored in depth. A detailed psychosocial history, such as that attained through a family constellation interview from a lifestyle assessment, can help explore how the client reacted to key life situations during his or her formative years (Powers & Griffith, 1987; Shulman, 1973). Such data can be used to help determine the client's particular lifestyle in great specificity. Tools such as the Basic Adlerian Scales for Interpersonal Success—Adult form, a 65-question normed and standardized test that asks clients to respond to sentences about their early childhood situations, can be used to supplement data collection and facilitate research on the nomothetic level, should that be desired (Kern, Wheeler, & Curlette, 1993).

Assessing and Testing the Current Style

After a detailed psychosocial history has been gathered, a more detailed analysis of the client's current style, as it operates in the here and now, needs to be undertaken. There are many ways to do this, ranging from least to most intrusive on the client's time and resources. Given the background, education, training, and preference of the clinician and the needs of the situation and client, early recollections, Thematic Apperception Test or Children's Apperceptive Storytelling Test (Schneider, 1989) stories, Rorschach Inkblot Test protocols, Minnesota Multiphasic Personality Inventory—2 profiles, projective drawings, intelligence testing, and/or neuropsychological testing may be needed, if not necessary, to manage the case and conduct the treatment (Maniacci, 1990).

A point of distinction will clarify the above. A lifestyle assessment is a subjective phenomenological technique. It has no norms and cannot be standardized. It is an idiographic tool *par excellence*, particularly in the hands of an experienced clinician. The Rorschach, on the other hand, is an objective phenomenological technique. Like the lifestyle assessment, it can describe the patient's phenomenological situation in detail, but unlike the lifestyle assessment, it has norms, frequency tables, and indexes that can serve to guide clinicians as to how the patient's phenomenology is used. The lifestyle assessment can describe, in exquisite detail, the client's subjective views but, lacking norms and nomothetic data, it is unable to tell clinicians how the particular convictions are being used. Tests like the Rorschach, because of its large sample size and frequency tables, can more accurately predict how such convictions might be used (Maniacci, 1990).

Summarizing the Data and Presenting
It to the Patient–Patient System

At this stage of the treatment, usually 3 to 5 sessions into the process, the treatment plan has been agreed on by the client. The idiographic dynamics have been investigated along the two dimensions specified above (i.e., early childhood situation and current style), and the data need to be summarized and presented to the client and, potentially, the client system, should the referral come from another clinician who will be involved in the case, concerned parents or significant others, or third-party payers. The sharing of the summaries is important. Clinicians should be sensitive to the feelings and attitudes of all involved, yet mindful that they may have to report data that are difficult, if not alarming, to concerned parties. Professionalism needs to be uppermost in the clinician's demeanor, and at all times an encouraging attitude should be maintained that appreciates not only the patient's deficits but his or her assets and strengths.

☐ The Dynamic Formulation

The last phase of the assessment process involves what is called the dynamic formulation (Strupp & Binder, 1984). Clinicians work along two dimensions. First, given the aforementioned dynamics, clinicians examine how the above-derived data will affect out-of-session tasks assigned to the clients. For example, if a detailed assessment shows that Mark is a competitive, hard-driven man with superior intellect and conceptualization skills, out-of-session tasks that he believes are "below" him may not be attempted. Similarly, should he believe that his superiority is being "challenged" or "threatened" by assigning tasks or designing intervention strategies that he believes encourage him to give up some of that superiority too early in the treatment process, compliance might become an issue. Couple and family interventions, or medical interventions, in which Mark's key value system is too forcefully challenged too abruptly, will most likely fail.

Second, the data derived from the assessment need to be examined for their impact on in-session tasks. "Transference" issues need to be taken into account, even in what might traditionally be considered nonanalytically oriented contexts (Mosak, 1977). To return to the example of Mark, working with him to help him monitor his blood sugar level and adjust his insulin accordingly may prove much more beneficial than having a physician do it for him. He may interpret the physician's "taking control" as a threat to his superiority, and he may challenge the physician's competence and engage in power struggles. Asking Mark to help design his own treatment interventions may be more useful than designing them for him.

Whereas the treatment plan (with its five levels of intervention) and the problem list (derived from the lifestyle interview and testing) tell clinicians *what* has to be worked on, the dynamic formulation tells clinicians *how* to work on it. Knowing Martha has self-esteem issues related to her abusive childhood is what has to be worked on, but how the clinician should approach that issue is a whole different matter, and is best derived through the dynamic formulation.

☐ The Practice of Clinical Therapy

The actual practice of clinical therapy is straightforward, if the assessment has been thorough and the negotiation process attempted. A multistage approach begins that follows the treatment plan. Roughly conceptualized, it involves three components (see also Pinsof, 1995; Sperry, 1995):

1. Modify behavior through skill building, psychoeducation, and training.
2. Alter cognitions (i.e., challenge, dispute, etc.) as they adversely affect skill acquisition.
3. Modify motivation through exploration and reconstruction of early learning as it affects cognitions, emotions, and behavior.

A more detailed analysis will clarify each component. Number 1, "modify behavior," entails direct manipulation of client functioning. Whatever behavioral deficits exist are targeted and exercises are designed to remediate them. For instance, Carl may lack basic communication skills. The most efficient manner would be to teach such skills. Should the acquisition of those skills improve his overall functioning and decrease his subjective distress, little if any further intervention may be needed.

Number 2, "alter cognitions," becomes the targeted treatment goal should Carl be hesitant to either learn or use the communication skills. It may become apparent that his "resistance" is due to his belief that such skills are for "women" and that "real men" do not need such "fancy stuff." Cognitive disputation (Ellis, 1971), reading materials, and observational assignments where he watches others he might potentially admire use such skills may increase compliance.

Number 3, "motivation modification," may be needed as well. Carl may have come from a traditional, masculine-oriented home where male dominance and female compliance was the norm. His identity issues and worldview may be so wrapped up in such early learning that without a more detailed exploration into his motivation for maintaining such a stance, even in the face of potentially adverse consequences from his social network he may not realize the need to challenge such early learning and acquire new skills.

Keeping in mind the treatment plan–dynamic formulation distinction made above, a review of the three components is in order. Identifying a communication deficit is part of the assessment process, and targeting it is part of the treatment plan. How that communication deficit is approached is part and parcel of the dynamic formulation. Carl may have to be approached in a straightforward, no-nonsense manner with little of what he calls "psychocrap" thrown in. "Two good old boys" sitting and discussing the day may be much more therapeutic for Carl than a traditional client–therapist relationship. Any of the above three components can be approached in such a conversational style, if the clinician is aware of it from the start.

☐ Focused Treatment Sessions

If the clients are aware of the treatment plan and have had a say in formulating it (to whatever extent they desire or can manage), the stage is set for the treatment to begin. After some casual small talk to begin each session and help participants "warm up," clients are asked what they would like to work on this session. "What would you like to learn today?" or "What do you think we should work on next?" can be offered as typical session starters. Ideally, clients should select something from the treatment plan. Many times, they do, and the process outlined above begins (1, skill building; 2, alter cognitions; or 3, modify motivation). Many other times, however, it is not so smooth.

On either the micro or macro level, that is, within each individual session or the treatment as a whole, clients' compliance with the treatment plan is regularly assessed (Maniacci, 1996a). Most often, they stick to the plan. When they do not, it is typically for one of three reasons. First and most obviously, there may be real, commonsense reasons for hesitancy or even noncompliance. It may have been a bad day, and they might not want to do anything other than receive support. Intercurrent events may (temporarily) disrupt the treatment plan, such as family crises or medical illnesses that need to be addressed. Second, "insight" or new information may have occurred, and they may have "put some things together" and therefore want to modify the treatment plan. Third, they may be displaying in-session dynamics that mirror their out-of-session issues, in which case a different tactic is required. In this case, not following the treatment plan is truly indicative of their core lifestyle issues, and their deviancy from the plan is typically a case of their lifestyle issues playing out in session. The clinical approach to this type of behavior is different from the above two scenarios.

☐ Movement Within Treatment

For heuristic purposes, a map of the potential movement clients may exhibit in treatment can be constructed. If a treatment is goal is established at the beginning of every session, their movement can be assessed with regards to a fixed reference point. They can move toward it, near it, or away from it. A detailed examination of each is called for (Maniacci, 1996a).

Movement Toward the Treatment Goal

If a goal is established, derived from the treatment plan, that for this session assertiveness skills will be worked on, clients that engage in that process are considered moving toward that goal. The primary treatment strategy is counseling and education, with skill building and behavior modification the principal techniques. The clinicians typically provide supportive and encouraging feedback to clients. They are primarily working as teachers and facilitators.

Movement near the Treatment Goal

Once the goal is set, for example, assertiveness training, clients are assessed as to their movement. If they follow it, but not in a productive manner, or only partially, they are considered to be moving near the goal. The clinicians act like psychotherapists, explore the beliefs around the goal, and work to modify any cognitive distortions that might be interfering with the task. The process is primarily redirective and interpretive, with clinicians acting as therapists.

Movement away from Goals

If clients move away from the goal, and it is not for either of the first two reasons articulated above (i.e., intercurrent events or their desire to modify the plan because of new information), then it is most probably a direct result of their stylistic movement through life. Analysis and exploration is undertaken, classically through process work (e.g., an in-session focus), and the motivation for deviating from the plan is the focus. Confrontation and goal realignment are undertaken, and the clinician acts primarily as a psychoanalyst. In this mode of functioning, two dynamics are explored:

1. What safeguarding operations are being used when clients are asked why they deviated from the plan? These are nonjudgmentally clarified and explored for their origin and utility to the maintenance of the presenting problem.
2. How does the clients' handling of the in-session therapeutic relationship potentially mirror their handling of out-of-session relationships? This is clarified, and links are made to the presenting problem and their relevant social networks and family of origin dynamics.

In summary, clinicians first attempt to modify behavior. Should they be blocked in their attempt, cognitive exploration and disputation is undertaken. Finally, should that prove ineffective, a more detailed analysis of the motivation for maintaining such a stance is undertaken, typically by exploring the early learning of such patterns in the family of origin. Goals are established for each session that are derived from the treatment plan and are approached according to the dynamic formulation. Movement within each session is assessed on a continuing basis to determine compliance, here conceptualized as movement toward, near, or away from treatment goals. When movement is toward, clinicians primarily function as teachers and provide support and encouragement. When movement is near, clinicians principally operate as therapists and redirect and interpret cognitive distortions. When movement is away, particularly for stylistic reasons, clinicians act psychoanalytically, explore and confront safeguarding operations, examine in-session dynamics, and make links to early learning and presenting problem maintenance.

☐ Movement within Modalities

As stated in the beginning of this chapter, clinicians engaged in what is here referred to as clinical therapy work with complex cases. More than one modality is usually required. There are typically five modalities of which clinicians need to be aware: (a) consultations with other professionals; (b) supervision; (c) multiple therapy and/or coordinated concurrent treatment; (d) systemic, group, couple, and individual foci; and (d) somatic–medical interventions.

It is highly doubtful if any one clinician can provide expert treatment along each of the above modalities, and no clinician should be his or her own supervisor. An example demonstrates the process.

Billy is 16 years old and probably learning disabled. He has been using drugs and is intermittently violent and in trouble with the police. He has a family history of substance abuse and mental illness. For him, each of the modalities may look as follows.

I.   Consultations
   A.   Speech, language, and learning assessment along with intelligence and neuropsychological screening
   B.   Contact with his teachers and administration at school
   C.   Assessment by a drug and alcoholism counselor
   D.   Contact with relevant police personnel

II. Supervision—Periodic supervision with a senior colleague who has experience in such cases

III. Multiple therapy and/or coordinated treatment: More than one person is likely going to be involved with this case, and communication should be clear, ongoing, and professionally maintained

IV. Systemic, group, couple, and individual foci
   A.   Billy is seen for individual therapy
   B.   Billy's family is seen (with a cotherapist)
   C.   Billy's parents are periodically seen to help them with their marriage
   D.   Billy is engaged in group therapy at the school; this treatment is coordinated with individual and family treatment

V.   Somatic–medical interventions
   A.   A psychiatric consult is used to screen for psychotropic medication
   B.   A general medical workup is undertaken to assess Billy's overall health
   C.   An exercise and relaxation program is developed

To the uninitiated, this may seem complex, overwhelming, and beyond the scope of most practitioners. It can be complex, but if handled by a treatment team, who may or may not be affiliated with the primary clinician, it can run smoothly. Billy may need all of the above services, and more, in order to get back on track. Adler's work in Vienna after World War I probably involved many such cases, and his establishment of experimental schools, community clinics, and family education programs attests to his awareness of the many needs of the community where he lived and worked (Hoffman, 1994; Terner & Pew, 1978).

Although any one clinician could probably not handle all aspects of Billy's case, it is not uncommon for one (primary) clinician to handle the individual, couple, and family consultations, perhaps even some of the testing, and refer to others for the rest.

Over the course of many months, if not years, there may be serial contacts with various subsets of Billy's family. Especially in the era of managed care, rather than tackling the entire case, only parts of it may be worked on over a long period of time. Nonetheless, an overall assessment of the needs of the case would take place as stated above, whereas only parts of the treatment plan may be implemented at any one time (Bedrosian & Bozicas, 1994).

☐ Clinical Example: The Case of Jane

"Jane" came to see the clinician for outpatient, individual psychotherapy after dissatisfaction with her two previous therapists. She had been in psychoanalytically oriented therapy for close to 18 months with a clinical psychologist. This had been her second attempt at individual treatment, and it, like her first, had proved frustrating. She was still depressed, had mood swings, and contemplated suicide on several occasions. A thorough initial interview was undertaken, and the accompanying write-up follows the six key areas outlined above from the initial interview.

Sessions 1–2: Summary of the Initial Interview and Treatment Plan

Identifying Information.   Jane is a 34-year-old woman who has been married for 11 years to her current husband, who is 3 years her senior. This is her second marriage (and his first), with her first having lasted for barely 3 years and producing one child, a girl. Her current marriage had produced one child as well, a boy, and both children, ages 13 and 9, respectively, live with her and her current husband. The first husband has no involvement or contact with them. She is employed as a technical worker for a large communication company and resides near her place of employment. Jane was raised Catholic but no longer practices any religion (though she reports being spiritual). She is high-school educated and currently working on her BA in health and human services. She is the third of four children, the older two being from her mother's first marriage (that ended in divorce). Both parents are deceased and died at relatively young ages, her mother from a stroke and her father from complications due to advanced alcoholism. Psychologically, Jane is the elder of two in her subgroup. She is on no medication and reports good physical health, other than mild problems with overeating and weight.

Presenting Problem.   Jane presents as depressed, lethargic, and anhedonic. She finds no meaning in her life, is considering dropping out of school, and has had periods of suicidal ideation and severe mood swings. She avoids any and all alcohol and drugs but tends to overeat to manage her moods. This has been her state for the past 2 years. She reports that her marriage is conflictual, with her husband being overcontrolling, intimidating, and absent a great deal of the time due to managing his own business. Her daughter is withdrawn, shy, and uninvolved, and her son is physically aggressive, failing in school, and increasingly unmanageable. She reports feeling burned out, hopeless, and on the verge of ending it all. When she gets most depressed, she reports that her whole family is affected, her husband "takes over," things settle down for a while, and the process begins all over again as her schedule becomes too busy, her son too aggressive, and her husband too absent. She reports she needs him more involved, is very afraid of being alone, and yet feels no man has ever lived up to her expectations. She ends up feeling disappointed, frustrated, and angry at them, pushes them away, and overeats.

Background Data.   Jane reports being social as a child, spending most of her time with one or two good friends who were always there for her and knew just what she wanted. She loved the teachers who went out of their way for her, took extra time to work with her, and sought her out. She came from an alcoholic, abusive family and frequently found refuge with boys who promised to take her away from her troubles. They never did. Her two previous therapists reportedly were not very helpful and were too nondirective, and she believed they were not caring enough. Nonetheless, she had trouble leaving them, would get angry with them, stop treatment for awhile, and then wait for them to contact her. Her first therapist rarely did, and she lost interest in him. Her second regularly sought her out, but Jane believed that although this woman cared, she (the therapist) was not directive enough.

Current Functioning.   She values her work, which she described as keeping people in touch. She has worked at her current job since shortly after high school and has done well. She feels her supervisors are available, her job is sufficiently structured, and the pay is reasonable. She would like more help with her tasks at times, but overall work is one of the few areas of her life where she finds stability.

Her social life is limited. Between school and work and the managing of the home and kids, she does not go out much. She still has one or two close friends from childhood she "clings" to and uses for support and nurturance. She has little contact with her family of origin.

Her sex life is very unsatisfactory. She experiences no pleasure with her husband and reports that he is insensitive. Jane would like a better relationship with him, but she is afraid of "rocking the boat," displeasing him, and losing him. That, she reports, would be devastating.

Treatment Expectations.   When asked what would be different if she could get rid of her symptoms, she responded that she would be stronger, more self-confident, and able to manage for herself. She is not sure why she is having such trouble and would like the clinician to help her put her life together. Jane believes it will take a very long time. Maybe, at some time in the future, she would like her husband to be involved, but she hopes that this treatment will be mostly for her. Finally, she believes that the most famous person of all time is God, because he is loving and caring and protects those who follow him.

Clinical Summary.   Jane is a depressed woman with a dependent, borderline style of personality who comes from a dysfunctional, abusive family. She has been looking most of her life for support and an "ideal" figure who will organize, structure, and support her development. She is a kind, hard-working individual who lacks many skills, such as assertiveness and parenting, and believes she needs others to take care of her. It is probable that many of these skills were not modeled for her as a child and that she grew up wishing that powerful, assertive men would also be caring and considerate, but she tends to find that they are controlling and overbearing instead. She uses her depression in order to keep others by her side, in her service, and to prevent herself from developing too many skills that her husband may perceive as threatening. She manages to work and do well in school, both of which are structured and highly supportive, but cannot allow herself to be too confident, for that might demonstrate that she is wrong in her opinion of herself, and that she does not need a man, which would lead her to panic. Her *DSM* diagnosis is as follows:

> Axis I—296.32 major depression, recurrent, moderate (principal diagnosis); V61.20 Parent–child relational problem; V61.2 Partner relational problem
>
> Axis II—301.6 Dependent personality disorder (with borderline features)
>
> Axis III—None reported, but mild weight problems (per history)
>
> Axis IV—Marital, family, and family-of-origin problems, chronic, severe
>
> Axis V—Current GAF: 51; highest GAF past year: 61

Treatment Plan.

A. Crisis stabilization
    1. Sign a suicide emergency contract, specifying procedures to be taken should Jane feel suicidal. A 24-hour crisis line number was given to her, as was a contract for involvement with her close friends and family if needed.
    2. The procedures for emergency contact of the clinician and hospitalization (if needed) were outlined.

B. Medical–somatic
    1. A consult was established with a psychiatrist for evaluation of an antidepressant. Because of her suicidal ideation, only a small number of pills were provided at any one time.
    2. A general medical workup was requested as she had not had a thorough physical examination in almost 2 years.

C. Short-term goals
    1. Family counseling to set limits, bring some order, and stabilize the situation with the children, in particular, the son
    2. Concurrent individual counseling for Jane to foster a therapeutic relationship with the clinician. The focus will be supportive and nonconfrontational initially, focusing on strengths and building skills.

3.   Marital counseling to elicit support and improve the general atmosphere with the couple

D.   Long-term goals
1.   Individual therapy to focus on family-of-origin issues, identity issues, and her dependent style

E.   Ancillary services
1.   Referral to a parent education group at a local child guidance center
2.   A lifestyle assessment of Jane to better understand her style

Jane readily agreed to the contract. She believed that no one had taken such an interest in her in a very long time. She reported that she believed the clinician seemed to know his "stuff" and that she thought she was in good hands.

Sessions 3–20: Concurrent Individual and Family Counseling

Jane was seen every other week for individual sessions, with the intervening sessions scheduled for family counseling. Two individual sessions were spent collecting lifestyle interview material. Her summary of the family constellation was the following.

Jane was the third of four children, but psychologically the firstborn of two in her subgroup, having a younger sister. This was a conflictual, violent family. The central family values were power, indulgence, and taking care of oneself. Father was an alcoholic tyrant who abused his wife when he was drunk and had little to do with the family when he was not. Mother was a beaten woman who suffered and complained due to his mistreatment. Jane tried to take care of her sister, but to no avail. She believed her sister was favored, pampered, and loved more than she was, and she felt rejected, alone, and decided to make her mission in life to find her Prince Charming, but unfortunately she wound up finding frogs instead. She grew up thinking that life was unfair, men had all the power and none of the responsibility, and she was being victimized, like her mother.

Jane provided seven early recollections and one childhood reoccurring dream:

1.   Age 4. I'm playing in the yard. Me and my friends took this huge box and made a fort. We were playing. Most vivid moment (MV): alone, in the box, safe. Feeling (F): safe.

2.   Age 5. In the hospital for tests. My parents dropped me off. I'm eating green Jell-O. Mom says she's going to get cigarettes and never came back. MV: She lied to me. F: abandoned, deceived.

3.   Age 9. Dad had a seizure in the bathroom. Somebody came and tried to help him. I thought he would die and didn't know what to do. He came out of it. MV: He's helpless, out of control. F: really scared (crying as she reports this memory).

4.   Age 9. My older brother came to visit and got into a fist fight with dad on the front lawn. I'm standing , watching. MV: the fight. F: scared, hiding out as I watched.

5.   Age 7. Our neighbors were on vacation and I thought they were rich snobs. We found some dead rabbits in their yard that a cat or something had killed, and I scooped them

up and threw them onto their patio. MV: sneaking over and throwing the dead rabbits in. F: fun at first, but very guilty later.

6. Age 4–5. I was standing on the swing set, trying to get real high, and I flew off. Blood started gushing all over after I hit the ground. MV: completely shocked—I lost control. F: pain, it hurt to fly off.

7. Age 3—4. Mom was walking me downtown. I was holding her hand when all of a sudden a boy riding his bike real fast came, and I got thrown to the sidewalk. He was so careless! MV: one minute walking with mom, and the next knocked down unexpectedly. F: fear.

8. Childhood dream. I am flying above the trees, above the poles, and wires. It's easy most of the time, but every now and then it gets real hard. I'm trying to get away from something, away from some animals and men out to get me.

Her summary of the early recollections (and dream) was as follows:

There is danger in the world, and I never know when I'm safe. People are hard to trust. Life requires the ability to rise above, but that is risky. I should be in control, for with it comes safety. I'm vulnerable, and angry, and I would like to give back to those that are insensitive and indifferent, but I'm afraid and too guilty to do it. Men can be violent, and the only time I'm truly safe is when I'm alone, but that is scary too, for I don't want to be abandoned.

She wholeheartedly agreed with the assessment. At this point, two lists were generated. The first detailed the convictions she had that caused difficulty for her; the second, a list of assets that served her well.

Interfering attitudes, beliefs, and behaviors:

1. Jane cannot decide between being in control and out of control.
2. She has a hard time trusting, especially men.
3. She waits for the bad to happen and feels unable to prevent it.
4. Jane feels too vulnerable and in need of either hiding out or being taken care of.

Assets and strengths:

1. She can loosen up and have fun.
2. She can strive for great heights.
3. She has a conscience.
4. Jane can be flexible.
5. Jane is willing to fight back, if she is mad enough.

The dynamic formulation was constructed. Jane is someone who enjoys being taken care of, but beneath her depressed, helpless exterior is strength and a great deal of anger. She will initially allow someone to take over, but should she feel unjustly treated, she will strike back, in vengeance, passively. Jane will probably look for the clinician to take over, but wrestle with him for control. If she wins the struggle, she will feel abandoned and threatened, but if she loses, she will feel even more vulnerable, depressed, and alone. Initial successes should not be surprising, for she can rise to great heights, but her ability to maintain such gains is the question.

Jane's initial individual sessions were spent working on these dynamics in a supportive, encouraging way. The main focus was to relieve the stress at home. Natural and logical consequences, family (council) meetings, and techniques for dealing with the four goals of children's misbehavior were instituted (Dreikurs, 1958; Mosak & Maniacci, 1993b; Sherman & Dinkmeyer, 1987). Jane, without her husband, started attending a weekend parent study group. The situation at home began to settle down. Her son was seen by the clinician for neuropsychological screening and the results shared with the family and school. He had some diffuse impairment that affected his ability to process language and express himself verbally. A referral was made to his school's special education department, where a speech, language, and learning assessment was made. He was learning disabled. Father reported having similar problems as a child, and although he was encouraged to undergo similar tests, he declined, and stayed on the periphery of the family counseling process. Jane's son was placed in a special learning environment, given a tutor, and over the course of the next few months, improved dramatically. Within 20 sessions, Jane was reporting feeling much improved, more peaceful at home, and ready to try it on her own. Her husband was more involved, and she believed she was ready to "make a go of it." After negotiation, it was agreed to try it for a while, but Jane was encouraged to continue with her medication and parent study group and to keep in periodic contact.

Sessions 21–28

Eight months later, Jane called, in crisis. Although the home situation remained stable with the children, the marriage was in "grave danger." Her husband had begun drinking again, a fact that had not been emphasized during the first series of interviews. The couple agreed to a 10-session contract to work on their marital issues. She believed that her husband had not learned enough from the initial sessions and was not willing to work on his part in their marriage and family life. He had been reluctant to be in treatment of any kind, and he dropped out of therapy after three sessions, claiming she was the main problem and that she needed to be "tougher." Five more sessions were spent working with Jane alone to help her cope with what she considered a challenging but workable situation. She did not love him, but she did want him to stay. She was not seen again for almost a year.

Sessions 29–45

Almost a year later, Jane's marriage ended in divorce. She was handling it well, but her son was not. Jane had stopped her medication, was completing her degree, and felt more powerful and self-confident. She sought treatment for herself and her son. The following 16 sessions were spent working with Jane and her son and, on occasion, her daughter.

Family-of-origin issues were addressed with all of them (Bedrosian & Bozicas, 1994). Jane did not know how to deal with men, and her son, now almost an adolescent, was growing. She felt intimidated by him, and he imitated his father in his treatment of her. He could be controlling and demanding, but not abusive. He had begun experimenting with drinking. This frightened and confused her, stirring issues of her father's drinking. Through contracting, psychodrama, and the involvement of his paternal grandfather, her son settled down, understood the issues between his mother and father, and gladly took over the role of the "new man" of the house in a more peaceful, if not always cooperative, manner. Jane, once again, believed she was ready to try it on her own and stopped treatment.

Sessions 46–94

One year had passed since her last session with her son, and he was in good shape, but Jane was mildly depressed, worried, and confused about her future. She had met another man, was falling in love, and stated that she had a hard time "saying no" to him. She thought she was losing control. She thought that before she went too far into a depression and needed medication again, she might finally take some time for herself and work on some of her own issues in greater detail, if the clinician thought she needed to. It had been almost 3 years since her initial contact with the clinician. [Of note: Her daughter, until now a missing piece of the picture who was seen only occasionally, had previously begun treatment for individual issues with another clinician. She was now 17 years old and sought out the clinician for help before she went away to college. Her treatment was with the full knowledge and blessing of Jane, who managed to not get involved. Although she had some issues in common with her mother, her issues were her own, and she remained on good terms with Jane. Hence, her therapeutic contacts are not summarized here.]

Although Jane thought much of her lifestyle assessment was still valid, she believed she had grown. The Rorschach Inkblot Test was administered by the clinician, and the following is a detailed summary of her protocol.

This is a valid profile. Jane took the test in an open and honest manner and was willing to apply a good deal of effort. She worked hard to provide detailed responses. At the present time, she is managing well. If she is under stress, it is not adversely affecting her. Jane, under most situations, is a cautious, hesitant person who carefully examines what she does. Her style of problem solving is a mixture of thoughtful deliberation and trial-and-error processing. At times, she jumps right in, but often not too far for too long before she backs off and debates (usually with herself) what she has just done. She's prone to "on-again, off-again" situations and may have a hard time firmly committing herself to issues. Overall, she is a person who can be unusual, if not idiosyncratic, in her thinking. She often bites off more than she can chew, and although she works very hard at what she does, she frequently overcommits and fails to clearly think through what she begins. She can be very ambitious and active, and although she often starts out with common sense, she can be impulsive. She wants things to happen faster than they do, and that is when she jumps ahead and makes guesses and connections that might not be helpful. Jane can be empathic and lively, trusting her feelings to lead her. Her self-esteem is not as high as she presents, and she frequently is guarded with people and looks to isolate and hold back. Specifically, she seems to be dealing with several issues. She is a bit scared of confronting someone or something, and is unsure whether to speak up or keep quiet and hold back, appearing in control. She is probably looking for a cooperative relationship but would be surprised by what it entailed. Men seem to worry her, and she is looking for support and a helping hand.

The test protocol seemed to confirm the dynamics noted almost 3 years earlier in Jane's lifestyle assessment. Although her confidence had improved, many of the same issues were reemerging. Jane agreed to a more protracted contract that would explore her lifestyle issues in greater detail. The following is a summary of a year's worth of work.

The focus of the sessions was primarily Jane's attitudes, expectations, and beliefs about how she navigated her way through the world. Her behavior was primarily adaptive, now more so than ever. Her need for skill building and support had decreased considerably. Her feelings about herself and her situation still seemed to lead her to trouble. A more detailed exploration began under the supervision of a senior colleague.

A basic principle guiding this stage of the work entailed examining her current situations, assessing how she perceived them, and deciding what she wanted to do about them. Quite often, Jane had a hard time separating what she expected to happen from what actually happened. Even if the best worked out, the tension and effort she put into "controlling" herself and her reactions wore her out. Once a particular dynamic was identified in the here and now, its roots in the past were located. This was more than an archeological process, however, in that the past was used to determine not what happened to her, but the meaning she ascribed to the event and, most important, the conclusion she came to about how to deal with such issues in the future. A particularly poignant example came from the middle period of this work.

Jane was curious about why she had had such serial contact with the clinician over the course of almost 3 years. After a brief review of the chart and past notes, it was discovered that she came back almost every summer, by late summer, to be exact, with the same feelings of helplessness and despair. We explored this time of year and realized that it was the anniversary of not only her father's death, but her mother's as well. Without realizing it, she was expecting to be abandoned at this time every year and, ironically enough, had "arranged" just such events throughout her life. Her breakups almost always happened near the end of summer, as did her major fights with significant others. She would feel edgy, as if she were going to be abandoned, and become either too clingy or too withdrawn and aloof, pushing people away. Jane believed that by "hitting" them first before they hit her, she would be safe, for if she could not prevent the worst from happening, at least it could be under her control. She would always break off therapeutic contacts around the same time as well, or shortly thereafter.

Such insight opened the door to processing some of her most frequent safeguarding operations. Jane would use anxiety as one of her most effective tactics. By being scared, she could enlist others to take care of her. It also justified her getting mad, for if she were scared, others seemed to be more patient with her.

Another safeguarding operation was to see herself as a helpless, unintelligent little girl. By all outward appearances, more often than not, especially during the past 2 years or so, she had been functioning relatively well. Yet why did she still see herself as a child? The answer took a long time to unravel. If Jane saw herself as too competent, it might mean being disloyal to her feminine guiding line. If she were to feel like a "real woman," she had to see herself as uneducated, weak, and in need of support, like her mother. Still, she had wanted to act like the mother of one of her childhood friends, a strong, capable woman who could manage. To do that, however, might mean to not fit in with her family. Hence, Jane arranged the following. She would act like her childhood friend's mother, yet feel like her own mother. Although behaviorally it might be acceptable to be successful, in her private logic, her attitude toward herself, she still had to see herself as like her mother. Now she could have the "best of both worlds," so to speak; she could act one way but arrange to feel another, and hence maintain her view of herself and her place in the world and still achieve some of the success she so desperately wanted.

Our relationship became a key focus as well. The more we identified various dynamics in out-of-session situations, the more apparent some of the in-session dynamics became. Jane saw therapy, and me in particular, as replacing her family, and more specifically, the men in her life who could not live up to her expectations. Gradually, she was able to explore the times I either let her down or lived up to her expectations, and we began a process of mutual exploration regarding how therapy was to be conducted without her becoming too dependent on her latest "prince."

Case Conclusion

Jane has finished her therapy, for now. Over the course of about 4 years, just over 90 sessions were used, or approximately 22 sessions per year. Individual, couple, family, and group psychoeducation were used. In addition, psychological and neuropsychological testing proved crucial, as were consultations with physicians and special education professionals. Antidepressant medication proved extremely useful in pulling Jane out of the depths of a moderate and quickly worsening recurrent depression and gave her the improved concentration and attention to engage in treatment. Over the course of the 4 years, clinical interventions ranged from skill building and encouragement to cognitive disputation and analytically oriented process work. She feels free to come back should she need to but confident enough to try it alone. She is still single, with her daughter in college and her son graduating high school. Although there are no signs of depression, she still has a tendency toward mild mood fluctuations, and she can be overly needy with her social network or the men she may be dating. She is not diagnostically a dependent personality disorder any longer, but she still has clear traits of it.

☐ Summary and Conclusion

Clinical therapy is the application of Adlerian psychotherapy with complex, difficult cases. Linear, unidimensional treatment strategies with such populations often are limited in effectiveness and frustrating for both clinicians and patients. Adler, in his work at the turn of the century, practiced along many dimensions, and his work displays facets of a biopsychosocial approach that belies its apparent simplicity. He wrote as a physician, psychoanalyst, family therapist, and educator and social reformer. For clinicians to be prepared for the next century, what is needed is an integrated, multidimensional treatment approach that takes into account current diagnostic language and research issues, along with an idiographic, treatment-tailored approach. Both aspects of a case need to be considered.

For such an approach to be developed and used, a thorough assessment has to take place. Treatment decisions need to be planned, and clinical style needs to be adjusted not only according to specific client dynamics but according to specific client timetables and needs. What may be right at one time in the course of a treatment may not be right at another, and what may work in one format may not work in another.

Clinicians need to be trained in different treatment styles and formats. Although a unified assessment perspective seems crucial in order to not confuse treatment issues, a diverse treatment application seems necessary. Adlerian principles and dynamics are commonsensical, integrative, and adaptable. They easily allow for integration with other observations and techniques. If clinical practice is to continue into the next century, such flexibility is required. If clinicians believe such flexibility is a benchmark of mental health in patients, it needs to be considered a benchmark of good clinical practice as well.

☐ References

Adler, A. (1917). *Study of organ inferiority and its psychical compensation: A contribution to clinical medicine* (S. E. Jelliffe, Trans.). New York: Nervous and Mental Disease. (Original work published 1907)

Adler, A. (1931). *What life should mean to you* (A. Porter, Ed.). New York: Blue Ribbon Books.

Adler, A. (1956). *The individual psychology of Alfred Adler* (H. L. Ansbacher & R. R. Ansbacher, Eds.). New York: Basic Books.

Adler, A. (1964). Physical manifestations of psychic disturbances. In *Superiority and social interest: A collection of later writings* (H. L. Ansbacher & R. R. Ansbacher, Eds.). New York: Northwestern University Press. (Original work published 1934)

Adler, A. (1978). *Co-operation between the sexes: Writings on women, love and marriage, sexuality and its disorders* (H. L. Ansbacher & R. R. Ansbacher, Eds. & Trans.). New York: Anchor Books.

Adler, A. (1982). *The pattern of life* (2nd ed.; W. B. Wolfe, Ed.). Chicago: Alfred Adler Institute. (Original work published 1930)

Adler, A. (1983). *The neurotic constitution: Outlines of a comparative individualistic psychology and psychotherapy* (B. Glueck & J. Lind, Trans.). Salem, NH: Ayer. (Original work published 1912)

Adler, A., & Associates. (1930). *Guiding the child: On the principles of individual psychology* (B. Ginzburg, Trans.). London: George Allen & Unwin.

Adler, K. A. (1972). Techniques that shorten psychotherapy: Illustrated with five cases. *Journal of Individual Psychology, 28*, 155–168.

American Psychiatric Association. (1994). *Diagnostic and statistical manual of mental disorders* (4th ed.). Washington, DC: Author.

Bedrosian, R. C., & Bozicas, G. D. (1994). *Treating family of origin problems: A cognitive approach.* New York: Guilford Press.

Dreikurs, R. (1958). *The challenge of parenthood* (rev. ed.). New York: Hawthorn.

Dreikurs, R. (1967). *Psychodynamics, psychotherapy, and counseling.* Chicago: Alfred Adler Institute.

Ellenberger, H. F. (1970). *The discovery of the unconscious: The history and evolution of dynamic psychiatry.* New York: Basic Books.

Ellis, A. (1971). Reason and emotion in the individual psychology of Adler. *Journal of Individual Psychology, 27*, 50–64.

Hoffman, E. (1994). *The drive for self: Alfred Adler and the founding of individual psychology.* New York: Addison-Wesley.

Huber, C. H. (Ed.). (1991). On beyond Adler [Special issue]. *Individual Psychology: The Journal of Adlerian Theory, Research & Practice, 47*.

Kern, R. M., Wheeler, M. S., & Curlette, W. L. (1993). *BASIS-A inventory interpretive manual: A psychological theory.* Highlands, NC: TRT Associates.

Lombardi, D. L. (1973). Eight avenues of life style consistency. *Individual Psychologist, 10*(2), 5–9.

Maniacci, M. P. (1990). *An Adlerian interpretation of the comprehensive system of the Rorschach Inkblot test.* Unpublished doctoral dissertation, Alfred Adler Institute (Adler School of Professional Psychology), Chicago.

Maniacci, M. P. (1996a). An introduction to brief therapy of the personality disorders. *Individual Psychology: The Journal of Adlerian Theory, Research & Practice, 52,* 158–168.

Maniacci, M. P. (1996b). Mental disorders due to a general medical condition and other cognitive disorders. In L. Sperry & J. Carlson (Eds.), *Psychopathology and psychotherapy: From DSM-IV diagnosis to treatment* (2nd ed., pp. 51–75). Washington, DC: Accelerated Development.

Maniacci, M. P. (in press). The psychotic couple. In L. Sperry & J. Carlson (Eds.), *The disordered couple.* New York: Brunner/Mazel.

Mosak, H. H. (1977). *On purpose.* Chicago: Alfred Adler Institute.

Mosak, H. H. (1995). Adlerian psychotherapy. In R. J. Corsini & D. Wedding (Eds.), *Current psychotherapies* (5th ed., pp. 51–94). Itasca, IL: F. E. Peacock.

Mosak, H. H., & Maniacci, M. P. (1993a). Adlerian child psychotherapy. In T. R. Kratochwill & R. J. Morris (Eds.), *Handbook of psychotherapy with children and adolescents* (pp. 162–184). Boston: Allyn & Bacon.

Mosak, H. H., & Maniacci, M. (1993b). An "Adlerian" approach to humor and psychotherapy. In W. F. Fry & W. A. Salameh (Eds.), *Advances in humor and psychotherapy* (pp. 1–18). Sarasota, FL: Professional Resource Press.

Mosak, H. H., & Maniacci, M. (1995). The case of Roger. In D. Wedding & R. J. Corsini (Eds.), *Case studies in psychotherapy* (2nd ed., pp. 23–49). Itasca, IL: F. E. Peacock.

Nikelly, A. G. (Ed.). (1971). *Techniques for behavior change: Applications of Adlerian theory.* Springfield, IL: Charles C Thomas.

Norcross, J. C., & Goldfried, M. R. (Eds.). (1992). *Handbook of psychotherapy integration.* New York: Basic Books.

Pinsof, W. M. (1995). *Integrative problem-centered therapy: A synthesis of family, individual and biological therapies.* New York: Basic Books.

Powers, R. L., & Griffith, J. (1987). *Understanding life-style: The psycho-clarity process.* Chicago: Americas Institute of Adlerian Studies.

Schneider, M. F. (1989). *CAST: Children's Apperceptive Storytelling Test.* Austin, TX: Pro-Ed.

Sherman, R., & Dinkmeyer, D. (1987). *Systems of family therapy: An Adlerian integration.* New York: Brunner/Mazel.

Shulman, B. H. (1973). *Contributions to individual psychology.* Chicago: Alfred Adler Institute.

Shulman, B. H., & Mosak, H. H. (1988). *Manual for life style assessment.* Muncie, IN: Accelerated Development.

Sicher, L. (1991). *The collected works of Lydia Sicher: An Adlerian perspective* (A. K. Davidson, Ed.). Ft. Bragg, CA: QED Press.

Sperry, L. (1995). *Handbook of diagnosis and treatment of the DSM-IV personality disorders.* New York: Brunner/Mazel.

Sperry, L., & Carlson, J. (Eds.). (1996). *Psychopathology and psychotherapy: From DSM-IV diagnosis to treatment* (2nd ed.). Washington, DC: Accelerated Development.

Sperry, L., & Maniacci, M. P. (1992). An integration of DSM-III-R diagnosis and Adlerian case formulations. *Individual Psychology: The Journal of Adlerian Theory, Research & Practice, 48,* 175–181.

Strupp, H. H., & Binder, J. L. (1984). *Psychotherapy in a new key: A guide to time-limited dynamic psychotherapy.* New York: Basic Books.

Terner, J., & Pew, W. L. (1978). *The courage to be imperfect: The life and work of Rudolf Dreikurs.* New York: Hawthorn.

Wexberg, E. (1970). *Individual psychological treatment* (Rev. ed.; A. Eiloart, Trans.; B. H. Shulman, Ed.). Chicago: Alfred Adler Institute. (Original work published 1929)

Jon Carlson
Don Dinkmeyer, Sr.

Couple Therapy

It was once appropriate to treat all couples in essentially the same fashion according to one's theoretical position. For the most part, all approaches worked fairly effectively because of the high level of functioning of the couples who traditionally sought out psychotherapy services. Couples requesting therapy tended to get better regardless of the type of therapy used (Sperry & Carlson, 1991).

Today's clientele, however, has changed markedly. This population is very resistant to change and seldom responds to traditional therapeutic methods (Huber, 1992). Couple therapists need to base treatment on a sound theoretical model that allows for this diversity of clientele, a model that can clearly assess the uniqueness of each couple system and develop a tailored treatment plan for each (Sperry, 1992). The treatment and interventions of necessity will be as varied as the couples, and therefore, therapists must be able to use any of the available strategies in an integrative fashion (Carlson, Sperry, & Lewis, 1997).

The Individual Psychology of Alfred Adler provides the necessary basis to work effectively with the full spectrum of today's couples (Sherman & Dinkmeyer, 1987). In this chapter, the principles of Adlerian psychology, as they apply to couples therapy, are described and the assessment tools and techniques used to produce a treatment plan that is able to integrate methods from a variety of approaches are discussed.

☐ Adlerian Principles

Adlerian psychology is a systems theory. It is holistic, purposive, cognitive, and social and focuses on the relationship or the patterns of interaction between partners. Adler realized that people are social beings and, therefore, all problems are social problems. He believed that problems between couples were not serious disorders but rather problems with cooperation between the partners.

Adlerian psychology provides a number of principles that serve as the basis for an integrated approach to couples therapy. The following principles undergird the process of therapy.

1. The couple relationship is understood as an interpersonal social system in which input from each partner either (a) improves the relationship or (b) stimulates dissonance and conflict.

2. "Trust only movement": The interaction, communication, and movement between the partners are purposive and goal directed. The movement reveals intentions, feelings, and values that influence the system. It is essential to understand the psychological movement between the couple that creates cooperation or conflict.

3. Therapists must concentrate on observing and understanding what partners do instead of focusing on what they say. There has historically been too much interest in verbal communication between the couple. Although communication is important, movement is more revealing. Notice movement that is cooperative and movement that is resistive.

4. Each person is an individual, social, decision-making human being whose actions have a purpose.

> The attitude of every individual towards marriage is one of the expressions of his [her] style of life: we can understand it if we understand the whole individual, not otherwise. (Ansbacher & Ansbacher, 1956, p. 434)

The communication and movement between partners express the intentions and goals of each partner. There are some relationship-destroying goals that may include attention, power, vengeance, or displaying inadequacy in order to be excused (Dinkmeyer & Carlson, 1984; Huber & Baruth, 1981). These goals are diagnosed by observing the feelings expressed by the partner. The feeling experienced indicates the purpose of the transactions (i.e., feelings of annoyance may indicate attention, feelings of anger may indicate power, feelings of "wanting to get even" may indicate revenge, and feelings of "giving up" and discouragement may indicate displays of inadequacy). The therapist guides communication toward positive interaction, with the goal of increasing the potential for involvement, trust, and caring.

5. Each partner has the creative capacity to choose and to create his or her own perceptions and meaning. The couple is helped to see that their goals and the ensuing conflict are chosen. Choice is an essential component of all behavior but is frequently denied in human relationships. Couples are helped to see that by their beliefs, behavior, and attitudes they can make new choices.

6. Each partner has the responsibility to decide. Each person is responsible for his or her own behavior. When each person is responsible, equilibrium and solutions exist instead of dysfunction and blaming.

7. Change in the relationship always begins with one's self, not with one's partner.

8. The beliefs, behavior, and feelings that exist in the system between the partners are the result of subjective perception. Behavior is a function of one's perception or of what experiences mean to a person. The therapist helps the partners understand the meaning they are giving to their experiences. Relationships have the potential for continuous miscommunication because each partner anticipates—or thinks he or she knows—what the other will say, and so thinks he or she does not need to wait and listen.

9. A couple's happiness (CH) is based on each person's self-esteem (SE), social interest (SI; capacity to give and to take), and sense of humor (SH). These are the ingredients of a happy relationship. Self-esteem is the individual's sense of worth and acceptance. Social interest is the desire to cooperate, and sense of humor is the ability to see the relationship in perspective.

$$CH = SE = SI = SH$$

10. Relationships are also strongly influenced by the couple's belief systems. The belief systems are related to priorities (Kern, 1990). Some of the priorities significant in the marital relationship include the following: control, perfection, pleasing, self-esteem, and expectations. The personality priorities are based on perceptions and reveal what people believe they must do to belong and be accepted (Dinkmeyer, 1991).

11. An important factor in understanding couple relationships is how the lifestyles of each partner fit together. This interaction, according to Dreikurs (1946), is evident with the choice of a partner. We choose a partner "who offers us an opportunity to realize our personal pattern, who responds to outlook and conceptions of life, who permits us to continue or to revive plans which we have carried since childhood" (Dreikurs, 1946, pp. 68–69).

Adlerians see this complementarity in the give and take of the lifestyles of two people. A couple relationship "is not merely one of a conscious choice and logical conclusions; it is based more profoundly upon the integration of the two personalities" (Dreikurs, 1946, p. 83). This involves the fitting together of both their similarities and difference.

☐ Couple System

A relationship system is created by the couple. The system and the partner constantly influence each other. Problems in the relationship often serve the purpose of maintaining a type of equilibrium. Problems or symptoms result when too much pressure for change is occurring. This is often viewed as discouragement about being valued or counting.

When people feel their self-esteem threatened in any way, the energy they would spend in developing cooperation with their partner may be used to blame each other, make excuses,

or defend themselves. None of this behavior brings them closer together or invites cooperation between them. (Bettner & Lew, 1993, p. 372)

The system is developed and influenced by choices. Behavior is always influenced by the subjective meanings assigned to an experience and the conclusions and
beliefs that come from these experiences. What partners think and how partners feel
influence the choices they make and the kind of direction and behavior they pursue.
These choices create the organization and pattern for relationships we call *the system*.
For example, one partner may decide to control the relationship, which can lead to a
conflict over some issue. The conflict is not about the issue or symptom but rather the
real concern—control.

The goal of the system is to seek a relationship with communication and respect
as equals. The system is a unified whole. The therapist understands the couple system
by understanding each partner and how the partners influence the system and how the
couple system influences them.

The Adlerian system is organized by the purposes of behavior. There is an underlying private logic (rules) unique in each system that guides the system to organize and
function in a particular fashion. Once the therapist understands the logic of the system,
the behavior begins to make logical sense, even though it may be confusing to those
outside the system.

Private logic is defined by the subjective perceptions of the couple and each partner. The logic may be, for example, "I must control," I am right," or "My partner should
always please me."

Psychological movement is influenced by the goals and priorities of the system
and by the cooperation and the competition between the partners and the consequences
of their behavior. To be effective in couples therapy, it is necessary to understand and
comprehend each partner. It is even more important, however, to recognize the significance and essential nature of understanding and fostering the development of a healthy
and cooperative system (Carlson & Dinkmeyer, 1987).

☐ Assessment

Assessment is used to help the therapist understand the couple system while revealing
to the partners forces and motives that maintain the conflict and dysfunctional behavior. By assessing the system, the process of change is initiated, and each partner becomes aware of his or her role in creating dissonance. Adlerians use traditional psy-
chodiagnostic procedures and data-gathering instruments, as well as several unique
procedures including lifestyle, marital inventory, early recollections, strength assessment, and mini-lifestyle.

Lifestyle

Assessment in couples therapy, although dealing with individuals, is always focused
on understanding the system between the partners. This begins by understanding the

individual lifestyle of each partner. The lifestyle is the characteristic and unique pattern of thinking, feeling, and acting.

As the relationship develops, a couple lifestyle also develops. This is the characteristic pattern the couple uses in relating to each other. The couple lifestyle is based on perceptions, beliefs, expectations that influence choices, and behavior in areas such as social interaction between the couple, the sexual relationship, friendships, and finances.

Couple lifestyles influence what is discussed and communicated, responsibilities, and who takes the role of being passive or aggressive in certain situations. The choices and behaviors in the major areas of the relationship form the lifestyle that becomes patterned and predictable. This predictable pattern results in expectations and self-fulfilling prophesies (i.e., "I knew you would").

When assessing the partners, the therapist recognizes that their psychological movement explains the intentions and purposes of each partner and the couple system. The psychological movement will explain why and how the system works and why there is conflict. From the very first contact with the couple, the therapist observes the psychological movement, the way the couple enters the room, the nonverbal communication, who speaks first, what they say, and what issues they defer to their partner. These observations reveal the system, the purposes, the beliefs, and the values that are being expressed.

As Adlerian therapists listen, they realize the importance of understanding the priorities that are being expressed. The priorities may be for control, perfectionism, superiority, or being a victim or martyr. We use the Lifestyle Scale (Kern, 1990) as part of the intake process before the first interview to identify each partner's beliefs and priorities. Priorities indicate what partners believe they need to do to belong or to be accepted. Priorities are used to understand core convictions and goals. The priorities and beliefs on Kern's (1990) Lifestyle Scale include the following: controller—I must be in control and get my way; perfectionist—I control myself and others by being perfect; pleaser—I must please others at all costs; victim—I am not responsible; and martyr—I am overburdened and people expect too much.

As each partner's priorities are identified, the therapist becomes aware of the forces that maintain the system. The pairing of a controller and pleaser, for example, can produce a predictable couple system.

Marital Inventory

Another scale that is used early in the assessment process is the Marital Inventory (MI; Dinkmeyer & Dinkmeyer, 1983). Each partner completes the MI before beginning treatment. The MI is arranged systematically to acquire the kind of information that will help the therapist understand the couple's goals, strengths, and preferences. The MI helps the therapist distinguish between what may be complaints, symptoms, and real issues by identifying the purpose of the symptoms.

The MI emphasizes a positive approach to couple assessment through questions such as "What is positive or right about this marriage?" and "Where are the resources for improving this relationship?" By being positive and encouraging, the partners can assess their own individual strengths and identify the strengths of their couple system.

In the early stages of the interview, Adlerian therapists do not emphasize dissatisfaction and complaints. Instead, strengths, assets, and resources are identified to improve the relationship system. The MI identifies patterns such as who seeks to be in control, who is concerned with getting even, who is the peacemaker, who is the compromiser, and who is interested in change.

The MI begins by asking about the symptoms or issues that bring the couple to therapy. It then identifies the goals of the relationship. Couples often had goals when they first married; however, they may not have a clear goal when in therapy. The therapist is concerned with identifying what the couple wants to have happen in the relationship. The couple often wants to focus on what needs to be changed. They know what they do not want. The therapist needs to help the couple be clear on what it is they do want.

Finally, the MI identifies the three most important strengths for building and improving the relationship. The couple is asked to identify their own strengths and what they believe are their partner's strengths.

Mini-Lifestyle

The mini-lifestyle (Dinkmeyer, 1988) is used in couple therapy. Because the couple is usually seen together, there is not sufficient time to do the traditional intensive, detailed lifestyle work (Shulman & Mosak, 1988) for each partner. Detailed lifestyle work involves collecting data over a period of several meetings. The mini-lifestyle interview helps the therapist understand the family of origin and the family atmosphere in which each person developed. The analysis of the psychological position of the birth order helps the therapist to identify traits the partners bring to the marital system. For example, if one partner's priority is perfectionism with high standards and the other partner's priority is pleasing, the potential interaction is reasonably predictable. The mini-lifestyle also provides an opportunity for each partner to spontaneously identify his or her assets, satisfactions, strengths, and challenges in the couple system.

Early Recollections

Early recollections (ERs), which are specific incidents the individual remembers that occurred preferably before the age of nine, represent a unique resource for gaining access to each partner's perceptions of self, relationships, and the couple system. ERs are a creative interpretation of life that explains in essence the following: "I believe relationships are . . . As a result, I . . . " ERs provide a theme that explains each partner's movement, goals, beliefs, and attitudes. ERs tell of ways in which the individual tends to respond as a person who is passive, solves problems, seeks revenge, suffers, manipulates, seeks excitement, cooperates, or provides resistance. By understanding the basic perceptions and goals, the therapist can develop an understanding of strengths and resources in the system, as well as limitations and liabilities.

A tentative hypothesis based on ERs is developed and shared with the partner. The therapist asks each partner for feedback on this understanding of their beliefs and perceptions that are summarized as basic perceptions. The couple participates and collaborates in every phase of the therapy. It is only when the couple understands, believes, accepts, and owns suggestions that the therapy can be effective. The therapeutic process involves regular feedback from the couple.

Goals for the Relationship

Next we explore the goals of the relationship. What would they like to see happen? How would they make it happen? What are they willing to give up to get greater satisfaction? Will they reduce their need to control or get their way? Are they willing to change or modify some of their expectations of their spouse?

Each person is asked to describe the relationship as if it were better, and to think of it as a video or short vignette that describes what partners would be doing to make it better. Clients are asked what they are willing to do to make this picture a reality. This gives the couple a clear picture of what they would like to see and provides direction for the marriage therapist.

As we know, communication in the marital system is often dysfunctional, ineffective, and a major hindrance to the development of cooperation. We have found one way that is usually most effective to improve communication is to ask the partners to reverse roles. Each partner is asked to speak as if they were their spouse and assign a specific topic:

1. How do you see the relationship?
2. How does the relationship work? What are you getting from it? What does your partner get from it?
3. What are the most important strengths you believe you have to help build this relationship?
4. What are the most positive things about our marital life and system when it is working well?

Identifying Areas of Satisfaction and Areas of Dissonance

This list of marital tasks identifies current satisfaction and dissatisfaction. The areas of dissatisfaction allow the couple to identify what in that area of dissatisfaction appears to be working satisfactorily. The areas investigated are (a) work, (b) participation in household chores, (c) social interaction with each other, (d) socialization and friendships extending beyond the couple, (e) demonstrations of affection, (f) sexual relationship, (g) meaning of life and spirituality, (h) parenting, (i) leisure and recreation, (j) family finances, and (k) health and fitness.

Often couples lack a picture of an effective, cooperating, and satisfying marital system. Table 6.1 will help you understand strengths and limitations in a relationship.

☐ Summarizing the System

An important aspect of Adlerian couple therapy is that once the assessment has been completed, the therapist summarizes the system by identifying what seems to be the following: (a) the real issues of the relationship, (b) the strengths the couple brings to these issues, (c) the ways in which the couple has learned to belong or be significant, (d)

TABLE 6.1

Marriage is...	Marriage is not...
Listening (being heard)	Tuning out
Caring	Ignoring
Encouraging	Criticizing
Resolving problems	Giving up
Believing	Doubting
Courage	Quitting
Trusting	Fearing
Making the effort to cooperate	Fighting or quarreling
Being responsible	Blaming
Finding solutions	Making excuses
Win–win (each satisfied)	I win–you lose
We are both right	You are wrong
Cooperative and independent	Being dependent
Courage to be imperfect	High standards, perfection
Commitment to each other	Me first
Commitment to work out problem	Hopeless or why try
Forgiving	Carrying grudges, emotional baggage
Loving unconditionally	Bargaining, keeping score
Respect	Being disrespectful
Patience	Insisting on my way now
Confidence in partner	Distrust
Pride in partner	Ridicule of partner
Forgiving	Withholding forgiveness, feeling revengeful
Appreciating	Resenting
Allowing differences	I'm right, you're wrong
Supportive	Noncaring

the liabilities in the relationship that need to be modified, and (e) the psychoeducational needs for reading, training, or skills that are evident or deficient.

☐ Couple Therapy Techniques

The therapist focuses on aligning goals between the partners while developing a relationship with mutual respect. The partners are asked what they want and expect and what they are willing to do to achieve their goals. The initial agreement is developed by having each partner describe the situation as he or she sees it. Current feelings are discussed rather than going into a lengthy history of the relationship that could include the venting of old grievances. The purpose of therapy is either to find a way to maintain and improve the relationship or to work toward an agreeable separation. Cooperation is essential in the therapeutic relationship. Many couples have learned to cooperate only by fighting. The paradox that fighting requires cooperation can lead to seeing the conflict and relationship in perspective. The emphasis is placed on having the couple learn to live as equals. They need to be aware that unless they are cooperating with social interest (Dreikurs, 1946) in a give-and-take relationship, they are probably working against each other.

The Adlerian couple therapist is able to use techniques from other schools of therapy. The Adlerian theory allows the therapist to integrate a variety of approaches (Sherman & Dinkmeyer, 1987). The following are four techniques that are unique to Adlerian therapy (Carlson & Slavik, 1997).

Catching Oneself

The therapist asks the partners to practice catching themselves in any behavior they want to change. In the beginning, they will have difficulty in catching themselves before falling into their old traps such as seeking revenge, playing inferior, or being powerful or controlling. They can learn to anticipate, then practice avoiding situations that provoke their undesirable behavior. This technique requires the partners' ability to laugh at their own behaviors rather than become discouraged when they do not catch themselves (Dinkmeyer, Dinkmeyer, & Sperry, 1987).

Hidden Reason

Searching for a hidden reason for behavior is a technique developed by Dreikurs (1967) and is used to help the individual look at the thinking process used when deciding on activities. When the therapist asks one partner, for example, why she is acting a certain way, the answer may be an honest "I don't know." Both the therapist and the other partner may then offer guesses as to the reason behind the behavior. After several guesses, the first partner is asked, "Could it be that one of these ideas makes any sense?" At this point, the first partner will begin to understand and recognize the hidden reason. This technique enables both partners to gain a greater understanding of the purposiveness of their own and their partner's behavior (Dinkmeyer et al., 1987).

Switching Roles

Switching roles is an effective technique when the couple is in conflict and both partners are taking a firm stand. Each partner is asked to take the opposing position on an issue and to discuss it as if it were his or her own viewpoint. This must be done seriously and not sarcastically. Each partner is encouraged to share as many reasons as possible to try to convince their partner that their viewpoint—which in reality is their partner's—is correct. The technique provides insight into the other person's beliefs and encourages more open-mindedness in resolving conflicts.

Paradoxical Intention

Adlerians believe that to maintain any symptom, one has to fight it. By encouraging the couple to develop and maintain a symptom, even in exaggerated form, the therapist is instructing them to stop fighting the symptom. Thus, the couple becomes more aware of the reality of the situation and sees that the consequences of the behavior must be accepted. The paradoxical recommendation is given as an experiment: "See what you can learn" (Dinkmeyer et al., 1987). Often couples do not follow through with the recommendation. They feel the task is ridiculous. It soon becomes apparent to them, however, that maintaining their symptom is equally ridiculous.

☐ Case Example

James (26) and Sandra (24) have been married for 4 years and have two children, Robert (3) and Lisa (1). The couple requested treatment as a result of learning that Robert has been diagnosed with Tourette's Syndrome and further testing is currently underway to see if additional neurological or medical problems exist. The couple each completed the following inventories before the initial visit.

- Demographic data sheets requesting information on such things as education, problems within marriage, problems with children, names and ages of siblings, relationship with parents, medical status including present use of medication, listing of previous therapy involvement, and a statement about goals for treatment and degree of optimism of treatment being successful
- Kern (1990) Lifestyle Scale
- MI (Dinkmeyer & Dinkmeyer, 1983)
- Mini-lifestyle (Dinkmeyer, 1988)
- Millon Clinical Multiaxial Inventory—III (Millon, 1994)

A review of these assessment procedures gave the therapist considerable insight into this couple before the first session.

Sandra indicated that she had been crying all the time since learning about her son's medical condition. She reports being the fifth child out of nine children. She was the sixth out of seven girls. She reports that she is not close to her parents and that she finds them to be very controlling. The parents are very devout Roman Catholics and not physically demonstrative with the children or each other. Sandra reported that she found her place in the family through her obedience, intelligence, good grades, lack of rebelliousness, lack of temper, lack of selfishness, and being punished the least. She attended 2 years of college before getting married to James and has never worked outside the home. She describes herself as "quiet, reserved, shy, organized, hard working, but having a hard time accomplishing goals." Her ER was this: "It was the first day of kindergarten and I was wearing my favorite red shirt. I felt special and smart going to school for the first time." Her scores on the MCMI–III showed someone who has both obsessive and depressive personality disorder features. Her Kern Lifestyle Scale showed extreme stress.

James indicated that he has been confused lately with all the changes in their lives and has been having problems with his work and children. He reports being the youngest of four children. The oldest was his brother, followed by two sisters and then James. His parents were not physically demonstrative and divorced when he was a teenager. He has regular contact with his parents but does not feel close to either. He reports finding his place through being spoiled, having a temper, and being critical. He did not help around the house or make good grades (compared with his siblings). He reports having an MBA in a family that values education. He currently works as a middle-level manager for a large national company. He describes himself as "someone who likes to make people feel good about themselves." His ER was "I would do cartwheels, etc., to ease the tension and pain when my parents would fight as my other siblings would sit and watch. I was scared, lonely, helpless and sad." His scores on the MCMI–III showed someone who is experiencing considerable anxiety and depression. He additionally showed as someone who has both dependent and depressive personality disorder features. His Kern Lifestyle Scale also showed extreme stress.

A summary of the assessment shows a young couple experiencing considerable stress as a result of having young children, one of whom has a major medical–psychiatric disorder. Both are experiencing personality disorders that stress submission, pleasing, and depression on James's part and doing what one should do and depression on Sandra's part. It appears that neither is living the type of life that they would personally want to; however, neither seems very clear as to what that chosen life would look like.

First Session

The therapist began the first session by going over the data collected and verifying the data with both partners present. Both indicated considerable stress in their life, indicating that they had never felt so alone and powerless.

Therapist: How comfortable are you with the medical treatment that your son is receiving?

James: I think we feel very confident with the university hospital. They are doing all that they can.

Sandra: *(nodding)* They have been really great.

Therapist: So it sounds like you are comfortable with your son's medical treatment and believe that you are doing all you can for now.

Both nod in agreement. It appeared to the therapist that the obvious presenting stressor was being dealt with effectively but the stress level was still too high.

Therapist: Where do you guys receive support? How helpful have your families been through this crisis?

James: I can't count on my Dad. I have to take care of him, and my Mom's new husband won't allow us to bring the kids over.

Sandra: I can't tell my parents about Robert's problem. We are suppose to be strong and deal with our own problems. If I told them I would just begin to cry and really upset them.

Therapist: So if I understand the situation correctly, neither of you have support except from each other.

Both acknowledge the accuracy of this observation and describe how fortunate they are to have one another. The pattern seems consistent with their personality profiles in that she does what she is supposed to and he tries to please others. Both need to become in touch with their own lives and goals and to create the life that they want. The therapist urges Sandra to honestly express herself to her parents because it is very likely that if she does not break this pattern, she will soon keep things from James. She indicated she could already see this happening. James, on the other hand, was urged to talk to his father and ask for help—in essence, allowing his father to be a father. He was also urged to tell his mother that he wanted his children to have a grandmother. Both indicated that they could see the importance of doing this; however, they doubted that they could.

Therapist: So it sounds like you are choosing to stay stuck in your problems and to pass them onto your children and their future relationships.

Both responded quickly to this paradoxical statement that they did not want this to happen.

Therapist: How about giving each other and the kids an early Christmas gift?

Both looked puzzled.

Therapist: How about doing your respective homework as a gift for your partner? You can do it for them.

This assignment was too difficult for either to refuse. James needed to please (i.e., his wife and children) and Sandra had to do what she was suppose to do (i.e., be a good mother and wife). The couple agreed to do this in the next 2 weeks before the second session.

Second Session

Both returned indicating that they had done their homework. James was amazed that his father (a very popular schoolteacher) could actually be a father to him. He asked for his dad's help and advice. His father has been to their home on two occasions and has been a source of support for his son. His mother proved to be a different story. She indicated that she would really like to be more involved with her grandchildren but really could not as her new husband wants a life without children. Sandra was visibly changed at this session. Her parents could not believe that she had not told them about their grandson and would do whatever they could to be of help. She indicated that she was not only able to cry in front of them but also with them as she and her parents got in touch with their loss and fear for Robert's future.

The couple returned for several more sessions to work out changing patterns in their relationships with others and with themselves. Their stress level decreased as they were able to obtain support from their family and from each other. The brief intervention and solution became possible through effective assessment and effective intervention tools.

☐ Summary

Adlerian psychology provides a meaningful and practical theoretical base for couple therapy. Therapy is viewed as a collaboration between the couple and therapist. By incorporating the principles, the therapist has a comprehensive system for building therapeutic change. The purpose of the therapy is to assess current beliefs and behaviors while educating the couple in new procedures that can help them establish new goals.

☐ References

Ansbacher, H. L., & Ansbacher, R. R. (Eds.). (1956). *The individual psychology of Alfred Adler: A systematic presentation in selections from his writings*. New York: Basic Books.

Bettner, B. L., & Lew, A. (1993). The Connexions focusing technique for couple therapy: A model for understanding lifestyle and complementarity in couples. *Individual Psychology, 49*(3/4), 372–391.

Carlson, J., & Dinkmeyer, D. (1987). Adlerian marriage therapy. *The American Journal of Family Therapy, 15*(4), 326–332.

Carlson, J., & Slavik, S. (1997). *Techniques in Adlerian psychology*. Washington, DC: Accelerated Development.

Carlson, J., Sperry, L., & Lewis, J. (1997). *Family therapy: Ensuring treatment efficacy*. Pacific Grove, CA: Brooks/Cole.

Dinkmeyer, D. (1988). *The mini-lifestyle*. Coral Springs, FL: CMTI Press.

Dinkmeyer, D. (1991). *The basics of understanding your lifestyle*. Coral Springs, FL: CMTI Press.

Dinkmeyer, D., & Carlson, J. (1984). *Time for a better marriage*. Circle Pines, MN: American Guidance Service.

Dinkmeyer, D., & Dinkmeyer, J. (1983). *Marital inventory*. Coral Springs, FL: CMTI Press.

Dinkmeyer, D. C., Dinkmeyer, D. C., Jr., & Sperry, L. (1987). *Adlerian counseling and psychotherapy* (2nd ed.). Columbus, OH: Merrill.

Dreikurs, R. (1946). *The challenge of marriage*. New York: Hawthorn.

Dreikurs, R. (1967). *Psychodynamic psychotherapy and counseling*. Chicago: Alfred Adler Institute.

Huber, C. (1992). Compulsory family counseling. *Topics in Family Psychology and Counseling, 1*(2), 1–81.

Huber, C. D., & Baruth, L. G. (1981). *Coping with marital conflict: An Adlerian approach to succeeding in marriage*. Champaign, IL: Stipes.

Kern, R. (1997). *Lifestyle scale*. Coral Springs, FL: CMTI Press.

Millon, T. (1994). *Millon multiaxial inventory—III*. Minneapolis, MN: National Computer Systems.

Sherman, R., & Dinkmeyer, D. (1987). *Systems of family therapy: An Adlerian integration*. New York: Brunner/Mazel.

Shulman, B., & Mosak, H. H. (1988). *Manual for lifestyle assessment*. Muncie, IN: Accelerated Development.

Sperry, L. (1992). Tailoring treatment for couples and families. *Topics in Family Psychology and Counseling, 1*(3), 1–79.

Sperry, L., & Carlson, J. (1991). *Marital therapy: Integrating theory and technique*. Denver, CO: Love.

CHAPTER

Robert Sherman

Family Therapy:
The Art of Integration

Adlerians have been formally doing professional family therapy since the 1920s. The objectives of such therapy are to help the family learn to understand its behavior, have the courage to correct its mistakes, and learn to perform in more constructive and desirable ways.

The ideal family is seen as well integrated, cohesive, democratic in its functioning, and neither enmeshed nor disengaged. There is equality between the spouses and among the genders. There is room for individual differences and collective, cooperative action. There is mutual respect and interest in each other and in the world at large. There is a climate of optimism, an openness to new ideas, and a willingness to change and deal with the impact of imposed changes. There is open, clear, and honest commu-

I wrote this chapter as an outcome of over 40 years of professional scholarship and clinical experience. The chapter represents my integration of available knowledge and experience. Although some of the ideas and materials include herein are original, most have been gleaned from a multitude of sources over the years and integrated into my perspective of Adlerian systems therapy. So, for example, the information in the beginning material on Adlerian history and principles can be found in many well-known Adlerian texts. Information about many of the techniques listed for changing roles and places can be found in the works of Salvador Minuchin (e.g., 1974) and many others. Concepts about systemic family therapies can be found in all the major texts in the field and are summarized in such sources as Gurman and Kniskern (1991) and Nicols and Schwartz (1998). Many of the important Adlerian sources are listed in the References and Suggested Resources. It is therefore assumed that this information available in the general literature of the field is already known to scholars and experts conversant with the field. The contribution here is to select, integrate, and order the information in a unique way, combined with some original ideas and techniques to be useful to all practitioners. I am most grateful to all the experts in this very rich field from whom I have learned and borrowed, and also to my clients and students, who taught me much about psychology, therapy, life, and what it means to be human. I take full responsibility for the contents of this chapter. Dialogue with others on the ideas contained herein is most welcome.

nication among the members. There is a sense of pride in self and in family and a belief that I and we have at least some power to influence and control our lives. Family members encourage one another rather than discount, demean, or negatively criticize each other.

Individual differences and needs are seen as family resources and potential strengths when appropriately recognized, synthesized, and integrated. Therefore, a major purpose of therapy is to assist the family to synthesize its differences into new and better family structures and behavior patterns in the same way as cross-pollinating plants may lead to sturdier varieties. The opposite are often fruitless efforts to overcome and defeat one another, each reciprocally finding methods to sabotage the other's efforts. Conflict establishes boundaries: I versus you. At best there can only be winners and losers, but more often everyone loses. Of course, the description in the previous paragraph is an ideal, and there probably are no totally ideal families in the real world. The ideal family as imagined by Adlerian psychology is based on a social democratic cultural tradition. Obviously, most cultures in the world are not bound by that tradition. In fact, most cultures stem from an entirely or largely authoritarian tradition. Immigrants coming to the United States bring their traditions with them and gradually acculturate to U.S. society. Cultural differences could pose a serious dilemma for Adlerian psychology and indeed all for American culturally based theories. The Adlerian answer is to recognize the uniqueness of every family and to build on the strengths inherent in every culture. But again, the art of synthesis and integration becomes urgent. Immigrants, to be successful, must find a way to live in this society that they have chosen to join for whatever reason, and this society must find a way to enable its immigrants to join with comfort and contribute constructively and successfully to society and maintain their own well-being in the process. Adlerians connect with what is and move forward together in a cooperative venture.

This chapter is divided into four parts. Part 1 addresses the history and the principles of Adlerian psychology relevant to Adlerian systems family therapy described in Part 2. Part 3 identifies the refinements in systemic thinking that govern the theory, briefly describes critical family dynamics to attend to, defines assessment and change, and briefly discusses six dimensions of the whole within which change can be brought about. Part 4 presents the outline of a general integrative model within which to conduct Adlerian systems family therapy. Many techniques for assessment and change or reeducation are listed in the outline. Unfortunately, space does not permit describing the techniques in detail. The reader is urged to use the list of resources at the end of the chapter to discover where to get detailed descriptions.

This approach to family therapy seeks to include rather than exclude. It is concerned with thinking (cognition), feeling (emotion), and doing (behavior); past, present, and future as a continuum; themes and transitions in development; individual and system; system and larger systems; individual and family uniqueness and the impact of culture and subcultures; purposiveness, intentionality, and chance events; and many more.

As an inclusive theory, the principles and practices of Adlerian psychology permit it to be well defined as a cognitive, behavioral, analytic, social constructive, and systems theory. Inclusiveness also means that it addresses a great deal of complexity. There are ways of negotiating that complexity effectively using the model presented later in this chapter and in other Adlerian models.

☐   History and Relevant Adlerian Concepts

History

Alfred Adler was an early advocate of social psychology and probably the first formal family therapist in the sense that he worked together with parents, children, teachers, and sometimes others involved in the life of the child as the identified patient. In that sense, he was also the first family systems therapist. Family therapy evolved in Adlerian psychology first within the process of open-forum counseling introduced by Adler in Austria after World War I. This involved seeing a client system observed by an audience of additional client systems; a client and therapist work together in the center of a circle of group participants. By the rise of the Nazis in the early 1930s, there were 32 Adlerian child guidance clinics doing open-forum counseling. However, teaching democratic principles and practices inherent in Adlerian psychology was obviously not well received in a totalitarian environment, and the clinics were closed and many of their professional staff fled to more hospitable countries or were caught up in the Holocaust. Those who emigrated carried the ideas and practices with them. Adler himself lectured in Great Britain and the United States until his untimely death in 1937. Thereby many people and professionals were exposed to Adlerian concepts and practices. Those who migrated set up Adlerian training programs in the various countries they inhabited, including the United States where Alexandra and Kurt Adler, Helena and Ernst Papanek, Danica Deutch, Rudolf Dreikurs, and many other students of Adler settled and organized training institutes and clinics. Open-forum counseling was particularly favored, refined, and taught by Dreikurs in the United States and spread widely by over four decades of Dreikurs' students, and now their students.

Relevant Adlerian Concepts for Family Therapy and Open-Forum Counseling

The following concepts help to explain why Adler chose to work in open forum with the family, teachers, and others as an advantageous modality, initiating the discipline of systemic family therapy.

Social Embeddedness.   Adler observed that people are born of a social connection and can survive and prosper only in a social milieu of care. People acquire their behavior in social interaction and develop dysfunctional behavior in a social context. Therefore, he concluded, more effective behavior is also best learned in a social interactive process in which the persons most involved in the interactive dysfunctional behavior participate together to bring about more effective desired behavior. He also believed that any behavior that exists is part of the human condition shared by others. Therefore, if one person or family has a problem, others probably experience something similar and could learn by sharing in the process of solving the first person's or family's problem. The act of constructively participating is an act of social interest and social feeling and contributes to the healing process of all involved. The act of sharing one's problem and life in order to be helpful to others as well as to receive help is likewise a manifestation of social interest and feeling as all join together in a cooperative venture. Such a venture reduces feelings of alienation and counteracts alienating behavior patterns that characterize most dysfunctional behavior.

Behavior Is Learned.   Adler believed that most dysfunctional behavior is learned like all other behavior and therefore does not represent an illness as such. Rather it is the result of mistaken ideas or imitated behaviors that are inappropriate to the situation. Adler was well aware for his time of the influence of genetics and stressed it in his theory of organ inferiority. However, he thought that people could learn or create effective ways of meeting the challenges of life, including those engendered by genetics, if they developed a healthy outlook on life and a positive lifestyle and remained optimistic and positively socially interested and connected.

Place, Belonging, and Significance.   We all occupy many places in various social systems, including the family. The rights, privileges, and reputation of each place determines our significance in each social system, including the family. It also determines how we view the world. The world looks substantially different to the small child among giants than it does to the chief of state ruling over millions. Our view, the meaning we assign to experience, is very much influenced, perhaps even determined, by our point of view, the beliefs and values we already hold, and the point of view is very much influenced by the places we occupy in the system. Along with self-actualization and completion (striving to fulfill and improve oneself and one's place), Adler identified the need to belong and feel significant as a major motivating force in human behavior and, we might add, in the behavior of human systems. To be accepted in an open-forum session or in a nuclear family therapy session is testimony that you are a recognized member of this community. You belong and are important enough for all the others to be here with you.

Mistakes Can Be Destructive or Useful for Creative Development.   Only if we have the courage to err can we risk trying new things and keeping an open mind. We all make mistakes. Therefore, identifying and correcting them is an integral part of growing. The problem arises when we incorporate mistaken ideas into our priority beliefs and values, set goals based on those ideas, and act on them. They become part of our very identity both as individuals and as families. Because they are so much a part of the self and the identity of the family, we ignore the evidence of negative consequences and negative feedback and continue to maintain the same mistakes rather than identifying and correcting them. That becomes dysfunctional and even destructive. People who must be right have difficulty accepting even ordinary mistakes. Working in open forum or family rather than depending on individual self-report makes it easier to observe and help to correct mistakes.

Lifestyle.   Lifestyle is based on subjective perception and includes perception of self, life, work, love, friendship, relationship to the environment and the cosmos, and one's characteristic ways of dealing with these perceptions. Included are belief systems of myths, attitudes, purposes, expectations, goals, worldview, view of self, and view of others—the core of how we think, feel, and behave. Families, institutions, and indeed cultures also develop and perceive the world subjectively through the lenses of their beliefs, values, worldview, self-view, and view of others and develop specific characteristic patterns of behavior to implement those views in dealing with life. Each and every system develops its own unique lifestyle. We can therefore readily work with the entire family and collaborative systems, not just one individual at a time.

Uniqueness, Holism, and Integration.   Adler believed very strongly that each lifestyle was idiosyncratic and idiographic even though there might be important overlapping with others who share similarities. Thus, each family and person must be observed and studied on its own terms in its specific contexts in order to understand and appreciate the behavior being expressed. Even though each part of the individual or system is likewise unique (one person's heart is somehow different from another person's heart), the parts are integrated into a unified, inseparable, functional whole. If a part is changed or missing, the whole must reorganize or perish.

It is evident that many of the major constructs of general systems theory such as holism, subjective perception, purposiveness of behavior, the interactive nature of behavior, and others were very much a part of Adler's thinking early in the 20th century, predating modern systems theories.

☐ Adlerian Family Therapy Today

Adlerian family therapy as it is practiced today builds on the principles advocated by Adler, refines the systemic aspects of the theory, and adds a repertory of techniques that can be used to undertake assessments and bring about change. Thinking holistically, the six different areas that can be approached to change the whole are identified, and specific techniques are related to each of the six areas. These are included later in the chapter, incorporated into a specific model offered for Adlerian systems family therapy.

Systemic Elements Requiring Further Attention

Definition of a System.   A human system is a group of separate individuals organized together into a unified interactive whole created, maintained, and changed by its members. The system acts on and is influenced by external elements such as the environment and larger culture in which it is embedded. It must deal with stages and transitions occurring in the members and environment such as birth, death, children, leaving home, war, and economic changes.

Individuals Create the Family System.   It is well recognized that human systems are created by people through their beliefs and performances, each interacting with the others to form the organized patterns of the human system. A human system is not a machine. An individual can greatly influence the system through his or her actions. The reader may recall an incident in 1995 in which a person called an airport in

New York and said a bomb had been planted on the premises. The airport closed down, and tens of thousands of lives and businesses were affected all over the world as flights were canceled and rerouted. Not all individual actions are so dramatic, but they all have systemic consequences. The system remains organized as it is only as long as the members continue behaving according to the same rules, roles, and patterns as before.

The System Helps Create and Influences the Individual. Similarly, the system acts to maintain itself and acts to force conformity on its members. It assigns places, roles, performances, identities, rights, privileges, and reputations to its members, greatly influencing individual lifestyle, personality, and behavior. The system incorporates who will behave how, when, where, and with whom and the value of those actions. The system includes the myths and values that its members are to live by. To maintain itself, the system acts to enforce all the above more often than to reward change. However, successful long-term systems have among their rules, myths, and values some mechanism to allow for or even encourage change. For example, Adlerians strongly encourage families to hold regular democratically organized family meetings to consider the needs of the members and to make future plans.

The Family System Is Part of Larger Cultural Systems. The family system is a major repository of the larger culture to which the family belongs, as it interprets, accepts, and imitates that culture and transmits it to its members. It may also transmit what it rejects in that culture. Each participant also interprets, accepts, rejects, and imitates what is transmitted.

Many other cultures and subcultures have an impact on the family as a unit and separately on each person in it, such as race, ethnicity, religion, school, occupation, job, peer group or gang, gender, education, community, organizations of which one is a member, and institutions such as the law and health care systems. Each of these cultures constitutes an organized system with its own myths, expectations, and visions; its own boundaries; its own rules, designated roles, and patterns of organization and communication. Each person who belongs and identifies with any given system must also be able to operate within it and negotiate it. Thus, each individual and family is also part of many other systems simultaneously, which he or she helps to create and which demand adherence to their particular systemic patterns. Many aspects of these different systems may well be different than, even antagonistic to, the other. For example, our economic system favors competition, whereas most religions emphasize cooperation and helpfulness. Allegiance to a gang may demand fighting with others, behavior forbidden in most schools and communities.

In such a heterogeneous world, clear and consistent definitions of beliefs, identities, values, and appropriate behavior are difficult to create for the individual and the family. Add to this that over 75% of marriages are interethnic, over 50% interfaith, and over 3% interracial (and these numbers are increasing). Thus, the degree to which culture influences individual and family lifestyle requires a great deal of integration and synthesis.

The Family System Moves Forward toward Systemic Goals. The line of movement of the individual and the system is toward the fulfillment of its known goals and those goals that are not overtly clear to the person or members. To the outside world, this movement may appear to be backwards or circular as when the family seems to avoid engaging in commonsense actions and continues to perform in the same dysfunctional repeating pattern, even when it appears they know better. When we understand the internal logic of the person or system, the purpose or the direction of the movement becomes obviously toward their goals. Typically, if the behavior is dysfunctional, then either the goal or the means for achieving the goal are mistakenly chosen. The implication here is that behavior is purposive, learned, and chosen for the purpose. Dysfunctional behavior patterns appear circular in that each participant's behavior reinforces the others' behavior, creating a repeating pattern of interaction. For example, mother is supposed to be a good mother and properly rear her children in this family. Her adolescent son constantly "forgets" to do his chores. Mother becomes increasingly nagging, critical, and punitive in trying to teach her son to be a good, responsible person in order for her to also be a good mother. An important family value is that sons are to grow up strong and independent. Mother's criticism and punishment threatens the son's sense of independence and personhood. He is not allowed, according to other family values, to hit or attack his mother, so he "forgets" in order to be strong and independent. Meanwhile, another culturally imbued family value accepted by all the members is that women are to take care of and listen to men who have the ultimate authority and independence. Mother, therefore, comes from a position of inferiority when making demands on her son, and this makes it easier for the son to defy her unless the father steps in with authority or backs mother's authority. Mother and son cooperate in continuing the fight, which is a further, if aggravating, way of toughening the son according to the family priority goal.

From the above example, it can be seen that a given pattern of behavior can be driven by multiple forces operating simultaneously in both individuals and in the system to create and maintain the repeating pattern that embodies one or more family goals.

A System Maneuvers on the Continua of Rigidity–Flexibility and Stability–Change. A system must be sufficiently rigid to maintain its boundaries with respect to all other entities in the world, particularly all other families, and yet maintain sufficient continuity to retain its continuing discrete identity in the face of constant change. It does these through the development of its own unique mythologies, values, beliefs, expectations, rules, roles, and patterns of communication. A positive, optimistic attitude prevailing in the family encourages openness and flexibility in meeting the challenges of life and in seeking out opportunities to be seized. A pessimistic set of beliefs and expectations leads the family to be overly rigid, tight, protective, and avoidant of change. They are governed by fear and anxiety rather than by excitement and curiosity. A family that is too open or ready to accept every new thing will have few guiding lines or rules for its members and little to hold them together as a discrete entity. There is a great deal of confusion and even chaos in such systems. There is also the possibility for a great deal of creativity in a chaotic, unstructured environment, but there is little structure available to guide and plan for the use of that creativity. It is probably safe to conclude that in addition to openness and flexibility, some level of resistance to external pressures, including those of the therapist, is essential to family and individual survival.

Flexibility. Of course, change is an inevitable given of life. We grow, age, and face constantly evolving situations in life as well as new demands and expectations from others. Sometimes change is sudden and catastrophic, such as death of a family member or the physical destruction of one's home and possessions. Flexibility is required to cope with ongoing processes of change. Family values that include interest in others and the importance of membership in the system of all humankind—social interest and social feeling—encourage openness and flexibility. The belief that we have some influence and ability to control events is another value that reinforces optimism, openness, and flexibility. Too great a need to try to control both events and others will lead to dysfunctional behavior as viewed by others and by the community. They will react to contain the controlling and domineering behavior. Therefore, there is a need for enough openness and interest in others to receive the feedback that is being given by others about the consequences and impact of the behavior.

Transitions.   Transitions are a major source of pressures to change. Birth, death, major illness, marriage, entering school, leaving home, divorce, a new job, loss of a job, retirement, illness, geographic moves, and war are among the transitions that demand major changes in the system. How these changes are perceived, assessed, and dealt with is determined by the individual lifestyles of the members and the lifestyle of the system. The members and family give meaning to the events in the light of the goals they strive for, their existing beliefs, the knowledge they have of alternatives available to them, and the skills they possess to choose and enact those alternatives.

Resistance.   In psychotherapy, resistance is usually defined as a negative that impedes progress. That may well be true. However, resistance is also necessary to place a boundary around any given entity in order to contain it as discrete from others. It is also necessary in order for a system to maintain its integrity by controlling the impact of external forces acting on the system. In this sense, resistance represents an important strength in the system that can be used by the therapist in constructive ways by recognizing the internal logic and value behind the resistant behavior. The greater the resistance, the greater the motivation to mount it, the greater the power mobilized to perform it. This power can in turn be tapped and directed toward constructive uses.

Culture Defines Systemic Territoriality and Boundaries.   Cultures
prescribe what is close, what is distant; what is within and what is without; what is part of and what is separate from; what is enmeshed and what is disengaged; and who are we and who are they. However, the family (and each member) interprets these prescriptions based on its own experiences, accepting and imitating the prescriptions after its own fashion, or rejecting them and creating other definitions for itself.

Territoriality.   We know that a traditional Italian family will insist that the newlyweds live close by, even in the same building; come every Sunday for dinner and fight out conflicts in the venue of the extended family, all of which Anglos would consider as enmeshed. We know that Latino families prefer to interact nose to nose at a distance of approximately 14 inches, whereas Anglo families prefer approximately 30 inches and therefore feel very intruded on by those who traditionally come physically closer. We know that many Asian families will avert the eyes rather than look directly at the other person, which is considered rude, whereas Anglos would interpret averted eyes as timid, inattentive, distant, or rude. As a group, it appears that men and women grow up in different gender cultures and have somewhat different definitions of intimacy. To oversimplify, for men intimacy is doing together and intercourse, and for women it is personal talk and being together. Men learn to compete to belong, to be somebody. Women are taught to relate in order to belong and be somebody. When a man ignores or does not fully discuss with a woman, she feels left out, distanced. When a woman criticizes or puts down a man, he feels demeaned and pushed away. Male and female roles are currently evolving and may look different in the future. Our culture often demands that a person work long hours in order to do the job or succeed in the vocation. The spouse or children may feel more and more abandoned by the worker who makes them a lower priority in his or her time, attention, and energy. American culture favors much education for our children. Some immigrant groups struggling for survival may favor putting their children to work at an early age or may not believe that females require an education.

Territoriality also extends to issues of privacy, possessions, touching, and emotional space. If a daughter borrows her mother's blouse, is that normal and okay or is it unacceptable "taking" of one's possessions? If a mother asks a daughter, "How did things go on your date last night?" is that intrusive or normal? If mother does not ask, does that mean that she does not care or that she is respectful of privacy? When and what kind of touching is acceptable and when and what kind is considered abuse? Some families are very physically affectionate and others are very reserved.

How Cohesive Should a Family System Be?   Cohesiveness involves belongingness, identity, felt similarities, and degree of interagreement among the members; how much do they stick together, identify themselves as members of the group, and believe that they belong together? This, too, is in part a matter of value and culture.

Boundaries are established to set this family off from all other entities. They define who and what is included or excluded within the boundaries, what credentials are needed to be included, and the rules of inclusion or ostracism. They further assert who participates in given activities and who can talk about what with whom.

Identity is a crucial element in human systems. Who are we and who am I? How do we define and affiliate ourselves? Identity includes a process of labeling or naming something and affiliating with that label. To one's self or in the larger society, the label may have either positive or negative connotations and may carry with it a range of privileges and obligations. It also assumes a set of relatively stable and recognizable characteristics. Identity also provides one with places within larger systems. What does it mean to be a garbage collector or physician in the community in which you live and in the nation at large; to be a Democrat or Republican; Catholic or Jew; physically challenged or a star athlete; the youngest or eldest child in the family; the family breadwinner or child care person; bright or special education pupil; tall or short; the person proposing new things to do or the one who wants to keep things as they are? Is your family an alcoholic, mentally retarded, or racially inferior family or is it a professional, wealthy, creative family? The value assigned to these labels by oneself and others has an enormous impact on the degree of pride we feel in carrying the labels and in our self-concept as one who is so identified. It may also influence our sense of optimism or pessimism and the degree to which we can be open or rigid. The labels may prescribe the bounds within which we are expected or allowed to behave or misbehave. The above are but a few examples of the impact of culture on territoriality, closeness, intimacy, belonging, and identity.

Additional Social Psychological Constructs to Understand Family Dynamics

A human system operationally consists of the patterns of interaction among the partici-pants of the organized group that constitutes the system. Many constructs such as ri-gidity, flexibility, resistance, territoriality, transitions, cohesiveness, boundaries, and identity have been discussed in the previous sections. Other constructs that are more directly related to the patterns of interaction within the system include the dimensions of power, alliances and collusions, closeness and distance, myths and beliefs, rules, roles, similarities, complementarities and differences, and patterns of communication. These provide us with tools for observing and understanding the behavior patterns in the family system. Similarly, by bringing about change in any of these dimensions we can bring about change in the system.

Power.   Power consists of the manner in which decisions are made in the system and how actions are elicited or coerced. Who in the family is able to influence whom to do what? The person who is overtly most aggressive or most pushing for change may not necessarily be exercising much power if others successfully defy, withhold, with-draw, or sabotage that person. Most obvious are efforts to be the boss and get one's own way. One who through weakness elicits others to do his or her bidding may be very powerful. Making noise is not enough; others must agree or comply. Adlerians stress that decisions are ideally best made collaboratively through discussion, agreement, and conformance with agreements. Conflicts in the family tend to be more visible in the power dimension of interaction, although their source may really lie in some of the following dimensions.

Alliances and Collusions.   Members make special connections with one an-other within the system. Thus, a father may collude with a rebellious daughter against his wife, with whom he does not know how to cope. Husband and wife may ally to-gether in the process of parenting. A wife may ally with her mother and father against her husband. Two siblings can gang up on a third. Each parent may ally with a differ-ent child who becomes somehow more his or her child. Alliances can be a source of strength that empowers the family, or they can create dysfunctional triangles that get in the way of more appropriate dyadic interactions, such as the collusion between father and daughter against the wife.

Beliefs.   The way in which the family and its individual members story their expe-riences in the world is included in the myths they create, the beliefs and expectations they hold, the attitudes they express, and the values they implement. These are the core of all cognitive psychologies, of which Adlerian psychology is one. Most individual and systemic behavior is shaped by and derived from this dimension. The majority of the principles of Adlerian psychology already discussed in this volume and earlier in this chapter refer to this cognitive dimension, and therefore are not repeated here. Suf-fice it to say that these myths and beliefs form the heart of the individual and family lifestyle.

Rules.   Rules are developed by the family to implement their beliefs and the goals that are derived from those beliefs. Rules involve who is to do what with whom and how. An example is that "We believe in education, therefore the rule is that the children must do well in school." A second belief might be that "We are good Christians and therefore the rules are that we all go to church on Sundays and we must help our less fortunate brothers by serving in the soup kitchen program." A third rule might be that "No one is allowed to make noise when we put the baby to sleep because we believe that the baby's needs come first." Individual members may also assert what they hope will be rules. Unless the others accept them, these assertions lead to family conflict. The rules may include the assignment of roles to each member of the family for the efficient enactment of the rules.

Roles.   Roles are reciprocal relationships in which each participant cooperates by performing expected behaviors. A leader cannot be a leader unless others agree to follow. A rescuer requires a victim or needy person who can be rescued. A peacemaker can only try to make peace if others are in conflict and allow the peacemaker to intervene; often they may combine and attack the peacemaker. A pursuer cannot pursue unless another distances. There are hundreds of common family roles from the one who does the finances to the gardener, historian, launderer, car washer, dog walker, homework helper, bully, big brother or sister, child partner for a parent, pal, confidante, sick one, helpless one, carrier of the family anger, compassionate one, contrary one, central switchboard through whom all communication must go, time clock who informs everyone when it is time to get up or do something, and so forth. If a member changes one's role, the system has to either force conformity somehow or reorganize to accommodate the change. If mom suddenly refuses to wake up Johnny every morning for school, Johnny will either try to enforce her role or get up by himself. Being able to count on one another's behavior in most situations produces the stable characteristics of the family. A couple who fight often probably does not even need to be present for the next fight if they could just put on a recording of the last one. A family member accepts or volunteers for those roles that are consistent with his or her lifestyle and that in turn become part of the family lifestyle. In addition, the system occasionally forces a role on a member, such as in child abuse.

Similarities.   The degree to which participants hold the same beliefs and values, behave in the same manner, and identify with each other is indicative of their similarities—the ways in which they are alike. "We like the same music, identify with the same religion, are vocationally ambitious, like to sleep late on weekends" are a few examples. We tend to feel more comfortable with those who are most similar to us and experience our commonalities. We do not have to like those commonalities in order to feel more comfortable with such persons. However, if we like ourselves and our identity, we probably will like those who are most similar to us. Those who dislike something about themselves will dislike those same things in another, including one's spouse or children. Nevertheless, for the most part, similarities provide the glue that binds relationships together.

So many couples are coming together from different cultures and subcultures that it requires a greater effort to find powerful similarities to keep in the foreground of their lives and to help them form the bases of new syntheses that can become new similarities. For example, in an Anglo–Italian interethnic marriage in which the Anglo wants to teach the children to grow up and out and maintain a good deal of independence from the nuclear family and the Italian wants to teach the children to stay very close physically and participate intimately in all the extended family's doings, we need to create a new family similarity, such as, perhaps, "Our children will learn to grow up and make their own independent lives, but live within a 30-minute commute of the parents, visit at least twice a month, and be involved in important extended family matters." Of course, the grandparents may have some things to say about such arrangements and may need to be included in accepting the new idea about "us." The children will need to agree and/or react.

If the family is too similar, there could be a lack of interpersonal excitement and options for change that comes with differences among the members. If the members are too dissimilar, it may be very difficult for them to develop any kind of cohesiveness or even to get to like each other.

Complementarities and Differences.   These are the opposite of similarities. Each individual, even those in the same family, is unique and has unique needs that may be different from and even contrary to those of other family members. What is good for one may not always be either good or desirable for another. Inevitable differences can be the gold mine of new constructive growth and change or the murky depths out of which arise the worst nightmarish conflicts of family life. Some differences are the basis for the formation of the reciprocal role relationships described above in the section on roles. Someone who needs to be needed has to find or teach another who is or will be needy. One who must be the boss seeks to engage others who perhaps are dependent and will submit and comply. People also do seek out persons who represent for them an ideal that they miss and/or wish for themselves, or who can fill a need that they have. If I am passive, I may choose to engage with someone who is more active. If I am shy, it would be nice to link up with another who is more socially outgoing and adept. Thus, the wife who is more social may become the social secretary of the family, and the husband who was taught to be more mechanically inclined becomes the Mr. Fix-It of the family and complies with his wife's social arrangements.

Patterns of Communication.   Every family is characterized by the manner in which the members communicate. Often the complaint brought to the therapist is "We don't communicate." This is an absolute impossibility. Even silence can be a very powerful communication, as can physical withdrawal or disengagement. Felt noncommunication is a potent message. Communication can be verbal, including tone and pitch of voice; touch; involvement with someone's perceived physical or emotional space or possessions; physical posture; physical signs such as shaking one's head in agreement or rejection, standing up or sitting down; making or averting eye contact; and symbolic signs such as the way one dresses, carrying a flag or banner, or keeping a door locked or open. We communicate by expressing moods such as joy, anger, intensity, or interest. We communicate by giving or withholding information, lying, creating double messages, or double binds. "Yes, but" is a typical kind of double message. Some theorists believe that every family dysfunctional pattern involves some kind of double bind. The communication is such that no matter what you do you lose. One parent says, "Why don't you ever put your clothes away?" The clothes are put away. "You only did it because I told you again and again to do it."

Patterns of communication consist of who can speak about what to whom and how. The patterns that emerge are governed by the rules of the family and are embedded in the structure of the roles within the family. "Children are to be seen and not heard" is a rule governing communication. "Don't fight in front of the children" is another example. A third example is "In this family, we don't show anger or yell at each other." However, most rules are not so explicit; they just evolve as the family evolves. Mother chooses her eldest son as her confidante about her problems with her husband, giving him also the role of surrogate partner. The eldest child is assigned child care responsibilities for the younger child. In that capacity, he or she communicates and teaches the younger child many things, favored and disfavored by the parents.

Assessment and Change

There are six dimensions of behavior that particularly lend themselves to examination and assessment and efforts to bring about change in family systems. These are (a) the belief systems; (b) patterns of interaction around roles and places; (c) available knowledge and skills; (d) social feeling and social interest; (e) feelings of optimism, empowerment, and hope; and (f) patterns of communication. Although the last three could be subsumed under the first three, they are of sufficient power to acknowledge them separately here. It is very fortunate that most of the structured techniques available in the literature simultaneously attend to and encompass all six of these dimensions. Examples are described below.

Assessment.   By assessment, we are seeking to discover what the patterns of individual and systemic behavior actually are, what they mean at several different levels, and what their consequences are, including in what ways they are dysfunctional. We would like to identify the strengths available in the system that we can build on in bringing about the desired changes. It is further useful to learn what other systems these clients are members of and affected by and see what strengths are available in schools, church, culture, community agencies, extended family, and many possible others that can be engaged to help, or which indeed may be creating the problem. Among the many frameworks of meaning that can be used to understand the family and its members are those of the many cultures they belong to, especially U.S. culture at large; the private logic of the family system; the private logic of each member; the private logic of the therapist viewing the behavior; and the theoretical school of the therapist that tells him or her how to look, what to look for, what tools to use, and what it means. In this text, Adlerian theory informs our work.

Change or Reeducation.   *Change* and *reeducation* refer to new behavior patterns instituted by the family as a group and by its individual members, especially the identified client, if one person is so labeled, and leading to more constructive and desired consequences. Change involves both new understandings and the practice of new actions. Knowledge and understanding by itself may or may not result in new behavior because competing values may inhibit the implementation of what is known to be better. For example, I may know the dangers inherent in taking drugs but feel less depressed when I am high and so continue to take drugs, all the while saying, "I must stop!" Adlerians believe that change is almost always with the express consent and agreement of the parties involved and not based on coercion or manipulation by the therapist. However, there are a few exceptions. On the basis of societal values, external controls might be used in cases of impending suicide, violence to others, or uncontrolled use of destructive substances, but only if unsuccessful in otherwise gaining the people's cooperation. The therapist's use of paradox is sometimes criticized as manipulative. However, paradox when used appropriately to dramatize existing dysfunctional behavior or to state the truth of that behavior so that the clients can see it more clearly from a new perspective is no different ethically from other forms of interpretation. When we think holistically, we can focus our attention on any one or more of the six areas for change listed above and help to bring about a change in that arena. The person and family will then have to reorganize as a whole to accommodate to the new situation. The caveat is that the family must commit to practice the new behavior.

An example is the Expressing and Experiencing Love Exercise (Sherman, Oresky, & Rountree, 1991) used with a couple in conflict to help them understand their goals and styles in loving and being loved. The couple is asked to cooperate and answer four questions and also to listen attentively to the spouse's answers. The questions are the following: "What things does your partner have to do concretely so that you will know that you are being loved?" "What things do you do concretely to let your partner know that you are being loving?" "What interactions were most pleasant in your family growing up?" "What kind of interactions were most negative or missing in your family growing up?" "Please rank order your answers, 1 for the most important, and so forth." The answers are examined to identify the priority beliefs and goals, where they came from, and how they lead to disappointment even when both partners are expressing love to one another based on their own priorities, which are different from the other's. They compare and contrast their lists to discover the basis of their misunderstanding and to familiarize one another with their needs and expectations and the reasons for them, of which most people are unaware. The exercise provides the couple with the opportunity to evaluate their beliefs and priorities from a new perspective. As a result, they may choose to change some of their ideas and then change some of their goals. They observe their own roles in the conflict by pushing for the original priorities and also for the sources of their disappointment in the roles taken by the partner. They learn that they can behave differently by paying attention to and being interested in the partner's language of loving and show love more often according to the partner's priorities, once those have been evaluated and clarified. They discover the partner's efforts at loving and feel more encouraged and optimistic about the relationship. Learning that they can target their loving behavior more accurately provides further encouragement and a sense of empowerment. They practice cooperation in order to perform the exercise, which provides evidence that they do not have to fight. This too is encouraging. When each partner is paying closer positive attention, they feel closer to one another, which increases optimism about the relationship. They need to communicate their own list clearly to the therapist and partner, and they need to demonstrate that they have heard and understand where the partner is coming from. They are therefore practicing effective communication skills that can be used as a model for further communication. Throughout the process, the counselor may question or coach the couple; interpret, reframe, or restory the material; acknowledge, validate, reinforce, or confront behavior; or use any number of other tactics during the exercise to bring about change.

☐ Outline of an Integrative Therapeutic Model for Family Therapy

Introduction

The model offered here stresses four major stages that function both sequentially and interactively over the course of each session and over the entire course of the therapy. One or more of the stages may receive greater or lesser attention at any given time or session. This outline is not intended as a step-by-step process for conducting the counseling interviews. Rather, it suggests many techniques and tactics for achieving the goals of each of the four major stages of the therapy. So, for example, in Stage 1, Defining, Joining, Contracting, and Structuring, it is suggested that the therapist acknowledge each member's stated definition of the problem, and several methods for joining with the clients are identified. For a step-by-step description of the conduct of an interview, see Dinkmeyer and Sherman (1989) and a very brief summary after the description of the model.

The model and the suggested techniques and tactics are not offered as a cookbook approach. Every family is considered unique, and it is the practitioner's obligation to design a therapy suited to the particular family. Also, for economy of time, the therapist focuses on only those techniques and processes necessary to help the family. Therefore, the model offered here is to be considered a resource that the therapist can use as a guide to design a given therapeutic process.

Most families arrive in therapy in the midst of a power struggle, frustrated, carrying the individual perceptions of their lifestyles and culture and their own images of the therapist as a potential friend, foe, helper, rescuer, interferer, judge, mediator, expert, or ally, thus posing a considerable challenge to the therapist. Many cultures do not view psychotherapy as a viable or appropriate problem-solving or curative treatment. These issues, among others, need to be addressed in the first stage of the therapy. The four major stages of the model are (a) defining, joining, contracting, and structuring the therapeutic system; (b) assessing and understanding the motivation and behavior of the members and the family; (c) changing, reorienting, and reeducating the family members and the family system; and (d) evaluating and reinforcing the changes, planning next steps, and terminating.

The Four-Stage Model: Techniques and Tactics

Defining, Goal Setting, Joining, Contracting, and Structuring the Therapeutic System.

Welcome the Clients. Welcome the clients and invite them to describe what brought them into the meeting. Inquire if any member is there involuntarily. Thank that person for the opportunity to meet him or her.

Invite Each Client to State What the Problem Is in the Family. Acknowledge each one's point of view about the problems as stated so that each feels heard and understood. Clarify the stated problems in terms of what it means to each individual and its impact on that person. Underneath conflicting statements of the problem is often to be discovered a common basic need such as to be heard, understood, counted, or feel loved. Often the members in conflict are experiencing the same underlying need. In other words, they are in agreement and want the same thing. Pointing this out to them can be a surprising dynamic. The therapist then validates the needs as important to each.

Ask Clients to State What Each Thinks Will Make It Better, Insisting on Positive Statements of Dos Rather Than Don'ts. Second, it is even more powerful if each can then be encouraged to say what he or she could do to make it better rather than demanding change of the others.

Formulate a Common Problem Stated in the Positive that Cuts Across Their Multiple Concerns. Some examples are "You would like to create a more respectful environment with less fighting" or "You would like to figure out how each person can get more of what he or she wants without hurting the others." Stating it in the positive opens the way to formulating positive goals for the therapy. It is also useful, when possible, to reframe the criticized patterns of behavior from the negative to the positive. In the case of the nagging wife and resistant husband, one can reframe it as, "Is it possible that we have here a woman who readily sees the need and opportunities for change and therefore takes on the difficult job of being the change agent and boat rocker and a husband who more favors stability and the status quo and would like to protect the family by moving more slowly and cautiously toward changes, trying to keep the boat from tipping over?"

Discuss in Concrete Positive Terms What Outcomes Would Make the Work Together a Successful Enterprise. Help the clients identify goals that are realistically attainable within the constraints of time, finances, resources, and obstacles likely to come up. Explore with the family what the consequences of obtaining those outcomes are likely to be on the family, on each member, and on others outside of the family system. Attuning them to the consequences of their actions is important therapeutic work.

Prescribe an In-Session Task to Work on an Agreed-On Small Subgoal. Some examples of subgoals may be "What shall we do as a family this weekend?" "How shall we prepare and clean up after dinner tonight?" or "In a nondemanding, noncommanding, noncriticizing way can you each tell the others what happens to you when [the symptomatic behavior] is occurring?" By observing the behavior, the therapist can see how the family operates, the degree of cooperation, the family's skills in performing, and the sources of resistance. This is an assessment technique as well as a way to help clarify the chosen goals.

Joining with the Clients Is Essential and Is Ongoing from the Moment of First Contact. Techniques and tactics can range from a smile of recognition or welcome to body language indicating careful attention, finding something in common with one or more members, and admiring a pin or article of clothing to a mutual connection with the person who made the referral. Especially important is to acknowledge each person's presence, contribution, feelings, and wishes. If appropriate, it is even more potent to validate or at least show appreciation of the person's position or the family's plight. Often the identified client may also be the family scapegoat. The person pressing hard to "correct" the situation may sometimes also not be very popular in the family. The therapist needs to join especially with those two individuals.

Joining with the Involuntary Client Who Is Personally Oppositional or Culturally Oppositional Requires Additional Methods.   The therapist can take a one-down position. "Tell me how people in your group would try to solve a problem like this?" "Would it help to invite one or more family elders to join us?" "You have already demonstrated that no one can make you do anything. Now what do you want to do with that power?" "You're the boss. What would you like to do?"

The therapist can take an authoritative position. "This [state the problem as it is referred to you] is the problem that has brought us together. I have some ideas and I'm sure you will have some too." "The court has put us together. Let's make the best of it. Our meetings might even turn out to be useful because I've been with many families in the same boat." "At what age did you learn to play dumb? You are very good at it. You're probably a very talented person." "Others are sharply criticizing you. I've learned that each person experiences the same events very differently. I would really like to hear your side of the story; how you see it; how you feel about it." The therapist can lead in brainstorming ideas.

The therapist can join with the opposition. "If I were in your shoes, I would be pretty angry [upset, inconvenienced, humiliated, feeling put down, etc.] by this situation." The therapist can move indirectly, especially with adolescents who are withholding. "Could you please tell me something about your brother [mother, father, family, culture, school, neighborhood]?" The person is often happy to speak about someone or thing other than the self and thereby both becomes involved and reveals the self through projection onto the subject being discussed. This could also be incorporated within the framework of circular questioning that reveals systemic patterns of interaction as perceived and described by one member.

Structuring and Contracting Provide the Framework of the Therapeutic System.   Some things the therapist carefully spells out, and others are simply modeled. The therapist carefully describes any fee and payment rules, meeting times and places, insurance policies, number of sessions, cancellation and termination policies, records required, rules of confidentiality, rules of communication in sessions, and perhaps some rules of respect and courtesy. More subtly, the therapist structures the therapeutic system by the various roles and positions he or she assumes. The Adlerian therapist is most typically an authoritative, not authoritarian, democratic leader who seeks cooperation and consent for all decisions. She or he models careful attention, listening, understanding, honesty, dependability, respect, and courtesy. Special respect and consideration will be afforded to the "leader" of the family, whoever that may be, culturally or dynamically determined, while maintaining the therapist's leadership position. For therapeutic purposes, the therapist can shift roles from leader to follower, to coach–teacher, good parent or grandparent or adult child, neutral member, or authoritarian rule setter as in stopping violence; can be intense or cool, cheerful or sad, humorous or serious, self-disclosing or detouring of questions about the self; can be leaning forward or backwards, standing or sitting, choose whom to sit next to, move the seats around; can dress casually or formally; and can suggest inviting additional members to join the session or see subgroups of family members. Each stance affects the structure of the group and the patterns of communication and interaction in different ways.

Assessing and Understanding the Motivation and Behavior Patterns of the Members and the Family.

Track the Interactive Pattern of Behavior Encompassing the Symptoms or the Defined Problem. Who does what, then who does what, and so forth until the reciprocal pattern of how each reinforces the behavior of the others is manifest. Who takes on what roles? Who communicates how with whom?

Uncover the Subjective Belief Systems of the Members and the Family as a Unit. What are their priority beliefs and the purposes around which they organize their behavior? The symptom or problem is likely to be organized around one to three central cognitive themes that give meaning to the behavior. The themes are also structural in that the people occupy places and then take on roles in relation to the themes. The direction and apparent goal of the behavior provide good clues as to the cognitive sources driving the behavior, often by looking toward the approximate opposite. For example, running away may signal that the family is too enmeshed and in need of further individuation of and respect for its members.

Observe What Roles the Participants Assume in the Interactions. What is the meaning of those roles in this specific system and to each member?

Explore the Context in Which the Family and the Symptom or Problem Are Operating. Who lives in the household or has a special place in it, such as a boyfriend? What is the constellation of the multigenerational family? What are the family gender guiding lines? What are the family guiding lines in relation to the problem area, that is, vocations, sexuality, intimacy, perfectionism, chronic illness, and so forth? What are the cultural and religious backgrounds of the family members? What are their vocations, interests, and time involvements? What is their socioeconomic and educational status? What are the characteristics of the community they live in? To what degree do they interact with others outside of the family, and what kind of external resources are available to them for support or assistance? What other resources are available to help them deal with these problems?

Discover the Strengths of the Family. These strengths should be discovered in relation to the above resources and in terms of intelligence, health, physical characteristics, problem-solving skills, information, talents, finances, optimism, tolerance, persistence, friends, social skills, and any others that may be relevant to the problem. Note particularly the great courage being displayed in dealing with the difficulties being faced by this family. The above strengths and resources can be used to encourage the family and bring about constructive change.

Observe the Following Dynamics.   These dynamics are (a) the distribution and use of power and decision making based on conformance; (b) the interplay around closeness, distance, territoriality, and intimacy; (c) the boundaries that include and exclude or are too rigid or too permeable; (d) the coalitions formed among the members and between the members and outsiders for or against other members; (e) the myths and beliefs that govern the system; (f) the rules devised to enforce and operationalize those myths and beliefs; (g) the roles assumed to carry out the rules; (h) the similarities and history that bind the family together and provide for its stability; (i) the complementarities that help fashion reciprocal roles and provide the excitement and resource of differences; and (j) the patterns of communication through which all the above are expressed and transmitted.

Ask If the Family Has Successfully Dealt with this Problem in the Past.   If so, why is it different now, or could they recycle their former successful solutions?

To summarize, find out what the specific problem patterns of behavior are; the meaning, goals, and context of the behavior; the strengths and resources available for change; the dynamics of the interactive process; and what previous successes can be built on. Collectively, these constitute the family lifestyle.

General Techniques and Tactics for Assessment.   Following many of the techniques listed below is provided a reference whereby the reader may find a detailed description of the technique.

- Questioning—open ended, structured, circular

- Tests, inventories, and questionnaires (Fredman & Sherman, 1987; Touliotos, Perlmutter, & Straus, 1990; Kern et al., 1995; Sherman, 1994).

- Observation of in-session behavior—dress, posture, seating patterns, tone of voice, metaphors of speech, subjects stressed, evidence of anxiety, fear, joy, satisfaction, pride, leadership, roles assumed, implicit rules followed

- Structured exercises—tracking, the day, family floor plan, ecomap, early individual or couple recollections, expressing and experiencing love, family photographs, and the name game (Sherman & Fredman, 1986; Sherman et al., 1991)

- Family constellation and genogram (Dinkmeyer, Dinkmeyer, & Sperry, 1987; McGoldrick & Gerson, 1985)

- Sculpting—intimacy sculpture, animal–object sculpture, perceived actual and ideal sculptures (Sherman, 1993; Sherman & Fredman, 1986)

- Metaphorical methods—writing autobiographies and diaries, composing and completing stories, making drawings, analysis of dreams, reading and writing poetry, choosing music, using the multitude of imagery techniques (Kopp, 1995; Pearce, 1996; Sherman & Fredman, 1986)

Some Methods for Organizing the Data Accumulated in the Assessment Process. Some methods for organizing these data in order to discover the central organizing tendencies and get to the "essence" of what is going on are described below. It is not possible in the time available, especially in short-term therapy, to deal with all issues that may be uncovered. It is necessary to focus on a select few that seem to be the central organizing tendencies around the symptomatic behavior and that inhibit further growth and development.

1. See the symptom as a metaphor for what is happening in the family. For example, does a child running away signal that most family members are somehow running away from an atmosphere in which individuality is not respected? Does compulsive behavior signal fear, insecurity, or a sense of powerlessness in the current family or family of origin? Asking questions about related behavior in nonsymptomatic members may elicit the central family dynamics, for example, "How do each of you manage to stay away from the family?"

2. Project a word, phrase, or caption to capture the theme of the family interaction pattern, such as "fighting for air," "teaching mom to take father on," "need for appreciation," "never enough to go around," or "becoming independent at any price."

3. Notice what you the therapist are feeling when working with this system. Do you feel like rescuing, running, attacking, attaching yourself to, frustrated, confused, or pitying? What are you doing in response to those feelings? This is how you are invited to participate in the system. Others in the system are probably experiencing similar feelings and interacting in similar ways.

4. Carefully track the repeating pattern of behavior around the symptom to see how each person reinforces the behavior of the others to maintain the repeating pattern.

5. Identify the individual and family priorities and goals that drive the behavior such as the need for appreciation, attention, domination, protection, respect, being heard, or maintaining a critical tradition or myth.

6. Examine the reciprocal role relationships to see how the pattern is evoked and maintained. Among the common patterns are pursuer–distancer, rescuer–victim, active–passive, aggressive–violent, depressed–sick, and overresponsible–underresponsible ones. People may be in competition to occupy the same role such as dominant one or sickest one. In "remarital" families, there may be considerable competition for specific roles and places formerly accustomed to, such as eldest son, surrogate parental partner, or boss.

7. Observe the direction of the behavior (the line of movement) and its approximate opposite. The direction of the behavior can be inferred from the consequences that

repeatedly occur in a repeating pattern of behavior, such as the symptom. The person who says "I cannot do it" and gets others to do for him or her is obviously successful in avoiding particular categories of behavior. What categories others do for the person will indicate both the goal and the fear or need driving it. From the consequences, one derives the purpose. Similarly, what are the consequences for the persons who are so helpful? Do they need to be needed, nice, in charge? In this sense, we are all enablers.

Assessment goes on all throughout the therapeutic relationship as we observe clients' behaviors, their impact on the therapist, and the therapist's impact on the clients. However, therapy does not end with assessment. Clients must behave differently in a revised or new systemic pattern that is more effective for them in their own view and in their relationships with larger systems. This could pose an interesting ethical and moral dilemma. Suppose in the largest scheme of things in the human drama, it is the larger system declaring the symptomatic behavior of the individual or family to be dysfunctional when it is really the larger system that is dysfunctional through oppression, unreasoned hatred, distorted values of the moment, or dysfunctional patterns in the larger system that creates problems for its members? Who decides? We need to look at the symptom in its larger contexts to better understand the difficulties. In all cases, the individual and family are responsible for how they meet the challenges of life.

Remember, change and reeducation processes are ongoing throughout the assessment process. Techniques and tactics to help bring about behavior change follow.

Changing the System

The therapist and clients are working on behavior change from the very first contact. Techniques and tactics are listed here to accomplish changes through each of the dimensions described above: modify beliefs and increase feelings of optimism and empowerment, establish different places and roles based on community feeling and social interest, and acquire new knowledge and skills, including more effective communication. It is worth repeating that although specific techniques are given for each dimension, most complex structured techniques will involve all of the dimensions simultaneously. Sources may be found in the references at the end of this chapter in which these and many other techniques and tactics are described in detail.

Changing Beliefs, Myths, Values, Expectations, Attitudes, and Increasing Optimism and Social Feeling.

1. *Interpret the dysfunctional beliefs to the clients so that they perceive them in context and understand the meaning and purpose of their behavior.*

2. *Describe to the clients the consequences of their beliefs.* ("Is it possible that when everything must be perfect you often wind up with 0% instead of 80% of what you want?")

3. *Dramatize the beliefs to show their inappropriateness through exaggeration.* ("You're so weak and indecisive. How do you manage to get dressed in the morning?")

4. *Match a strongly held belief with a strongly held opposite belief to weaken the first one.* ("I'm confused. You say that family closeness is a vital family value, yet by being so angry and critical of your family you seem to chase the others away. What can you do with that?")

5. *Introduce a new positive belief to expand the system.* ("Now that you are older, wiser, and bigger and soon to start high school, do you think there may be some new things you want to attend to?" or "In spite of all the fighting, the members of this family are extremely caring and protective of one another. Look at [give examples of protective behavior].") Reframe an existing negative idea by giving it a positive meaning in a new perspective. ("So when your husband gets you angry it helps to mobilize you from a passive person and gets you to practice flexing your muscles.")

6. *Encourage rebellion against an old dysfunctional belief.* (To a father who believes in beating his children: "You said you were a bit wild growing up. Did you stop misbehaving when *your* father beat *you* regularly?") The old belief can be externalized. ("It's not your idea. That's your mother's voice criticizing you.") The old belief can be countered by using standard cognitive therapy countering techniques of using positive self-talk to replace negative ideas. Finally, use Socratic questioning to attack the logic of an existing belief.

7. *Tell stories.* Have the clients repeat their stories multiple times and highlight and reinforce the positive aspects in each retelling. Have them write a new, more favorable ending for the family story. Make up a fairy tale that puts the family situation in a new perspective. Have the family make up a fairy tale for the family.

8. *Use analogical techniques.* Imagery, poetry, art, music, sculpting, projective tests, and games help the clients discover new possibilities within themselves and new ideas. Objective tests and inventories are often a digital source of new ideas.

9. *Use traditional analytic techniques.* Help clients gain insight into their beliefs and emotions by using free association, analysis of dreams, early recollections, and interpreting the resistance.

10. *Increase the sense of optimism and empowerment that each member experiences in self and in the family as a unit.* As discussed earlier in the chapter, optimism facilitates change and the willingness to risk new behaviors. The therapist can accomplish this by affirming the family and each member; helping them to identify their strengths and successes; promoting positive concrete operational proposals, assertions, and mutually respectful negotiations rather than aggression, hostility, and demeaning criticism; working to make cooperative choices and decisions in a positive atmosphere such as a family meeting or couple conference; developing common workable goals; identifying and emphasizing positive changes made—catching each other being good rather than bad; and reframing negative ideas, feelings, and events into a more positive framework. These can be done in session and as homework tasks.

11. *Develop increased social interest and social feeling.* Again, as discussed earlier in the chapter, a system of beliefs that includes the importance and value of others, the recognition that one is a part of larger social wholes, and the necessity of connecting and cooperating with others is vital to effective living. The therapist can assist the family members to truly pay attention to each other, the family, and to others outside the family to get to know them more fully. Help the members to evaluate the consequences of their behavior in terms of its impact on the others. Define differences as strong possible assets that foster growth and add to the family rather than as liabilities. Teach conflict resolution and negotiating skills based on mutual respect. Prescribe positive exchange–type tasks such as "Decide on three things you can do this week that will make the family or one family member feel good." Prescribe the encouragement meeting as a regular family ritual in which each person is given positive feedback about the self as a person and about specific behaviors. Organize the family as a self-help group that will work together to help each member deal with specific challenges of life. Initiate fun games or cooperative tasks in session or at home to teach and reinforce cooperation. Have the family identify or create cultural traditions or customs or some unique to the family such as family dinner every Sunday, holiday observances, a family story time.

Changing Places and Roles.

1. *Assign new positions and roles directly.* "Jane [the overresponsible critic], can you this week accept being in charge of planning fun for the family?" and "Joe [the underresponsible fun lover], could you accept being in charge of the work assignments this week?"

2. *Strengthen existing natural roles.* ("Tim, you're very good at keeping track of the family history and what you folks have done in the past," "Sadie, you really do try to help your parents see that they could also have some fun as well as work," or "Father, are you pleased with your son's behavior right now? If not, what can you do about it?")

3. *Positively relabel existing roles to give them a more constructive place in the system.* This is similar to reframing ideas. ("Is it possible that Mary keeps interfering because she is a peacemaker and is trying to make peace between the two of you?")

4. *Prescribe role reversals.* This can be done by having each take on the other's part in session and role-play being the other. It can also be done by having members reverse roles between sessions as an experiment or by relabeling the roles. For example, the overadequate parent can be sent on "vacation," and the father and children, who are constantly berated for their lack of performance, can take charge of the household in mother's absence.

5. *Block inappropriate roles or role behavior.* Interrupt the existing pattern by prescribing or coaching a new pattern of behavior. ("Instead of criticizing again, could you put your pointed finger behind your back and try something new? Could you identify something that your son did that is right?")

6. *Spread out the symptomatic role among multiple family members.* Show the prevalence of the symptom in the system and defuse the identified client as the family scapegoat. For example, the oppositional child may be manifesting only one way of being a rebel in the family system. Father may be a rebel by staying away from home, brother by withdrawing from family affairs as much as possible, and mother by portraying herself as the family victim, rebelling by constantly complaining. No one *wants* to obey. The question then becomes what new roles can they assume to make this a more inviting, cooperating family?

7. *Establish, strengthen, or weaken boundaries among the family roles.* Help form more effective role relationships. ("Father, would it be alright for you now to tell Peter directly what you would like rather than telling your wife to speak to him?" or "Susan, you are a very responsible and helpful older sister, but it is really your parents' job to discipline your younger siblings and you must be tired of so hard a job; don't you agree, Mom and Dad?")

8. *Fashion new alliances to adjust the balance of power and improve communication.* ("As a single parent, would it be helpful for you to join with other single parents in a support group for adult companionship, sharing problems and brainstorming solutions?") The therapist might temporarily ally with a given family member to strengthen that person in relation to another or the entire family in the case of the scapegoat. Therapist to a domineering critic: "When did you acquire the job of being the family inspector general?"

9. *Provide more structure in a chaotic system.* ("Who will be responsible for each of the following tasks? When and how will they get done? Who will be included? Who should butt out?") Organize a regular family meeting as a family ritual. Revive or introduce customs and traditions to be performed as rituals with the family's agreement, based on their background and perceived needs.

10. *Introduce greater flexibility of roles in an inflexible, rigid system.* Because most dysfunctional families are stuck in a rigid, unsatisfying pattern, at least around the symptom, reducing rigidity is central to therapists' work in most cases. We work on it as well in modifying rigid beliefs and introducing new knowledge and skills. In terms of roles, family members can be asked to try some "experiments" in which they modify their existing roles or try on some new ones in limited, prescribed ways. The therapist can describe, interpret, or challenge an existing role or reciprocal roles in very pragmatic terms: Is it working? If not, would the persons be willing to try something different? Because rigidity is often a response to perceived threat, setting rules and modeling behavior within the therapeutic system that allow the family members to feel safe may give them greater confidence to experiment wiht new roles. Introducing some fun activities, suggesting that members violate some less serious family rules in an outrageous way, or pointing out that one family member is already breaking some rule and it is working out quite well are some of the tactics available. The therapist can also recommend powerful intensification and exaggeration of existing rigid roles and patterns make them so onerous or ridiculous that the members will recoil and rebel and do something different.

Increase Knowledge and Skills. A family cannot consider information or use skills that it either does not possess or does not know it possesses. It cannot make choices or choose options that are unknown to it. Just as dysfunctional behavior is in part a product of learning, so too is behavior change often a matter of learning new facts, ideas, options, and skills. Knowing something does not automatically imply that I know how to do something. If I am shy and the therapist encourages me to go to a party without first learning new social skills, ways of conducting myself at a party, the event may turn into a miserable, discouraging failure for me. Following are some examples of methods that can be used to enhance and empower clients with new assets to facilitate both problem solving and personal growth.

1. *Provide or teach the information directly as needed.* ("You can discuss this with Alice's teacher by calling and arranging a parent conference with her. She will be available.")

2. *Coach the clients during a problem-solving activity or sculpting or in performance of an in-session task by correcting or suggesting specific behavior.* ("Could you allow Tiffany to finish her point before answering?" "Could you please say the same thing in one sentence?" "Would you be willing to practice intimacy right now by sharing something that is personal and important to you with your family?")

3. *Suggest new ideas, options, or tasks for the family's consideration.*

4. *Refer clients to appropriate resources.* They may learn what is needed by seeing an attorney, physician, clergyman, or other expert. They can be referred to specific readings, artwork, music, movies, or TV programs to obtain some information or new perspectives, overtly demonstrated skills, or vicariously acquired skills.

5. *Recommend enrollment in a training program, a psychoeducational program, or a support group* such as parent education, marriage enrichment, Recovery, Alcoholics Anonymous, Alanon, Parents Without Partners, and hundreds more as an adjunct to the therapy.

6. *Use circular questioning,* in which members are asked to provide information about other members rather than to speak for themselves in order to put information into the system. It is also possible to build new premises into the questions that the therapist asks. ("Now that you have demonstrated to all how powerful you are, you are ready to use that power as a constructive, positive leader in your family and among your peers.") If all accept the premise that the person is a leader rather than a rebel and that constructive behavior is to be expected, this is both new information and a new role in the system.

7. *Interpret to the family the possible meanings of their patterns of behavior.* The therapist can also compare the behavior with that of other families and with what is common in their cultural background and the impact that it has on each member and the family as a whole.

8. *Use imagery* to help the family discover ideas within themselves and new insights and to practice new behavior by visualizing a situation and performing in it.

9. *Model skills by the therapist's own behavior in therapy.* For example, the therapist can model cooperation, attentiveness, constructive use of anger, assertiveness, rules of communication, appreciation and respect for others, and a host of other performances.

10. *Adjust patterns of communication.* Everything listed above will affect the patterns of communication. In addition, the therapist can videotape or audiotape the session and play back all or parts to show the family how they are engaging. The therapist can identify vertical (one-up or one-down) or controlling messages. The therapist can directly teach or coach good communication skills such as speaking for the self and psychoactive listening; giving clear messages; checking out what the other said and the others' intentionality rather than projecting one's own meanings onto the other; challenging double binds and double messages such as "yes, but"; and proposing rather than commanding. The therapist can change seating arrangements or who comes to a given session, request that clients speak to one another in arranged pairs, and even suggest the subject content. Clients can be taught to inform rather than expecting others to know without being told.

Evaluation, Termination, and Follow-Up.   As the therapy draws to a close, it is relevant to summarize and assess together what has happened and where the family is going. New effective behaviors need to be reinforced and commitments to continue the new behavior secured from each member. Future goals need to be clarified. It is also useful to check back with them in the future to see what has become of them and the possible influence of the therapy experience in their lives.

Termination of successful relationships can be difficult. Even brief therapy can be an intimate process. It is best at the beginning to make it clear that this is a time-limited relationship. The therapist is a current caring helper, not a best friend, lover, or permanent parent, nor one who will always be there and do for you. Premature termination can also be difficult. In such cases, the therapist tries to make the best possible arrangements for the family through future assigned and accepted tasks, referral to other experts, or a follow-up telephone call. The object usually is to end in an encouraging way. Sometimes clients will come up with new problems to avoid ending the therapy. The therapist reassures them that they have demonstrated the skills and courage to go on and deal with those problems on their own and that the therapist can become available in case of future unresolved difficulties.

Evaluation.   Quantitatively and qualitatively how has the family changed in relation to the presenting problems, contract, and goals for change?

1. *Questioning for self-report.* The family is asked questions to help them summarize the presenting problems, goals, and activities of the therapy and to compare those with their present feelings and behaviors individually and as a family. The therapist can contribute what she or he thinks may have been important omissions based on her

or his observations and check those out with the family. To what degree were the presenting problems alleviated and the stated goals attained? What other things may have been achieved along the way? What were the failures that require some further effort? The therapist also evaluates in terms of more constructive behavior, greater optimism and community feeling, more effective communication, and any pertinent factors considered of importance to the therapist.

2. *Before-and-after administration of tests and inventories.* There are hundreds of objective and clinical instruments that the practitioner can use to measure virtually any array of behaviors. Before- and after-therapy administration provides a measure of the differences that may or may not be actually attributable to the therapy unless controlled samples are used. Similarly, before and after performance of selected structured techniques may provide an observable measure of differences in performance, for example, such techniques as sculptures; sociograms; early recollections; the family floor plan; the ecomap; selection and discussion of family photographs, films, or videotapes; interpretation of dreams or daydreams; story completions; imagining a family picture on the wall with an underlying caption, and many more.

3. *Observation of changes in in-session behavior patterns over time.*

4. *Behavioral reports from collaborative sources.* Teachers, relatives, clergymen, friends, or other sources can provide direct evidence. Did the child's attendance and grades in school improve? Did a member get a new job? Is the depressed person back to performing normal routines? Does the family have regular family meetings or eat dinner together, with no TV on? These kinds of specific concrete changes are very significant indicators of progress or the lack thereof.

Commitment.   A major aspect of change is the performance of new patterns of behavior. The therapist secures a commitment from each family member and the family as a whole that they will continue to practice the new behaviors that they have found desirable during the therapy and that they will actively pursue the next steps agreed on toward their future goals. Predicting that family members will sometimes fall back into old patterns is used to reassure them that they are human and may fall back, but can catch themselves and get back on the desired track.

Follow-Up.   A time and method is scheduled for a review of the family's progress. This can be a therapy session, a mailed questionnaire, a telephone questionnaire, or a telephone interview. Activities similar to those performed in the evaluation process are repeated at this time to try to gauge the family's progress over time and the therapy's effectiveness, to provide an opportunity to reinforce elements of the therapy, and to reassess goals and future steps for the family. When this is scheduled as part of the therapy, there is a greater probability that the family will participate in such a follow-up process. It provides a sense of importance to the family, who see the therapist as continuing to care about them. It is also an incentive to the family to implement the goals and commitments agreed on in the therapy because the therapist will be inquiring of them as to their performance.

☐ Outline Summary of Sequential Steps in Therapy

Identify Early and Maintain a Clear Central Focus throughout the Therapy

1. Elicit the problem as presented by the family, as interpreted by the therapist, and as manifested in a specific pattern of interaction.

2. Join by acknowledging the behavior described and by validating its impact on each member.

3. Assess the direction, purpose, and meaning of the behavior in this system and formulate and present a tentative hypothesis.

4. Look for strengths, positive exceptions, and previously successful solutions.

5. Identify together achievable positive common goals and their possible consequences to the members and others.

6. Overcome obstacles to achievement of the goals by developing new beliefs and meanings, new places and roles, and new knowledge and skills based on increased optimism and empowerment and increased social feeling.

7. Evaluate the changes by observing, questioning, summarizing, and using before-and-after tests and techniques.

8. Reinforce the changes and get a commitment to practice the changes and to engage in a follow-up procedure.

9. Terminate in as positive a manner as possible.

10. Follow up the case to evaluate the family's progress and needs.

☐ Case Example

Presenting Problems

The Ben Zion family (fictitious name) of Michael (37), Hannah (35), Aaron (8), and Miriam (6) living in New York City were referred by a school counselor because the children were oppositional and demanding. The parents confirmed that they behaved the same way at home and that there was a good deal of fighting between the two children. The children readily admitted that they wanted things their own way and said they enjoyed fighting. Father said that he was a big "worrier" and had little time with the family. Mother reported that she wished she could be her old self and not be so depressed.

The Assessment Process

Questions about the family constellation revealed that Michael was an Israeli Jewish immigrant who married Hannah when she was on an extended visit to Israel, and they subsequently came to the United States. His parents were survivors of the Holocaust originally from Germany and Czechoslovakia. Michael, the eldest of two brothers, had been in combat in two wars in Israel as a tank commander. Many of his friends had been killed or wounded. He became a computer engineer and longed to return to Israel to be with his family for whom he felt responsible. Men were supposed to be responsible for their families and protect and provide for them. Education, competence, creativity, and self-reliance were major family values. Women were to conform to those family values and be "equal partners," work, and be responsible for the home. The loss of so many extended family members during the Holocaust made family loyalty an imperative value. Children were cherished, but had to be tough. The family perceived itself as close, but intimate conversations were rare, and discussion of past and present traumas was even rarer. He experienced himself as a much valued, respected, underpaid, and exploited computer engineer who wanted to create his own company. He did so on a part-time basis in his garage with a partner. He complained he just did not have enough time in his life. He also stated firmly that he very much loved his wife and children and was fearful for them.

Hannah was also of the Jewish faith and came from a family of the children of immigrants from Poland and Russia who had survived several slaughters of Jewish communities and who settled in New York shortly before World War I. Her parents as a young couple struggled through the Depression, and her father served in combat during World War II. Beginning a family was delayed until the couple could settle in after the war. Hannah was the youngest of three children; the two elder were brothers. She was very ambitious, perfectionistic, lively, and "a bit spoiled." Her mother was frequently ill, and Hannah often took care of her. Hannah became a nurse. Family values included high expectations for education and achievement, family loyalty, and the primacy of the husband–father in family affairs, although women were expected to work, achieve, and be "equal partners." The children were greatly valued and given a great deal of latitude in behavior and decision making. However, mother constantly "second-guessed" Hannah and thereby criticized many of her decisions so that she was never sure that she was doing the right thing, and she very much wanted to be perfect. Hannah did not want her children to suffer from the anxieties that beset her. She proclaims that she very much loves her husband and her children. She experiences herself as not tough or assertive enough and as somehow failing in life.

Child-rearing was usually permissive, with the parents occasionally getting tough when they felt the children needed correcting. But on many such occasions, the children did not take them very seriously unless they got really tough and demonstrated that they meant it.

Both Aaron and Miriam are very bright, active, verbal children who do well academically. They too admit their love for their parents and even some affection for one another. They periodically team up to fight a common adversary. They both want to do what they want to do when and how they want to do it and are willing to fight for the privilege. Aaron has no real friends in school or neighborhood and has little competence in athletics. He does read a great deal, especially science fiction, and dreams up many ideas that he is delighted to discuss. He counts himself superior to others and not needing their company. Yet he claims to have a few friends with whom he plays occasionally. Miriam is very playful, teasing, even a bit seductive. She has many friends but insists on being the boss most of the time, which creates some conflicts with them. However, she is very gay, personable, good humored, and attractive and so far has a strong sense of self, so people are attracted to her. She especially enjoys teasing her brother. Both children perceive themselves as smart and tough.

Assessment Techniques

The above data were gathered by interview questions, tracking both the behavior and the belief systems, tracking the routines of a typical day and a weekend day, observing the family's behavior in session, the construction of a family genogram, the completion of Sherman's Family Interaction Inventory (Sherman, 1994), gathering early recollections of the family members, getting reports from the school counselor and the children's teachers with parental permission, and a number of other techniques and tactics. The information above is distilled from much more data actually obtained through those methods. New information came out in every session from the beginning to the end of the therapy.

Hypotheses and Diagnosis

At an early stage, the therapist formed a tentative hypothesis that the line of movement in this family is a struggle to gain control of an uncertain and dangerous world. You must achieve at a very high level, being almost perfect in order to survive and compensate for multigenerational losses. The mother, father, and son are largely socially isolated, distrustful of others, with no real friends and distant family relationships. They feel thwarted in achieving their goals and are therefore depressed. The parents are essentially nice guys and pleasers. The children both rebel against and take advantage of this model of pleasing. Miriam further rejects the model of female weakness represented by her mother's depression.

However, the parents are very successful in accomplishing their most urgent goal in child-rearing: Their children are indeed independent, self-reliant, and tough.

Miriam also rebels against and is able to overcome the family pattern of social isolation. She therefore also escapes the direct pain of the family depression. She demonstrates a less dysfunctional, though still problematic, model of the family value system.

The Change and Reeducation Process

There are many directions for change based on the above hypotheses. The therapist elected to focus on the family's major symptom, which is feeling thwarted and depressed, and considered that all the other dysfunctional behavior patterns stem from those beliefs and feelings and are in their service.

The parents recognized that their goal was to become more assertive on their own behalf and to take the risks of being less pleasing to others in general and to their children in particular. Their belief systems, goals, and behavioral strategies were interpreted back to them as they emerged in sessions. Similarly, their respective roles in the family system were discussed as they emerged during the sessions. The parents were encouraged to undertake specific actions to accomplish their goals. Michael was seen by the therapist as the most likely person to begin to change behaviors that would affect the family system. He agreed to assert himself and made a variety of demands accepted by his employer with respect to his work projects and also secured a substantial raise in pay. This lifted his mood and self-confidence and made Hannah feel better as well. Mother then agreed to and did assert herself strongly with her husband to get him to reorganize his second job, get rid of his partner whom she detested, and spend more time with his family and with her in particular. The couple agreed, after practice with coaching in session, to schedule couple meetings on a regular basis to increase the intimacy and communication between them. The family also agreed to conduct weekly family meetings after practicing in session. This provided a democratic model for all to engage in the assertive and cooperative give-and-take of coming to agreements rather than just getting their own way; they also had to listen to others who are caring and trustworthy. The family explored their losses, vented their anger and sorrow with total validation from the therapist, and identified their strengths and opportunities. The family then decided to join a synagogue to find some sense of community and to get back in touch with their own feelings of rootedness. Michael began to write and telephone his family in Israel more frequently and to share more personal events, ideas, and feelings with them. Hannah then began to explore her anger toward her parents. After identifying and venting her negative feelings, she was encouraged by Michael and the children to see that her family of origin were complex people and her relationship with them contained both positives as well as negatives. She discovered what it was that she wanted from them, rehearsed in imagery and using empty chairs how to get it, and then brought her parents in for a session to work it out. Observing all the above, the children learned a lot more about their parents, extended family, roots, and life. The parents began to be more assertive with the children and to use the weight of their personalities to establish appropriate parental authority. Though they fought it at first, the children were reassured by their much more confident and less depressed parents. Aaron no longer had to sit home and be present for his "sick" mother and found that he could spend more time with new friends made in a religious instruction class. His search for friends who could connect with him around his creative ideas and experiments was less successful. He was encouraged to discuss these ideas with his parents, especially his father. This created a new bond between them. His fighting in school stopped, but he remained somewhat wary of his classmates given several previous years of negative interactions with them. The school agreed to give Aaron the chance to work on some of his ideas as special school projects and assigned him as a tutor to less able children with careful instruction on how to treat them. This gave Aaron a positive "place" in school.

As the household became more relaxed, Miriam became less "bossy" and more appropriately assertive. She began to bring her friends home to play. This both annoyed Aaron and gave him the chance to show some superiority to the younger children as the big brother. In the process, he also began to learn some new social skills.

As a result of the family meetings, the children developed specific agreed-upon roles around tasks and routines and specific agreed rules and boundaries around the use of space and possessions. This decreased but, of course, did not end the sibling rivalries.

Change Techniques

Some specific techniques and tactics were used to bring about the above changes in addition to those already described. The therapist formulated many questions, did some circular questioning, made many interpretations, and reframed many ideas to the positive. The therapist made concrete suggestions to undertake some of the particular tasks that the family engaged in; identified and reinforced such strengths as their mutual caringness, past achievements, obvious creativity, and ability to survive; and pointed out that they do have extended family, religious, and cultural roots, and community resources. Imagery was used for behavior rehearsal and reliving events surrounding losses. Role reversals were used, for example, to move parents from being protective to being assertive. Sculpting provided a model of their ideal family and helped them to rethink the family's origin. Coaching was initiated to teach skills of intimacy and of negotiating differences and to assert the weight of personality. Of course, other techniques and tactics came into play.

Objectives

The objective of all of the above change transactions was to substitute appropriate assertiveness for the need to control and to build new connections with others to overcome the feelings of isolation and fear after confronting the original beliefs, goals, and existing patterns of behavior.

Outcomes

The changes reported above are also the outcomes of the therapy as reported by the family, observed by the therapist, and reported by the school. A follow-up session 6 months later was attended only by the parents. They reported that their relationship was both much warmer and less conflictual; that the children were continuing to do well in school with no negative teacher reports; that relations with both extended families were more frequent and deeper; and that what the family unanimously really wanted and had agreed to was to return to Israel. They were busy making the necessary arrangements and lining up a good job. They were confident of their plan and expected to move within 3 months.

This case was successful in solving the presenting problems and helping the family to develop new beliefs, roles, places, and skills to meet the further challenges of life. Unfortunately, every therapist has failures—myself included—and is not successful with every case in terms of the above standards.

☐ Summary

The intent of this chapter was to present the thesis that Adlerian systems therapy is founded on an integration of both the principles of individual psychology and systemic thinking. The individuals create the system and the system and its members interact on and with each other. The underlying principles were discussed. A model for conducting this kind of integrative therapy was described and a case study reported to illustrate the model. The model is to be used as a guide rather than as a rigid formula. The model included many techniques and tactics to accomplish each major stage of the work. References are provided below wherein the reader can find more detailed descriptions of the principles and many of the techniques and tactics available, including those reported herein.

☐ References

Dinkmeyer, D. C., Dinkmeyer, D. C., Jr., & Sperry, L. (1987). *Adlerian counseling and psychotherapy* (2nd ed.). Columbus, OH: Merrill.

Dinkmeyer, D. C., & Sherman, R. (1989). Brief Adlerian family therapy. *Individual Psychology: The Journal of Adlerian Theory, Research, and Practice, 45*(1–2), 148–158.

Fredman, N., & Sherman, R. (1987). *Handbook of measurements in couple and family therapy.* New York: Brunner/Mazel.

Gurman, A. S., & Kniskern, D. P. (Eds.). (1991). *Handbook of family therapy. Volume II.* New York: Brunner/Mazel.

Kopp, R. R. (1995). *Metaphor therapy.* New York: Brunner/Mazel.

McGoldrick, M., & Gerson, R. (1985). *Genograms in family assessment.* New York: Norton.

Minuchin, S. (1974). *Families and family therapy.* Cambridge, MA: Harvard University Press.

Nichols, M. P., & Schwartz, R. C. (1998). *Family therapy: Concepts and methods* (4th ed.). Boston: Allyn & Bacon.

Pearce, S. S. (1996). *Flash of insight. Metaphor and narrative therapy.* Boston: Allyn & Bacon, Longwood.

Sherman, R. (1993). Intimacy genogram. *The Family Journal, 1,* 91–93.

Sherman, R. (1994). Family interaction profile. *The Family Journal, 2,* 262–265.

Sherman, R., & Dinkmeyer, D. C. (1987). *Systems of family therapy: An Adlerian integration.* New York: Brunner/Mazel.

Sherman, R., & Fredman, N. (1986). *Handbook of structured techniques in couple and family therapy.* New York: Brunner/Mazel.

Sherman, R., Oresky, P., & Rountree, Y. B. (1991). *Solving problems in couples and family therapy: Techniques and tactics.* New York: Brunner/Mazel.

Touliotos, J., Perlmutter, B. F., & Straus, M. A. (1990). *Handbook of family measurement techniques.* Newbury Park, CA: Sage.

☐ Suggested Resources

Adler, A. (1956). *Cooperation between the sexes; Writings on women, love and marriage, sexuality and its disorders* (H. L. Ansbacher & R. R. Ansbacher, Eds. and Trans.). Garden City, NY: Doubleday.

Adler, A. (1963). *The practice and theory of individual psychology.* Paterson, NJ: Littlefield, Adams.

Carlson, J., Sperry, L., & Lewis, J. A. (1997). *Family therapy. Ensuring treatment efficacy.* Pacific Grove, CA: Brooks/Cole.

Christensen, O. C., & Schramski, T. G. (Eds.). (1983). *Adlerian family counseling.* Minneapolis, MN: Educational Media.

Dinkmeyer, D. C. (1996). Adlerian family therapy. An integrative therapy. *Individual Psychology: The Journal of Adlerian Theory, Research, and Practice, 42,* 471–479.

Dinkmeyer, D. C, McKay, G., & Dinkmeyer, J. S. (1989). *Parenting young children*. Minneapolis, MN: American Guidance Associates.

Dreikurs, R., Corsini, R., Lowe, R., & Sonstegard, M. (Eds.). (1959). *Adlerian family therapy: A manual for counseling centers*. Eugene: University of Oregon University Press.

Grunwald, B. B., & McAbee, H. V. (1985). *Guiding the family*. Muncie, IN: Accelerated Development.

Hoffman, E. (1994). *The drive for self: Alfred Adler and the founding of individual psychology*. Reading, MA: Addison-Wesley.

Kern, R. M., Hawes, E. C., & Christensen, O. C. (Eds.). (1989). *Couple therapy: An Adlerian perspective*. Minneapolis, MN: Educational Media.

Manaster, G. J., & Corsini, R. J. (1982). *Individual psychology*. Itasca, IL: F. E. Peacock.

McManus, R., & Jennings, G. (Eds.). (1996). *Structured exercises for promoting family and group strengths*. New York: Haworth.

Mosak, H. H. (1987). *Ha ha and aha. The role of humor in psychotherapy*. Muncie, IN: Accelerated Development.

Popkin, M. (1987). *Active parenting: Teaching cooperation, courage and responsibility*. San Francisco: Harper & Row.

Sherman, R. (in press). Organizing the family as a self-help group. *The Family Journal*.

Sherman, R., Shumsky, A., & Rountree, Y. B. (1991). *Enlarging the therapeutic circle: The therapist's guide to collaborative therapy with families and schools*. New York: Brunner/Mazel.

Shorr, J. E., Robin, P., Connella, J. A., & Wolpin, M. (Eds.). (1989). *Imagery: Current perspectives*. New York: Plenum.

Shulman, B. H., & Mosak, H. H. (1988). *Manual for life style assessment*. Muncie, IN: Accelerated Development.

Sperry, L., & Carlson, J. (1996). *Marital therapy: Integrating theory and techniques*. Denver, CO: Love.

Starr, A. (1979). *Psychodrama: Rehearsal for living*. Chicago: Nelson Hall.

Toman, W. (1974). *Family constellation*. New York: Springer.

8
CHAPTER

Timothy D. Evans
Alan P. Milliren

Open–Forum Family Counseling

In 1922, Alfred Adler began the first child guidance clinic in Vienna, Austria. Instead of helping individuals in the seclusion of a private office, Adler adopted the daring practice of counseling families in public demonstrations. These sessions were called public because he conducted them in front of an audience consisting of his students, parents, members of the community, and other professionals. By involving the audience in the counseling session, Adler emphasized helping the family through education. These became the first open-forum family counseling sessions, and Adler's efforts pioneered the way for modern family and group therapy.

Adler's public counseling demonstrations challenged the then-traditional practices of individual therapy. Adler violated Freud's conviction that it was counterproductive, even dangerous, to deal with more than one member of a family. By interviewing the entire family in public, Adler challenged the concepts of the isolated individual, transference, and unconscious motivation and the mystery that surrounded client confidentiality. Instead, he offered a hopeful view of human nature and behavior that was based on choices and the observable interactions within the family.

Adler's goal was to create a commonsense psychology that would help all of humankind. "Adler viewed man as worthwhile, socially motivated, and capable of creative, independent action" (Sweeney, 1989, p. 2). This was in sharp contrast to Freud, who was primarily interested in solving the "riddles" of life (Progoff, 1969). Adler's concern was for humankind, as a whole, and his theory became oriented to helping people understand and improve their lot in life (Manaster & Corsini, 1982). He believed that therapy was not for an elite but should be made available to everyone. His public demonstrations reflected this desire to make psychology available to what Adler considered the "common man."

Adler's first centers were called *Erziehungberatungstellen*, which translates as "advice centers for bringing up children." By 1930, there were 32 community child guidance centers throughout Vienna. In his demonstrations, Adler emphasized the social embeddedness of human problems. Problems arise not from internal psychodynamic or genetic deficits but from problematic interactions originating in one's social context. Problem behavior is viewed as changeable when provided with proper information or education. Therefore, the "problem" child is not a victim of heredity or environment (disorder or deficits) but selects behaviors in response to his or her relationships with siblings and parents. The child's behavior, despite how "disturbed" it appears, is a logical answer to the situation in which he or she exists. As individual disturbance is a by-product of family conflict, it seems logical, then, that counseling be concerned with providing concrete guidance for parents (Sonstegard & Dreikurs, 1975).

In 1934, Fascism took hold of Austria. Remarkably, Adler maintained an optimistic view of human nature even in the face of human tragedy. Nazism finally forced the Vienna clinics to close, and many prominent Adlerians fled Europe, carrying with them the ideas and practices they had learned from Adler. After much difficulty, some of these Adlerians made their way to the United States, including Adler's children Alexandra and Kurt, both of whom have contributed to the development of Adlerian psychology in the United States. The best known and most prolific of Adler's students was Rudolf Dreikurs, who also immigrated to the United States. Dreikurs played a major role in popularizing Adlerian psychology in the United States. In 1939, Dreikurs opened the first child guidance center and Family Education Association center at the Abraham Lincoln Center in Chicago. This effort launched the open-forum family counseling and parent education model in the United States.

The necessity of doing educational and preventive work in family education has never been more evident. With the increase in the divorce rate, delinquency, juvenile crime and gang involvement, child abuse, and school-related problems; with increasing numbers of dual-career parents, single parents, and blended families; and with the overextension of our school systems with more students and fewer resources, the value of Adler's educational approach to family life becomes even more significant (Dinkmeyer & Dinkmeyer, 1981). This approach is efficient and effective, yet is both rehabilitative and preventive. Currently, open-forum family counseling is being used in cooperation with schools, universities, institutes, community groups, public agencies, child care facilities, Adlerian organizations, and churches. Adler may be pleased that his model continues to train professionals and, most of all, the "common man."

☐ A Case Example

With this background and the theme of the "common man" in mind, we begin an interview with parents that volunteered for family counseling in order to help their son who had been diagnosed with attention deficit–hyperactivity disorder (ADHD). This interview took place in front of an audience of over 200 people. The interview begins with the parents speaking to the counselor, Frank Walton, while the children are being supervised in the playroom (Walton, 1996, used by permission). At the beginning of the interview, it is important for the counselor to explain several routine procedures to the parents and audience. This introduction sets the tone for the entire interview. The counselor creates a relaxed and friendly atmosphere with the parents by explaining the nature of the family education process to the audience. In some cases, the counselor may explain to the audience and family the ground rules for the session.

Ground Rules

There are three essential ground rules for open-forum family counseling. First, the counselor explains that the process is educational and not therapy. Open-forum family counseling is made up of parents, teachers, and counselors interested in learning about families. This is best accomplished by interviewing families in front of an audience. The counselor may ask the audience, "Where do we learn to be parents? Most of us learn how to parent by the role modeling provided by our parents. At best, this was autocratic, resulted in conflict, and did not create friendly relations." Another question the counselor can ask the audience is "Does anyone here have a problem child?" This is usually met with laughter and a feeling of everyone needing help. The counselor wants to create an atmosphere where everyone participates as a colearner. This places the parents in focus in the position of helping those in the audience rather than being the troubled family there to receive help. As a result, the parents are more open about their concerns and willing to discuss what goes on at home.

Second, the counselor wants to establish that the information gathered during the interview does not pertain to pathology but to observable interpersonal relationships known as public behavior. The counselor is interested in the family's interpersonal dynamics. These dynamics may be observed in public. During the interview, the counselor wants to expose, explain, and suggest changes in this observable public behavior. For instance, if we go to the grocery store, we could observe the annoyance a mother displays as her child demands candy. The mother's annoyance and the child's tears are public behavior. This information would be pertinent to the counseling demonstration.

Third, the counselor wants to give a brief explanation on the commonality of problems experienced by families. The counselor may explain how Adler believed all problems are social problems and that the purpose of open-forum family counseling is to educate a large group of parents having similar child-rearing problems. Again, the parents in focus are put at ease when they realize that by discussing their problem they may help parents in the audience (Christensen & Marchant, 1983).

The Family Constellation

After the counselor has established the ground rules, the interview begins. The first phase of the interview involves formulating the problem and establishing rapport. This is achieved by the counselor, parents, and audience discussing the family constellation. The counselor begins by asking for the names and ages of the children in the family. The counselor also asks if there were any miscarriages, deaths of siblings, childhood illnesses, and grandparents, relatives, or other adults living in the home. All of this affects the way parents respond to a child and the child's view of the world.

Some counselors involve the audience in the interview by asking them to make guesses regarding each child's behavioral characteristics based on their birth order. The counselor also develops some hypotheses as to the behavioral characteristics of each child. Guesses that are accurate tend to build counselor credibility and rapport with the focus parents and the audience. The counselor immediately develops tentative hypotheses about the relationships that exist based on the family constellation. The parents are given the opportunity to modify the audience's and the counselor's guesses regarding the behavioral characteristics of each child.

Our session begins after Walton has reviewed the ground rules and is establishing the family constellation with the parents.

Counselor:	My objective is to first be a help to Mom and Dad, then the audience. I appreciate your helping us and the audience today. Please tell us the name and ages of the youngsters in your home?
Mom:	There is Rebecca, 10, and Darrel, 7.
Counselor:	Are you working outside the home, and in what field?
Mom:	I am in the medical field.
Dad:	I manage a restaurant.
Counselor:	Do you have any youngsters that have died? And if so where would they be in the family constellation.
Mom:	Yes. Before Rebecca, I had a miscarriage at 26.5 weeks. Darrel was premature at 35 weeks.
Counselor:	How far ahead of Rebecca was the miscarriage?
Mom:	Around 15 months.
Counselor:	*(Talking to audience.)* I want to put myself in the position of these parents. They had an experience of losing something precious. (To the parents.) How did you handle the loss?
Mom:	We were very pleased when Rebecca came along.
Counselor:	Was Darrel's pregnancy a concern?
Mom:	No, I was comfortable because Rebecca was not a problem, but then, Darrel turned out to be a problem.
Counselor:	Anyone else missing? Aunt? Grandmother that lives in the house or down the street? Someone who would have a prominent influence on your home?
Mom:	No.
Counselor:	Could you tell me about Rebecca?
Mom:	She is happy, gifted, and shy to begin with.
Counselor:	Anything else, Dad?
Dad:	She likes to help people. Is very sensitive and gifted in music.
Counselor:	Perhaps you have already answered this . . . but how would you complete this statement: Rebecca is the kid who always?
Mom:	Is very helpful, and gifted in music.
Counselor:	Is Darrel substantially different from Rebecca?

Dad: Oh, yes!

(Laughter from the audience.)

Counselor: How is he different?

Dad: Do you have an hour? He won't sit still, does not like to listen, but likes to take control, very affectionate.

Counselor: Is being affectionate different from Rebecca?

Mom: Rebecca is more so than Darrel.

Counselor: So affection is something of a family value for you both. Both of you are affectionate?

Dad: Yes.

Counselor: Anything else you would like to add?

Dad: He is very rambunctious, very, very smart. You will see this when you talk with him. He is not afraid to tell you what he feels.

Counselor: This is also different from Rebecca.

Counselor: *(Turning to the audience.)* What is going through my mind is the effort we all make to find our place in the family. We scout around to find our place. Rebecca finds for some reason to be shy, helpful, sensitive, reclusive, and still the affection comes through. She had 3 years to secure her place without Darrel. Darrel comes in, the second child, and needs to find a place for himself, like we all do. Our tendency is to be substantially different from the person with whom we are in competition. This does not mean we will be unkind, although that may take place. The point is, he is not going to be like Rebecca. He will be substantially different. He will maximize other things that are different from Rebecca. You can ask yourself, "among those siblings close to me in age, who is most different from me?" You will find there are areas of difference that are important to you. It may be hard to believe that decisions like this are being made so early in life, but I propose to you they are.

Problem Formation and Goal Alignment

Once the family constellation has been established along with some tentative hypotheses, the counselor will ask the parents for a specific concern. Parents usually identify this concern as the child with whom they have the most problems. This concern is often expressed as a generalized and vague diagnosis, such as my child has ADHD, is depressed, has dyslexia, or will not obey me. We look on these statements as expressions of discouragement and bankruptcy by the parents and professional community. Diagnostic evaluations do nothing for the child or the family.

     During the interview process, the counselor's job is to elicit specific examples of problem behavior from the parents so that patterns of interactions can emerge. The counselor must not allow the parents to be vague when describing these interactions. The success of counseling depends on the counselor's ability to recognize and define the problem in solvable terms and establish the terms for counseling based on specific patterns of interaction (Papp, 1984). This is facilitated when parents are required to report specific behavior that is observably going on in the present. Consequently, the counselor knows how to interview the parents so actual behavior is described—what family members are doing and saying. The counselor might ask the parents, "What would I see if I were there observing your family?"

The counselor will also inquire as to how the parents specifically respond to the problem situation. Because the session does not focus on the identified "problem child," but on the primary social context of the family, the counselor asks the parents, "And what did you do when your child misbehaved?" This question emphasizes the interpersonal nature of conflict between the parent and the child. Establishing how the parent responds is essential to understanding how the problem is maintained and identifying the pattern of relations that exist in the family.

The interview continues with Walton focusing on problem formation and goal alignment.

Counselor: How could I be of help to you? That may sound like a strange question since you volunteered to do this demonstration. You may be surprised I asked since your son has been diagnosed with ADHD. However, if you forgot the ADHD diagnosis and wanted to change behavior, what things would you want to change, what do you want to be different?

Mom: Just that he was easier to control in school situations, or when we are out and other people find his behavior distracting or unacceptable, that he would be easier to control. I would like it so the teachers find him to be controllable without placing him on medication, and are willing to work with him.

Counselor: Can you give me an example, in the home or when he is with you and he is difficult to control or distracted by other things that are troublesome?

Mom: When something does not interest him. If you are at church, or at a restaurant, and ask him to sit still, and it is something he does not want to do, he does not sit still.

Counselor: Okay, if I were there at church or at the restaurant, and I were watching, what would I see going on?

Mom: He may get up and go to the bathroom, walk around, talk, when he shouldn't be talking.

Counselor: If I were there watching, again what would I see Mom and Dad saying or doing? What do you do?

Mom: I would tell him to sit down. And he is doing what he wants. I may be coercive, to get him to do something. He is involved with the martial arts, and it is very disciplined. I may warn him at first, and, if he continues with his misbehavior, he will get an "x" if he does not respect or follow directions. He needs to do something and so I warn him at first, and, if he continues with his behavior, he gets an "x" in this area.

Counselor: You provide some rating, then, that you pass on to his instructor?

Dad: No, to his master!

(Audience laughs.)

Counselor: You threaten that you will do that?

Dad: No, we will do that!

Counselor: If I were watching, what would I see him doing?

Dad: He would start behaving better.

Counselor: So this is something that is of help to you.

Both
parents: Oh yeah!

Counselor: But if that were the answer, I guess you might not need to be here.

(Audience laughter.)

Mom: No, it doesn't always work.

Counselor: Most the time he gets up anyway.

Mom: Most times depend on if he is on his medication. On weekends I do not put him on his medication. I put him on medication for the teachers and the school. They, the psychiatrist, requested he be on medication after school, which I do not give him. I use the medication as I see fit, and not as it's prescribed. So, when he is medicated, he is a lot easier to control and . . . .

Counselor: Whether or not he is on medication, . . . let's just see. When he is distracted, he says, "I want to get out of here." And you say, "No, I don't want you to go. I want you to sit here. Come back and sit down." If I were watching, he would then do what?

Dad: Just take off.

Counselor: Take off? And, then finally, what happens?

Dad: We chase him.

(Audience laughter.)

Counselor: You do chase him. Who is most likely to be the chaser?

(Mom points to Dad.)

Dad: Whoever is closer.

Counselor: You are able to catch him?

Dad: Some of the time, he knows better. If I go outside, he knows if I say stop to stop.

Counselor: He knows better? Why is that?

Dad: Out of fear he is going to stop. We don't spank that much, but he stops because he's afraid we will spank him.

Counselor: You do not spank much but you do occasionally?

Dad: Oh, yeah!

(Audience laughter.)

Counselor: And the spanking *has* to occur only occasionally for people to live with the idea that they could be spanked. He, by and large, adheres when he hears your voice or sees you; he stops. But then again, nevertheless, he will still take off?

Dad: Yes, he will take off.

Counselor: So, is there something in your voice that when you say stop he will?

Dad: Yes.

Counselor: And, what about you, Mom?

Mom: He tends to listen better with Dad. He has a deeper, rougher voice.

Counselor: So, you get him to stop, . . . and take him by the hand? What are you likely to do after you get him to stop?

Dad: We will talk to him, ask him why he did this, and he usually answers, "I don't know."

Counselor: And he probably doesn't know. And so you ask him why you do this, and he says, "I don't know," and what finally happens?

Mom: Usually, he needs to stay in and is not allowed to go to a friend's house.

Counselor: If I were watching you bring him in the house, what do I see? How is he looking?

Mom: Angry.

Counselor: What will he do then? Sit down? Go to his room? Agitate?

Mom: Sometimes agitate and have a temper tantrum.

Counselor: And what do you do, Mom?

Mom: Tell him to go to his room and ignore him.

Counselor: And will he go?

Mom: Yeah, eventually I ignore him and he will stop.

Counselor: When you say go off to his room, I am trying my best to be in the house with you and observe it. So when he is going off to his room, when you say, "Go to your room," how does he look?

Mom: He is still angry.

Counselor: And how do you feel, Mom?

Mom: Frustrated.

Walton's next step is to further examine the family atmosphere, values, and inter-actions by exploring a typical day. However, before we move on to that aspect of the interview let us take a moment and examine the different kinds of family atmospheres and their effects on human development.

☐ A Democratic Psychology of Individuals

As demonstrated in this interview, most parents have little training or education in family relations or democratic living. Those who have discover that traditional parent education has little relevance for the improvement of parent–child relationships. Con-sequently, parents must rely on what they were taught by their parents, and this is usually autocratic, doing little to develop friendly and helpful relationships in a demo-cratically oriented society (Meredith, 1986). Some parents, in an attempt to be demo-cratic, merely stop being autocratic. This results in anarchy and, ultimately, a shift back to an autocratic approach. This constant shifting back and forth from autocracy to per-missiveness in human relations is part of our current dilemma in defining democracy (Dreikurs, 1971).

From an Adlerian viewpoint, family conflicts are related to inequality resulting in a vertical hierarchy. The superiors are pushing the inferiors around, and the inferiors are finding ways to push back. This is illustrated in the interview with the parents and in the son's uncontrollable behavior. As with the parents in the interview, when operat-ing in a vertical hierarchy, we stimulate the opposite of the very behaviors we intended to bring about. Instead of trust and honesty, we breed distrust and dishonesty; instead of compliance, we create rebellion or subversion; instead of openness, people become guarded; instead of satisfaction, people become dissatisfied; instead of cooperation, a competitive atmosphere develops. When family members are treated as if they are infe-rior, they soon resent the inequality and either fight back or behave helplessly. As we move to develop relationships of equals based on mutual trust and respect, we can no longer hold anyone's head higher or lower than our own

Psychology has provided little leadership for parents in resolving family con-flicts and creating democratic households. Adlerian psychology is one psychology that addresses the issue of democracy. Second-force psychology (behaviorism) has done little to address the issues of democracy in the family. Its system of token economy, rewards, and punishment creates a system of inequality. Those in a position of author-ity reward or punish those in a position of inferiority. A reward-and-punishment ap-proach to children puts them in an inferior position and creates power struggles be-tween those who are in control and those being rewarded. First-force psychology (psy-choanalysis) has been too busy searching for the causes of behavior. By looking to one's past, it was hoped that explanations could be found for the person's behavior and per-sonality. "Through reduction of guilt and by developing an ability to redirect or subli-mate his repressed desire, the patient was to conquer his mental disturbance" (Goble, 1970, p. 6). Freud seemed to have had little interest in the social application of his theo-ries and, thus, has had little influence on parent education or democratic processes in the family (Evans & Meredith, 1991).

Adlerian psychology is willing to wrestle with the ideal of equality and has pro-vided a model of counseling (open-forum family counseling) based on democratic prin-ciples. Democracy is usually characterized by some aspect of equality and fundamental human rights. Democracy only becomes problematic in human relationships when we associate equality with sameness. How can we treat a person as equal if that person is not the same but has inherent differences? Can an adult deal with a child based on equality if that child is not the same age or size? The answer is "yes" if equality does not mean sameness but equal worth (Cassel & Corsini, 1990). Although there are inherent differences among people, mutual respect, value, and dignity are the essential elements for democratic relationships.

The open-forum family counseling model is designed to create social equality within the family, where all members of a family and, consequently, society are recognized and treated as worthwhile human beings. Open-forum family counseling recognizes that the family, more than any other institution in our society, provides the opportunity for self-fulfillment and the development of social interest, Adler's criterion of good mental health (Ansbacher & Ansbacher, 1956; Mosak, 1995). For Adler, the demands of social living required that one develop the capacity to cooperate and contribute. Each of us has the innate potential for social interest and the function of education and training is converting the aptitude into an ability and skill. Social interest must be consciously developed until, as Bottome (1957) quoted Adler as stating, it becomes "as natural as breathing or the upright gait" (p. 168).

Thanks to the pioneering efforts of Adler and Dreikurs, we have the beginnings of effective principles and practices for creating democratic families and improving family living. We are also discovering a variety of methods for nurturing courage and social interest and creating mutual respect and dignity in the home, school, and workplace. However, much work still needs to be done—not only in terms of developing techniques for improving human relationships but in terms of communicating these to parents, teachers, and employers. The roots of social living are embedded in the concept of cooperation. To function adequately in a democratic setting, each person must develop those skills and attitudes appropriate to a give and take among equals (Milliren, Taylor, & Meredith, 1979). In accord with Adler's goal of creating a psychology for the common man, we must continue to find and define those practices that allow each of us to develop the skills for living in a democratic society. Of paramount importance within this goal is the need to help children develop the "psychological hardiness" required for effectively responding to the issues of life and living.

Four Styles of Family Relationships

There are four basic styles of family relationships that promote or inhibit respect in the family. These four patterns of parent–child relations are the following:

- Democratic—Everyone is considered a full-fledged human being and is given mutual respect and dignity in spite of differences in his or her inherent attributes.

- Authoritarianism—Some people have an inherent superiority and control and dictate what others, deemed inferior, will do.

- Indulgence—Those who are older and wiser must indulge those who are younger and weaker to show their love.

- Indifference—Everyone is an individual and must show their independence (Cassel & Corsini, 1990).

Democratic households require freedom with order and cannot function when one or the other of these qualities does not exist. Parents who are respectful of their children provide reasonable guidelines (order) while involving the children in the decision-making process (freedom). In democratic households, children share in decision making and through this involvement become responsible human beings. The family atmosphere is friendly and cooperative. Rewards and punishment are replaced with trust and hope in one's ability to learn from life's experiences. Parents are concerned with order but do not subdue, regiment, indulge, or control their children. They allow freedom, but not license. There is the existence of cooperation and routine in order for the family to function. Democratic families develop children who are problem solvers, have initiative, demonstrate emotional self-reliance, and are considerate of other human beings (Bettner & Lew, 1996).

For example, a child spills a glass of milk on the living room rug. A parent can scold or punish (order without freedom) the child by saying, "I told you to be careful; you never listen to me, now go to your room!" The parent could also say (freedom with order), "What do you need to do to solve this problem?" To be asked to restore the original condition is respectful and more conducive to the child's being careful and thoughtful the next time than if the child were punished or scolded. This type of question allows the child to make decisions and take responsibility for his or her behavior. It also invites an exchange of viewpoints, which trains the child to become morally autonomous (Kamii, 1984).

Autocratic households are based on *order without freedom*. Parents in this household demand compliance, and children are not involved in the decision-making process and have no power or right over their destiny. In this style of parenting, a responsible child is one who is an obedient child. Children are to obey their parents because parents are the authorities—"Do what I tell you because I am bigger, stronger, older, and wiser than you." It is a strict and coercive household that requires immediate obedience to parental authority. The story line is "So long as you live in our house, you will do just what we tell you. We are your parents, and we know what is best." Coercion thrives on inequality and is based on the belief that there are superiors who know what is best for those who are inferior and know very little. These parents believe they are superior to children and, therefore, have the right to control children through rewards and punishment (stimulus–response psychology). The evidence is overwhelming, however, that rewards and punishment are detrimental to children (Kohn, 1993, 1996).

Children who grow up in autocratic or coercive households have three courses of action. The first is blind conformity, to go along with the demands and rules. These compliant children find that by obeying the demands and rules, they never have to make decisions. Through their compliance, they are given a false sense of security and respect. The second course of action is to go along on the surface but to maintain dignity by doing as one pleases. Given this course of action, it becomes extremely important to not get caught. These children grow up not knowing how to be forthright and learn to excuse or blame others for their behavior and problems. The third choice is open rebellion. The choice with this course of action is to revolt and do the opposite of what the authority demands. In these households, there is often open warfare between the parents and child(ren). This open revolt is often identified as delinquency, and we then label these children as emotionally or behaviorally disturbed.

Indulgent and indifferent households are based on *freedom without order*. Indulgent parents mistake pampering for love. Unfortunately, pampering emotionally handicaps children and prevents them from learning how to solve problems. Pampering parents are ruled by children who force their parents to do everything for them. These parents help their children with homework, drive them to a different activity every night, play with them, and worry about them constantly. These parents might say, "My life is my kids; I do everything for them," and they do. Pampered children are free to do as they please, and there is no order. If the 2-year-old does not like her cheese sandwich for lunch, mom will provide a variety of choices and food until the youngster is satisfied. If the toddler returns home from child care with a cold, the parent is ready to quit work and protect the child from such inconvenience. Instead of being family centered, these parents are child centered. However, if these parents truly want to help their children, they must become family centered by making other life activities, including their marriage, a number-one priority.

The pampering approach is devastating for a child. It robs the child of initiative and self-confidence. In effect, it creates a vote of "no confidence" in the child's ability to solve life's problems. These children grow up expecting service from others, and because they believe they cannot handle life on their own, the world becomes a frightening place. Such children learn to avoid responsibility and develop few skills for cooperating with others. They approach life as if others are there to make things work for them, and they are experts at placing others in their service.

The indifferent household does not indulge the child; however, freedom without order prevails. Parents in the indifferent household disregard their children, allowing them to be free to do whatever they please as long as no demands are placed on the parents. Often these parents are preoccupied with their careers—their life is work. The family's motto might be "Do your own thing" or "Each person for him- or herself." No one ever eats together unless by accident, and the kitchen serves as a 24-hour snack bar. These parents have a distorted view of independence and for them cooperation means weakness, conformity, and inferiority. Cooperation is viewed as being bossed around by others, so in this family, Dad may be off to a board meeting, Mom may be going to school or to work, and each child is busy doing something different (Cassel & Corsini, 1990). The home serves more as a hotel rather than a place to nurture relationships and foster development.

Open-forum family counseling provides the parents (and audience) the opportunity to experience these differing family atmospheres while demonstrating more effective approaches to parenting. In addition, through the interview process, the counselor displays how an exchange of viewpoints with children encourages their development. The audience may observe how a 5-year-old who governs herself with respect to small decisions will become more capable in dealing with bigger issues and handling life challenges. Instead of giving 10 choices of food to a 2-year-old until she is satisfied, the parents and audience learn how offering limited choices creates freedom with order and responsibility taking. Here the parent may ask, "Do you want a cheese or peanut butter sandwich for lunch?" The child is involved in the decision making over food (freedom) and has the option not to choose or eat anything (order). Consequently, the interview provides a role model for parents, demonstrating how children learn to be responsible by making choices for themselves.

☐ A Typical Day

As the interview continues, Walton proceeds to explore the specific family interactions and dynamics by obtaining information regarding the nature of a typical day from the parents. Walton has the parents describe a typical day in their household. This technique is called *tracking* in the marriage and family literature. Tracking is a way for the family counselor to interact with the family members from a position of neutrality, primarily as a listener in search of information. The goal is to investigate the family atmosphere (as described above) and gain clarity on family interactions. Tracking allows the family themes and content to emerge, which verifies the counselor's earlier definition of the problem (Sherman, Oresky, & Rountree, 1991). Tracking a typical day is a safe way for the counselor and parents to discuss the interactions in the family and pinpoint the positive and negative patterns of interactions occurring between the children and the parents. This also helps the audience understand the dynamics of the parent–child relationship.

Now let us return to the interview:

Counselor: Let's go to your daily routine.

Dad: Talk to my wife.

Counselor: So, Mom, how does the day begin?

Mom: Usually I wake the kids up, between 6:30 and 6:45. They are supposed to lay things out the night before, so when they get up they can get dressed and eat breakfast. But it's a battle every morning. I am constantly nagging—hurry up, get dressed—because we have to leave by a certain time.

Counselor: *(To the audience.)* Does this also sound like your home on a typical morning?

(Audience laughs, and most people agree by raising their hands.)

Counselor: And what happens to Darrel and Rebecca?

Mom: Darrel gets out of bed and wants to play. He does what he wants but does not get dressed.

Counselor: So he wants to play, and you say, "Come on, we are going to be late"; and if I were watching what would I see him doing?

Mom: He keeps playing.

Counselor: And you are seeing some similar thing in Rebecca? What does she say or do?

Mom: If she gets out of bed, she does fairly well. Whereas Darrel likes to play, she tends to sleep. After maybe telling her once or twice she will get moving.

Counselor: If I were watching her, she would tend not to be so resistant or angry as Darrel?

Mom: She may make a face at you, but for the most part she would comply.

Counselor: So Darrel is playing and not coming along; how do you get him to comply? How do you get him to move?

Mom: I keep nagging him until he finally moves.

Counselor: Dad, from what you are hearing, does any of this surprise you?

Mom: No, because it wakes him up in the morning.

Counselor: What, do you put another pillow over your head or what?

Dad: Sometimes I get up and the room starts to shake.

Counselor: Mom can be a major league nagger, but you can be the heavy. When heavy artillery is needed to be called, it's Dad. So then people jump?

Mom: Yes, they know Dad's mad.

Counselor: Anything you want to add, Dad?

Dad: No.

Counselor: Now I want to be a help to the parents and myself, and to illustrate for the audience what is going through my mind. Early on we had a family with a compliant girl. Correct me if I am wrong. We had a family with a compliant girl, who received affection and went along with the program. But, what I did not know at first, was she may have been afraid not to go along with the program. Darrel is different. He is not going to be Rebecca. Part of how he is not going to be Rebecca is how he sizes up the situation. He can find his place by not going along with the program. We are dealing with some determined people, some forces to be reckoned with. Does that make sense? So it's not uncommon for someone in the family, especially a second born, someone behind a compliant sister, to say, "Maybe you are pretty controlling and forceful, but I bet I can show you that you can't make me do it your way." That is what I think is happening in your family. Dad and Mom come from this position for some good reason. I don't know what those reasons are, but I'd like to find out and help them find out.

Along with tracking, Walton wants to further understand the family dynamics by understanding how the parents arrive at their current positions in the family. He does this through their "most memorable observation."

Most Memorable Observation

The most memorable observation is a new Adlerian technique developed by Walton. This technique is an effective and efficient method of assessing the parents' hidden reasons found in their private logic. Adler's term *private logic* refers to the individual's cognitive constructs that are not in line with reality but that subjectively guide the individual. Our private logic contains hidden reasons that justify our thoughts and deeds for violating social interest (Evans & Kane, 1996). The most memorable observation allows the counselor and parents to understand their hidden reasons for maintaining ineffective parenting styles. The technique examines the conclusion each parent made about family life, whether that was positive or negative. This conclusion reveals what they each regard as a state of inferiority. The parents then compensate to avoid this imagined state in a way that contributes to the current family problem.

As the interview proceeds, Walton explores with the parents their most memorable observation in an effort to further understand the dynamics of the family.

Counselor: So Mom, somewhere between the ages of 12–15, you looked around your family life and drew some conclusion about it. The conclusion may have been positive, and you decided this is important. So when you become an adult you will do everything you can to make it this way in your family. Or, more commonly, it could have been distasteful. You may have thought that "when I become an adult, I am going to do everything I can to not have this happen in my family." What do you think you came up with?

Mom: I was a pretty compliant child. My father was controlling, and I was afraid of my father. Whereas my mother was a very affectionate person. Nothing sticks out in my mind about back then, although my mother was nagging, and I did not want to be nagging. Rebecca says she is not going to be nagging like me when she is an adult. But I find myself doing the same thing as my mother.

Counselor: You correct me if I am wrong; so your father could come on strong.

Mom: Very strong.

Counselor: What does that mean?

Mom: He used a belt.

Counselor: You did what you could to avoid it, or you took the belt?

Mom: Tried to avoid it.

Counselor: So that was a position of inferiority. You live life out of control. It was a position of inferiority that was there to be dealt with. You live life out of control.

Mom: Trying to please him.

Counselor: That can be seen as a minus. You live life as though you are renting space in a world run by other people. Now, as an adult, you are in control, you are not in a position of powerlessness. I propose to you that your memorable observation is "I don't have to feel like I am in a situation that I am out of control or other people are calling the shots." This would be a sensible position with a father who was overly controlling. You spent too much time pleasing people and being pushed around. So now you are going to prove that you are no longer going to be placed in that position. You have grown to be more assertive. That is a plus.

Mom: I agree.

Counselor: Except with children, I suspect it is overdone. You overcompensate. Yet it seems reasonable to you because you are not nearly as coercive as your father. Now, Dad, let me ask you the same question and what do you recall?

Dad: I did not see my mom and dad much because they were always working. So I had a babysitter or my brother babysat. So the power was in his hands.

Counselor: Tell us how he used this power.

Dad: He smacked me around a lot.

Counselor: He really punched you and beat you up.

Dad: Oh, yeah.

Counselor: He was how much older than you?

Dad: Five years older.

Counselor: So he was substantially older, and your effort was not to give up. Although he could overpower you.

Dad: Oh, yeah. I'd keep coming back at him.

Counselor: Does it make sense to you? That significant state of inferiority, the minus in this thread, to have someone else control you, to be out of control, is something you don't want to have in your life anymore?

Dad: That's correct. My family is nothing like how I was raised.

Counselor: That may be. But I propose to you that it is, in some significant ways. And when you talk about spanking, threaten to spank, that you have mastered or developed techniques to overcome your sense of inferiority and being out of control. Where people are going to dominate, you'll be damned if your kid is going to dominate you. It's not going to be that way. I see the fire in your eyes when you think about it.

Dad: *(Laughs)*

Counselor: Interesting that they have a lot of affection in the family. We have seen that.

Dad: Yes.

Counselor: So the resistance in this kind of situation is not direct, but your son is in a position to say no to you. He is in a stronger position. You're wanting him to say yes, and he is in a stronger position by denying you his cooperation. You walk slow when I want you to walk fast. You run out of the room when I want you to sit. I want you to get dressed for school and you stop and play. Darrel does anything to say "I will decide for me and you will not." Yet, if he could find out that no one is against him, if you could win him over, he may cooperate. We are not going to refine this now because I want some time to interview the kids. However, when you work with adults and kids, the ones mostly likely to make the first steps in change are the adults. I hope this makes sense to you. See, when you come on strong with Darrel, he feels duty bound to put his foot across the line. If you could back off and he could see that Mom and Dad like me, and the nagging stops, then some possible guidelines could be worked out. Choices are important to Darrel. More choices or limited choices would be of use to him. Encouragement would also be important. Maybe both of you could have a moment together where you could encourage him. Have a conversation with him, and if this rings true you could encourage him. You could say, "Son, I think we have made some mistakes and we would like to have your company in the living room so we can sit down and talk together." You could shock him by telling him how you have made the mistake of acting as if he would not be helpful unless you kept nagging, shouting, and even spanking him. You could tell him how you don't want to be so bossy. This has not been of help; and explain to him how you are going to work on that. Or, you may even want to pick a specific area like the morning routine where you are nagging, and you may want to pull back on the nagging. In the case where he runs out, I would suggest the value of letting him go. The running out is to get you to chase him, to get you angry and to defeat you. You're the parents, and if you're concerned about safety, you could go after him. But if it's a situation of who is the boss, you could realize the purpose is to defeat you. If you don't chase him, he is inclined to walk back in because it is not useful to him. So check yourself out. See if you call upon your anger and recognize when you use it as a weapon to hammer him in place. This is a violation of respect. It sets up a power relationship, and you are not winning his cooperation. You are forcing him to behave, and both of you have good reason to do this. You both don't want to be in a weak position, yet you are both out of control and both are losing control. So less is more, and that means less nagging, shouting, threatening, and he will test you. He will have to find out, "I don't feel like a guy who is at war with Mom and Dad. They treat me well, and I have choices and make input into the family."

At this time, Walton had the family and audience take a 10-minute break. He will begin the second half of the interview with the children. Before we present the interview with the children, it would beneficial to describe how and where the open-forum counseling demonstration takes place. In so doing, we describe what is known as the family education center.

☐ Family Education Centers

Family education centers are basic to the Adlerian family education model. A family education center consists of three primary components: volunteers, parent study groups, and the open-forum counseling interviews. Most family education centers operate by voluntary support. A group of parents, graduate students, mental health counselors, guidance counselors, or educators sponsor a center. These volunteers organize the center, providing a meeting room for the counseling demonstration and a separate supervised playroom for children.

The main function of a family education center is to provide opportunities for parent education. Parents involved in a family education center have the option of participating in a parent study group, being involved with the open-forum family counseling demonstrations, or both. Open-forum family counseling and parent study groups can operate independently and effectively; however, when combined they enhance the educational experience. For instance, the best way to find a family for the counseling demonstration is to select one from a parent study group and one that has already observed a family counseling demonstration.

It is recommended that parents who volunteer to be the family in focus observe other families being interviewed before they take their turn. This allows them to become acquainted with the procedures and observe the educational process that takes place. Consequently, parents feel more relaxed and in control and are not threatened by the upcoming experience.

Parent Study Groups

Parent study groups often form the nucleus of the center. The goal of a parent study group is to discuss and understand Adlerian psychology so it can be applied at home. Adlerian parent study groups emphasize purposive behavior, family constellation, logical and natural consequences, conflict resolution, and encouragement. The group helps parents develop an encouraging and cooperative family atmosphere.

Adlerian parent study groups may use books such as *Children: The Challenge* (Dreikurs & Soltz, 1964), *The Practical Parent* (Corsini & Painter, 1975), *Redirecting Children's Behavior* (Kohls, 1993), or *Positive Discipline* (Nelsen, 1981) or they may use educational programs such as *Raising Kids Who Can* (Bettner & Lew, 1996), *Systematic Training for Effective Parenting* (STEP; Dinkmeyer, McKay, & Dinkmeyer, 1997), *Systematic Training for Effective Parenting of Teens* (STEP/Teen; Dinkmeyer & McKay, 1990), *Active Parenting* (Popkin, 1987), or *Active Parenting of Teens* (Popkin, 1990). All of these are excellent materials for conducting parent study groups and include a manual or study guide that can provide the group leader considerable direction for conducting the group. In addition, some of these programs provide in-depth training in both the course content and leadership skills for study group facilitators. (For more in-depth information on parent study groups, please see Chapter 10.)

It is believed that the effect of parent study groups extends beyond the immediate group. The sessions have an influence on the participant's spouse, children, in-laws, and teachers. It is estimated that the direct or indirect influence of a parent study group that meets for 90 minutes each week can easily reach 50 outside people. Furthermore, research on Adlerian parent training has found that parental attitudes became more democratic and less restrictive and authoritarian through application of Adlerian principles and the STEP program (Mooney, 1995).

Parent study groups also provide excellent training for graduate students preparing to become family and school counselors. A prerequisite to doing any family counseling is to have graduate students conduct a parent study group. As group leaders, students learn how family systems operate and to field difficult questions asked by parents. This experience is excellent preparation for leading an open-forum family counseling session.

The Meeting Room

A family education center needs a meeting room, where the open-forum family counseling demonstrations can take place in front of an audience. In our case demonstration, the family was interviewed in a large auditorium. An empty classroom beside the auditorium was used as the playroom. To create a group atmosphere and avoid members of the audience acting like spectators, it is important to have a seating arrangement in which all participants sit close together. Where the audience sits influences their involvement in the interview. The interview works best when the family and counselor sit on a portable platform or stage that is only slightly elevated. When this arrangement is not possible, having the counselor and family sit on stools is a workable alternative. No member of the audience is allowed to sit in the back of the room and observe the interview. This is accomplished by arranging the chairs in a semicircle no more than four rows deep. The counselor and family are seated at the open end of the semicircle.

With a large group of 200 to 300, it is still best to use a modified version of this arrangement. If the interview takes place in an auditorium with fixed seating and a traditional stage, the group effect is lost and the quality of the interview is reduced.

Perhaps even more important than seating is sound. It is essential that each participant in the interview has a microphone, including the counselors, parents, and children. Taking turns and passing microphones during the interview becomes annoying and ineffective. Everyone should have a microphone so time is not wasted passing the microphone from person to person. Interviews that go poorly often occur because members of the audience cannot hear.

We recommend that a backup microphone system be available. Once, during a family interview with an audience of several hundred people, the microphone system blew a fuse. The fuse could not be replaced. The large audience had difficulty hearing, and people became impatient. The counselor could do nothing more than continue the interview. After this incident, the agency sponsoring the program bought its own portable microphone system. Many things can go wrong with the microphones, so it is best to have an alternate sound system.

Frequency and Duration of Interviews

Family education centers may hold open-forum family counseling sessions once a week, monthly, every other week, or sporadically. Most parents, and especially single parents, have difficulty attending during the week because they have to coordinate work, parenting, and other community activities. Saturday morning often works well for conducting open-forum family counseling. Agencies and universities may hold them during a particular time when a parenting class or family counseling course is being taught.

From our experience, 1-hour interviews are too short and tend to force the counselor to rush the process. Two-hour interviews work best because everyone has a chance to talk, and a break can be provided midway through the interview. Generally, 1.5 to 2 hours are recommended, depending on how actively the counselor seeks the audience's involvement.

The Playroom

There needs to be a playroom near the room in which the family interview takes place. While the parents are being interviewed, the children are in the playroom. This room is supervised by the playroom director and staff. The playroom director is trained in Adlerian principles, and the staff members are volunteers.

The playroom director needs to be creative and flexible as most open-forum counseling sessions take place in churches, school buildings, libraries, or community mental health facilities where there are no specifically designed playrooms. Often, the playroom director faces unexpected challenges that require problem-solving skills. For example, office space converted into a playroom may be difficult to control. In addition, the equipment available for a playroom may vary from toys, games, books, videos, computers, and puzzles to small amounts of paper and pencils provided by the playroom director.

The playroom serves two purposes. First, it provides a place for members of the audience to leave their children while they observe the interview. The playroom is designed to provide these children with interesting activities. The organization of the playroom is based on the same democratic principles presented in the parent study groups and the open-forum counseling demonstration. Children may participate in individual or group activities. The child is treated in a friendly manner and free to choose what he or she wants to do. Children are encouraged to be spontaneous and creative. The emphasis is on democratic responsibility through shared decision-making and choices. Order is created by the logic of social living and natural consequences.

Second, the playroom is a place where children participating in the open-forum counseling interview are observed in relationship to their siblings and other children. The behavior of a child during the counseling interview may differ considerably from that displayed in the playroom. The counseling that takes place in front of the audience creates a controlled atmosphere for a child. The playroom is an open atmosphere where the child is free to express his or her attitude and behavior. The playroom director's job is to observe the children who are participating in the interview and report this information to the counselor. The playroom director has been trained to recognize who takes a leadership role, plays inadequate, acts charming, has social skills, bullies, withdraws, or shows an interest in the other children.

Before the children enter the counseling room, the counselor and playroom director exchange observations in the presence of the audience and parents. This information is used to confirm and develop the basic dynamics of each child, identify how the family operates, and assess the child's attitudes and behavior in the playroom as compared with what the counselor has been told by the parents (Dreikurs, Corsini, Lowe, & Sonstegard, 1959).

Let us return to our case example. Walton's interview focuses on goal disclosure with the children.

☐ Interview with the Children: Goal Disclosure

One of the purposes for interviewing the children is to establish goal disclosure. By tracking the patterns of interaction (problem formation, typical day, memorable observation) with the parents, the Adlerian-trained counselor will pinpoint the child's goal of misbehavior (attention, power, revenge, inadequacy, or fun and excitement). The four goals of misbehavior are credited to Rudolf Dreikurs and have been described in the Adlerian literature (Dreikurs, 1964). The fifth goal—fun and excitement—was identified by Frank Walton in his work with adolescents (Walton, 1980). Children who behave unacceptably and pursue one or more of the goals of misbehavior are attempting to find their place of significance within the family or group in which they are functioning. Although children are not always aware of this purpose for their behavior, they often recognize it when it is disclosed to them. Children also have socially useful goals such as cooperation, friendship, autonomy, or contribution. However, the counselor is interested in the child's mistaken goals and how the parents maintain these goals with their responses to the child's behavior. By pinpointing the child's goal(s) of misbehavior, the counselor will suggest changes in the parent's responses.

Along with detailed descriptions of behavior, the counselor may ask the parents how the child's actions made them feel. Knowing the feelings generated on the part of the parents in response to the misbehavior offers significant clues as to the goal of misbehavior.

If we are annoyed by the behavior or if we feel like we have to remind and coax the child to get things done, the goal is probably attention getting. It is also attention getting if we feel we must constantly help him or her or if we are "delighted" by such a good child. When the goal is power, we feel provoked and generally engage in a power struggle with the child. We feel challenged by the power-oriented child and respond with "I'll show you" or "You can't get away with this!" The child whose goal is revenge usually affects us by making us feel hurt, and we react with comparable feelings of retaliation—"How can you do this to me? I'll get you for this!" Finally, the child who has given up leads us to feelings of despair and hopelessness so we give up with a "What's the use? I just don't know what to do" (Milliren et. al., 1979, p. 140).

Sometimes parents report a state of being like "nothing," "I did not feel anything," or "I did not do anything." The skilled counselor must train the parents to pinpoint their emotional response, such as they felt annoyed, angry, mad, vengeful, sad, or frustrated. Awareness of the goals of misbehavior allows the counselor to develop hypotheses about the dynamics of the family system. The counselor often shares these hypotheses with the family and the audience early in the interview. This adds to the anticipation that occurs during the interview with the children. When the counselor does goal disclosure with the children, everyone is interested in seeing if the counselor's hypotheses were correct.

While interviewing the children, the counselor is not conducting an inquisition or detecting who is correct. Instead, the counselor is attempting to understand each individual's perception of the present situation and how everyone contributes to the problem. The process of disclosing the goal to the child is always conducted in a tentative, questioning manner—"Could it be that you don't mind Mother and do what she asks because you want to be the boss and show her that you are in charge?"

> We must be careful not to confront the child with an accusation such as "You do it to get attention," because the child will only resent this and deny it. "Could it be . . . ?" is not an accusation; it is only a guess that may be correct or incorrect. If this is incorrect, we should guess again. (Dreikurs et al., 1959)

Goal disclosure occurs with the children once the parents leave and a brief playroom report has been given by the playroom director. In the case scenario presented, after the break the playroom director confirmed Rebecca's willingness to please and Darrel's unwillingness to cooperate. However, she noted that, when given a limited choice, Darrel was cooperative and pleasant.

We begin the second half of the interview with the children seated next to the counselor and the parents having left the room. Walton proceeded with the interview by moving toward the activity of goal disclosure with the children:

Counselor: We are teaching people about some ideas young people have. Rebecca, you have experience as a 10-year-old, and Darrel, you are how old?

Darrel: Seven.

Counselor: So you know how it is to be 7 in your family, and these people are inter-
             ested in how children look at life. Did you ever think you would be a
             teacher?

Children: No.

Counselor: Is there something that goes on in your family you wish was different?
             Any problem at home you wish you could change?

Rebecca: My brother hitting and kicking me.

Counselor: Darrel, do you recognize this problem?

Darrel: I am just hitting her back.

Counselor: What happens when you two punch and hit one another?

Darrel: We both get into trouble with Mom. We can't play with our friends for a
             week.

Counselor: Does that make you feel mad?

Darrel: (Nods in agreement.)

Counselor: And what do you do about it?

Darrel: (Smiles.)

Counselor: Can I tell you what I think you do, Darrel?

Darrel: Yes.

Counselor: Could it be you go and play with your friends anyway?

Darrel: *(Smiles.)*

Counselor: I talked with your folks and we had a friendly conversation, but I need
             your help. It seems to me you do not always feel like Mom and Dad are
             friendly.

Darrel: No.

Counselor: I know you love Mom and Dad a lot. But at times you both get mad at
             them. What do you get mad about?

Darrel: When I get put into timeout for an hour.

Counselor: Rebecca, does that happen?

Rebecca: Yes.

Counselor: And what do you do?

Darrel: I sit there and "plays" with my toys.

Counselor: It's hard to imagine you sit there. Darrel, it seems when someone tells you
             to do something you are determined that no one is going to boss you around.
             What do you think?

Darrel: Yeah.

Counselor: Could it be you hate to have people boss you around?

Darrel: (Smiling.) Yes.

Counselor: So when someone tells you to sit still you feel like not sitting still?

Darrel: Ask my sister.

Counselor: I wonder if you know you are both intelligent. Do you know that? I think you could have some good ideas, but I don't know if people ask you for your ideas.

Darrel: Nope. *(Laughter from audience.)*

Counselor: So people just tell you what they think?

Darrel: *(Shakes head in agreement.)*

Counselor: And you hate that. Would you like it if Mom and Dad ask you for your ideas more?

Darrel: Yes, but what do you mean?

Counselor: Your parents want to be good parents but get bossy sometimes and shout.

Darrel: Oh yeah, I hate that.

Counselor: I thought that, maybe, Darrel, you do not like them shouting and being bossy.

Rebecca: I do not like that.

Counselor: Well, we are going to work on Mom and Dad to see if they can stop being bossy and have them ask for your ideas. What do you think will happen? I believe you are going to get a chance. What do you think?

Darrel: Be great.

Counselor: What do you think, Rebecca?

Rebecca: Yeah.

Counselor: Rebecca, what do you do when they are bossy and yelling?

Rebecca: I do my work or what they want me to do and then go off to my room.

Counselor: So even though you do not like being bossed, you don't rebel; you do your stuff and go off to your room.

Rebecca: Yes.

Counselor: Okay. We are now going to send for Mom and Dad and have them join us. Could someone bring in Mom and Dad?

Parent Education and Recommendations

Typically, the children go back to the playroom and the parents return for the parent education and recommendation. This is the time when all the information is brought together and the parents gain a new understanding of the family. During this time, the counselor fine tunes his or her recommendations and asks for feedback from the audience. The counselor wants to give only one or two tasks for the family to work on during the next several weeks. In our case scenario, the counselor had the children stay when he brought the parents back in. Thus, the counselor made his recommendations to the entire family. With older children and adolescents, making recommendations to the entire family is often more effective.

In the concluding phase of the interview, the counselor shares his recommendations with the family.

Counselor: Mom and Dad, I think we are on the right track. During the interview Rebecca confirmed that she feels pushed around but that she goes along. She does not like it and would like to have something more to say about what happens to her. Darrel, go ahead and tell us how you feel. You told us pretty clearly that . . . .

Darrel: Mad!

Counselor: Maybe enough said on that! *(Audience laughs.)*

Dad: Darrel, what are you mad about?

Counselor: I want to sidestep some trouble here and say there is a sense of restraint. You now have the opportunity to allow your children to make choices and take responsibility for what they do. You have the opportunity for them to be a part of the family through shared decision making and limited choices. The more involved they become in the decision making, the more responsible they will become. I will mention one powerful technique that could be of help to you when you get started. It will be your decision to do this. You can remove yourself from the power struggle with Darrel. When you feel yourself get angry or wanting to make Darrel do something, you can remove yourself. This requires an attitude that says, "Wild horses could not make me respond if I did not want to." This is not unkind. It is being able to move off into the distance when someone is trying to defeat you. I would like to thank you very much for helping us. We had a good conversation with the kids. Parents, do you feel this makes sense to you?

Mom: Yes.

Counselor: We would like to stay in touch with you. I can do it by phone, but you have many folks trained in these ideas and there are resources here that you could use. I would now like to respond to questions from the audience for 5 or 10 minutes. Thanks, Rebecca and Darrel.

☐ Conclusion

The counselor conducting the open-forum family counseling session is trained in Adlerian psychology and considered a family educator. The emphasis is on creating a positive climate in which problem solving can be facilitated. The model does not view parents as abnormal or children as having disorders or deficits. Instead, the view is that the interpersonal nature of relationships creates problems within the family. Problems that exist in families are due to the dynamics of what goes on between the family members rather than the result of an individual deficit, disease, or addiction. Parents are viewed only as lacking the information they need to make appropriate changes in their behavior. Therefore, the family counselor educates the family. The counselor provides the information and experiences that create changes in how family members relate to one another. The emphasis is not on better ways to control children but on education for change in attitudes and behavior.

Counselors conducting open-forum family counseling are skilled group leaders. The counselor is sensitive to the dynamics of the family system while developing and attending to the group atmosphere created by the audience. The counselor does not treat members of the audience as passive spectators. Instead, the counselor involves the audience as helpers in the interview. For instance, the counselor may involve members of the audience by having them make guesses about the children's personalities based on the family constellation.

The counselor must also know when to use the audience to encourage the family while studying the interactions between family members. If done correctly, the counselor will create a supportive group atmosphere, an advantage not available in private counseling. During the demonstration, the counselor may even talk to the parents through the audience, especially if the parents are arguing or too stressed. The parents can listen and learn as observers while the counselor instructs and discusses a particular principle with the audience.

The open nature of the interviews and interaction between the audience and the family creates a sense of community. The interview brings out the commonality of problems among all participants. By focusing on observable interaction among family members (mealtime, bedtime, homework, or sibling fighting), 80% to 90% of the audience identifies with the family's problem. This recognition of shared similarities, despite the complexity of human problems, is called universality. When common denominators among people become evident, and the similarities are perceived by group members, universality occurs.

Universality pulls a group together and creates a feeling of belonging and cohesiveness. Universality and cohesiveness are recognized as two important curative factors in group dynamics (Yalom, 1995). When universality occurs, the family in focus and the audience move from a sense of isolation to connectedness. Group cohesion is formed, and parents learn they are not alone with their concerns for their children. The information provided for the family in focus is also of value to the audience as they share in the family's concerns. Consequently, almost everyone attending the open-forum family counseling demonstration benefits from the educational process (Christensen & Marchant, 1983).

☐ References

Ansbacher, H. L., & Ansbacher, R. R. (Eds.). (1956). *The individual psychology of Alfred Adler*. New York: Basic Books.

Bettner, B. L., & Lew, A. (1995). *Raising kids who can—Leader's guide*. Newton Centre, MA: Connexions Press.

Bottome, P. (1957). *Alfred Adler: A portrait from life*. New York: Vanguard Press.

Cassel, P., & Corsini, R. J. (1990). *Coping with teenagers in a democracy*. Toronto, Ontario, Canada: Lugus Productions.

Christensen, O. C., & Marchant, W. C. (1983). The family counseling process. In O. C. Christensen & T. G. Schramski (Eds.), *Adlerian family counseling* (pp. 29–56). Minneapolis, MN: Educational Media.

Corsini, R., & Painter, G. (1975). *The practical parent*. New York: Harper & Row.

Dinkmeyer, D., McKay, G. D., & Dinkmeyer, D., Jr. (1997). *Systematic training for effective parenting*. Circle Pines, MN: American Guidance Service.

Dinkmeyer, D., & McKay,. G. D. (1990). *Parenting teens*. Circle Pines, MN: American Guidance Service.

Dinkmeyer, D., Jr., & Dinkmeyer, D. (1981). A comprehensive and systematic approach to parent education. *The American Journal of Family Therapy, 9*, 46–40.

Dreikurs, R., & Soltz, V. (1964). *Children: The challenge*. New York: Hawthorn/Dutton.

Dreikurs, R. (1971). *Social equality: The challenge of today*. Chicago: Henry Regnery.

Dreikurs, R., Corsini, R., Lowe, R., & Sonstegard, M. (1959). *Adlerian family counseling*. Eugene: University of Oregon Press.

Evans, T. D., & Kane, D. P. (1996). Sophistry: A promising group technique for the involuntary client. *Journal for Specialist in Group Work, 21*, 110–117.

Evans, T. D., & Meredith, C. W. (1991). How far can we go and still be Adlerian. *Individual Psychology, 47*, 541–547.

Goble, F. (1970). *The third force: The psychology of Abraham Maslow*. New York: Grossman.

Kamii, C. (1984). Obedience is not enough. *Young Children, May*, 11–14.

Kohls, K. J. (1993). *Redirecting children's behavior*. Gainesville, FL: INCAF.

Kohn, A. (1993). *Punished by rewards*. New York: Houghton Mifflin.

Kohn, A. (1996). *Beyond discipline*. Alexandria, VA: Association for Curriculum Development.

Manaster, G. J., & Corsini, R. J. (1982). *Individual psychology: Theory and practice*. Itasca, IL: F. E. Peacock.

Meredith C. W. (1986). Democracy in the family. *Individual Psychology, 42*, 602–610.

Milliren, A., Taylor, F. A., & Meredith, C. W. (1979). *Child caring: Views and re-views*. Lexington, MA: Ginn Custom.

Mooney, S. (1995). Parent training: A review of Adlerian, parent effectiveness training, and behavioral research. *The Family Journal, 3*, 218–230.

Mosak, H.H. (1995). Adlerian therapy. In R. J. Corsini & D. Wedding (Eds.), *Current psychotherapies* (5th ed., pp. 51–94). Itasca, IL: F. E. Peacock.

Nelsen, J. (1987). *Positive discipline*. New York: Ballantine Books.

Papp, P. (1984). Setting the terms for therapy. *The Family Therapy Networker*, January/February, 42–47.

Popkin, M. (1987). *Active parenting*. San Francisco: Harper & Row.

Popkin, M. (1990). *Active parenting of teens*. Atlanta, GA: Active Parenting.

Progoff, I. (1969). *The death and rebirth of psychology*. St. Louis, MO: McGraw Hill.

Sherman, R., Oresky, P., & Roundtree, Y. (1991). *Solving problems in couples and family therapy*. New York: Brunner/Mazel.

Sonstegard, M., & Dreikurs, R. (1975). The teleoanalytic group counseling approach. In G. Gazda (Ed.), *Basic approaches to group psychotherapy and group counseling* (pp. 468–510). Springfield, IL: Charles C Thomas.

Sweeney, T. J. (1989). *Adlerian counseling: A practical approach for a new decade* (3rd ed.). Muncie, IN: Accelerated Development.

Walton, F. X. (1980). *Winning teenagers over in home and school*. Columbia, SC: Adlerian Child Care Books.

Walton, F. X. (Producer & Director). (1996). Initial counseling session with family of child diagnosed as ADHD with Francis X. Walton, Ph.D. [Video]. (Available from Adlerian Child Care Books, P. O. Box 210206, Columbia, S. C. 29211.)

Yalom, I. D. (1995). *The theory and practice of group psychotherapy*. New York: Basic Books.

CHAPTER 9

Terry Kottman

Play Therapy

From a developmental perspective, most children under the ages of 10 or 11 do not have the abstract verbal reasoning skills to articulate clearly all of their thoughts, feelings, reactions, and attitudes (Bettelheim, 1987; Piaget, 1962). Because of this consideration, many mental health professionals use toys and the process of play therapy to help them communicate with young children about the children's (a) experiences, (b) reactions to those experiences, (c) feelings about those experiences, (d) desires and goals, and (e) perceptions of themselves, others, and the world (Kottman, 1995; Landreth, 1991). This approach to counseling children allows them to use their own natural way of expressing themselves, without assuming that they are capable of using the more adult communication modality of conversation.

Although Adler (1963) and Dreikurs (Dreikurs & Grey, 1970; Dreikurs & Soltz, 1964) both discussed working with children from an Adlerian perspective, neither of them addressed the developmental constraints that may prevent children from being able to use language to communicate directly about their lives and their struggles. Most contemporary authors who have written about working with children using Individual Psychology as their theoretical foundation seem to work with children in the context of the family or the school—presenting Adlerian ideas for family therapy, parenting, or classroom management (Albert, 1989; Bettner & Lew, 1989; Christensen, 1993; Dinkmeyer & McKay, 1989; Glenn & Nelson, 1988; J. Nelson, 1987; Popkin, 1982, 1993). Even those Adlerian authors who have written directly about working with individual children using art or play (Borden, 1982; Dinkmeyer & Dinkmeyer, 1977, 1983; Lord, 1982; Nystul, 1980; Yura & Galassi, 1974) have not clearly described a concrete method for using play therapy from an Adlerian perspective. To remedy this void, I developed, on the basis of several years of working with children using a blend of Adlerian concepts and strategies and play therapy premises and techniques, Adlerian play therapy as an intervention approach to counseling children (Kottman, 1992, 1993, 1994, 1995; Kottman & Johnson, 1993; Kottman & Stiles, 1990; Kottman & Warlick, 1989, 1990).

In Adlerian play therapy, counselors use the principles of Individual Psychology to formulate their understanding of the client and his or her social context. The Adlerian foundation for conceptualizing the client is based on the definition of human nature that describes people as socially embedded, goal-directed, subjective, and creative beings who must be understood from a holistic perspective (Ansbacher & Ansbacher, 1956; Dinkmeyer, Dinkmeyer, & Sperry, 1987).

☐ Clients Appropriate for Adlerian Play Therapy

Adlerian play therapy is an appropriate strategy for counseling children between the ages of 4 and 11 or 12, depending on their development. It can be helpful with children who have a variety of different presenting problems but seems to work especially well with children who have (a) issues involving power and control (e.g., bullying; power struggles with teachers, parents, and siblings; temper tantrums), (b) experienced an event that they perceived as traumatic (e.g., sexual abuse, divorce of parents, adoption, death of a friend, pet, or family member), (c) negative self-concepts (e.g., being easily discouraged, not making an effort on work, making self-denigrating comments), (d) problems in cooperating with others (e.g., sibling conflicts, fights with parents, trouble with classmates), and (e) weak social skills (e.g., difficulty making and maintaining friends).

☐ Toys and the Playroom

To give children many different vehicles for communicating, Adlerian play therapists have toys from five distinct categories: (a) *family–nurturing toys* so that children can explore their relationships with family, friends, and peers and express their desire for nurturing and belonging; (b) *scary toys* so that children can explore their fears, perceived threats, past traumas, and mistaken beliefs; (c) *aggressive toys* so that children can explore trust and control issues and express their desire for protection; (d) *expressive toys* so that children can explore family relationships, mistaken beliefs, and feelings and express their creativity; and (e) *pretend–fantasy toys* so that children can explore relationships and practice new attitudes, feelings, and behaviors (Kottman, 1995). The following is a list of representative toys from each of these categories.

Family–nurturing can include toys like a doll house, baby dolls, animal families, people puppets, several families of bendable dolls, and kitchenware (such as pots, pans, dishes). Scary toys can include toys like snakes, rats, spiders, dinosaurs, a shark, a wolf doll or puppet, and a bear doll or puppet. Aggressive toys can include a stand-up punching bag, weapons (such as play pistols, swords, a dart gun), toy soldiers, and handcuffs. Expressive toys can include materials such as an easel, watercolors, crayons, markers, glue, scissors, pipe cleaners, clay, and construction paper. Pretend–fantasy toys can include toys such as masks, hats, costumes, puppets, transportation toys (like cars, trucks, airplanes), telephones, a doctor kit, and zoo and farm animals. Although it is not essential to have all of these toys, it is necessary to have representative play media from each of the five categories so that children will have the resources to express themselves fully in the play therapy process.

The toys should be arranged in an open space so that children can explore all of the play media available (Landreth, 1991). They need to be within easy reach of clients and should be kept in a predictable arrangement so that children will begin to experience the play therapy space as a place where they can expect consistency and safety (Kottman, 1995; Landreth, 1991).

Although the setting for play therapy would ideally be a large, custom-designed playroom with spaces for child-sized shelves, a kitchen area, bathroom, and sand box, this is rarely possible in the real world. Many counselors who work with children have limited funds or must share space with other professionals or travel from place to place (Landreth, 1991). It is essential to have a space in which to lay out the toys that is relatively quiet and private, with few distractions. In Adlerian play therapy, the primary factor in play therapy design is the comfort level of the counselor (Kottman, 1995). The play therapy space must be one in which the counselor feels comfortable and able to express his or her flexibility and creativity so that clients also feel comfortable and able to be flexible and creative.

☐ Phases of Adlerian Play Therapy

Adlerian play therapy progresses through the following phases: (a) building an egalitarian relationship, (b) exploring the child's lifestyle, (c) helping the child gain insight into his or her lifestyle, and (d) reorienting and reeducating the child. These phases frequently overlap—for example, the counselor will continue to build the relationship throughout the process. In addition to working with the child, the Adlerian play therapist also uses Adlerian principles to consult with parents and (if necessary and appropriate) teachers. Most Adlerian play therapists divide the time in a session between a play therapy segment with the child and a parent consultation segment with the parent(s). If this is not possible, the play therapist must work out another plan for working with the parent(s) on parenting skills and personal issues that might interfere with their ability to appropriately apply parenting skills in their relationship with their child.

Building a Relationship

In the first phase of Adlerian play therapy, the primary goal of the therapist is to build egalitarian relationships with both the child and the parent(s). In play therapy, the techniques used to build this partnership with the child include tracking, restating content, reflecting feelings, making tentative hypotheses, encouraging, asking and answering questions, actively interacting with the child, setting limits, and cleaning up the room together (Kottman, 1995).

In all of these relationship-enhancing techniques, the play therapist will need to tailor his or her decision on whether to be direct (talk to the child directly about what is going on in the child's life) or indirect (use the child's metaphor and what is going on in the play to build rapport with the child; Kottman, 1995). By listening to the child and his or her presentation of problem situations, the play therapist can usually determine which of these two methods of communication will be most comfortable for the child. For example, with a child who comes into the playroom, sits down, and starts telling the therapist that she is getting into trouble at school and that the teacher always yells at her, the therapist will usually choose to communicate directly about problem situations. With a child who comes into the playroom, asks to play school, and acts out a teacher who is always yelling at one specific, very sad child, the therapist might choose to communicate through the play and the child's metaphor rather than addressing the problem directly.

Tracking is a play therapy technique in which the therapist tells the child what the child is doing or what is happening with the play media (e.g., "You're picking that up." "The doll is moving up and down"; Landreth, personal communication, 1985). The purpose of tracking in Adlerian play therapy is for the therapist to communicate to the child that the therapist is noticing his or her behaviors (Kottman, 1995). This attention is meant to convey involvement and concern to the child.

Another technique designed to let the child know that the therapist is paying attention to him or her is restating content. When the therapist restates content (paraphrases the child's verbalizations, either about the child's life or about what is happening with the toys), he or she tries to convey that the child's words are important and worthy of attention. Quite frequently, in order to avoid sounding stilted or formulaic, the therapist may want to combine a tracking response and a restating content response with a reflection of feeling.

When an Adlerian play therapist reflects the child's feelings, his or her intention is to communicate acceptance of the affective content of the child's play and verbalizations (Kottman, 1995). The therapist tries to acknowledge obvious, surface feelings that the child has clearly expressed through play or talk and to use tentative hypotheses to make guesses about more subtle, underlying feelings, based on nonverbals and on background information about the child's life situation and lifestyle. For instance, if a child comes into the playroom and starts throwing the mother doll against the wall, saying "I hate my mother," the therapist might reflect the obvious feeling of anger by saying, "So you are feeling really mad at your mom." Then the therapist may make a guess about other feelings that the child might also be experiencing by saying something like "I'm guessing that you might also be disappointed that your mom didn't come to visit you this weekend like she promised that she would." The child does not have to answer any of these guesses verbally, but the play therapist must watch for nonverbal reactions, shifts in play, and/or recognition reflexes as possible responses to the reflection of feelings (Kottman, 1995).

In the play therapy relationship, encouragement has several different forms (Kottman, 1995). The therapist tries to make all of his or her interactions with the child encouraging. This strategy can involve avoiding doing things for the child that he or she can do for himself or herself, pointing out the child's efforts, acknowledging progress the child has made, and pointing out the child's assets. Essential elements of encouragement in Adlerian play therapy are the avoidance of judgmental language (like "good" and "well") and the emphasis on the child's feelings of pride and accomplishment.

Sometimes during the process of play therapy, a child will ask the therapist questions—about the relationship with the play therapist (e.g., "Do you like me?"), about play therapy procedures (e.g., "How often do I have to come here?"), about practical matters (e.g., "What time is it?"), or about the therapist's personal life (e.g., "Do you have a husband?"; Kottman, 1995; Landreth, 1991; O'Connor, 1991). The Adlerian play therapist can use the child's questions as another tool for building the relationship. Because Adlerians believe that the child has a purpose or goal in asking questions, the first thing an Adlerian play therapist does in response to such questions is to make a guess about the child's purpose in asking them. The play therapist then has a choice whether to answer the question factually or (if the question is inappropriate or too personal) to set a boundary by telling the child, "I choose not to answer that question."

Either way, the answer to the child's question will help to set the parameters of the relationship.

Another important technique in building rapport and getting to know the child is asking the child questions (Kottman, 1995). Rather than asking the questions in a formal interview, however, the Adlerian play therapist will try to weave the questions into the natural flow of the conversation and play. Again, it is important to remember that with some children, a direct way of asking questions is more appropriate and that with other children a more subtle, metaphoric way of asking questions about what is going on with the toys is more appropriate, depending on the child's usual way of interacting and developmental level.

In Adlerian play therapy, most of the questions that the counselor asks fit into one of two categories: (a) questions about the presenting problem or ongoing events in the child's life or (b) questions about the child's lifestyle and social context (Kottman, 1995). The first category consists of questions like "How is it going with your mother this week?" or "What happened when that big doll who yells at the baby doll hit her?" The second category consists of questions like "If you had to compare yourself to your brother and your sister, who is most different from you?" or "Which one of the kids in that doll family does that mom like the best?"

The rule of thumb in Adlerian play therapy is to limit the number of questions asked of the child to five or six per session. The purpose of this stricture is to ensure that the play therapy relationship is not hampered by the adult's assuming an interrogatory role. This is reinforced by the fact that the child does not have to answer any of the questions the therapist asks. When the child chooses not to answer verbally, the therapist must watch for nonverbal responses, such as a shift in the play or nods, shrugs, and so forth.

Another method of building a relationship with the child in Adlerian play therapy is interacting actively with the child (Kottman, 1995). The play therapist can play with the child at the child's request or initiate interactive play with the child. The play therapist can also role-play various situations with the child—allowing the child to control the direction of the role-play or assuming the control of the direction of the role-play himself or herself.

Limit setting is also a method of building the relationship in Adlerian play therapy (Kottman, 1993, 1995). By establishing that there are certain behaviors that are not appropriate in the playroom, the therapist can anchor the play therapy process to reality and communicate a sense of predictability and consistency to the child. There are several nonnegotiable rules in the playroom. These include a rule against the child's hurting himself or herself, the therapist, and any other children in the playroom. The child is also not allowed to purposely damage the toys or other parts of the playroom or to leave the play therapy session before the appointed time for the session has elapsed. The play therapist can also establish negotiable rules, such as how much water the child is allowed to pour in the sand, how many pipe cleaners the child can use in a project, how much time is spent in playing hide and seek during a session, and so forth. For these rules, the counselor and the child negotiate the limits.

When a child is about to break a playroom rule, the counselor starts the limiting procedure (Kottman, 1995). The first step in the procedure is to state the limit in a nonjudgmental voice (e.g., "It is against the playroom rule to . . . ."). The second step is to reflect the child's feeling (if there is one that is apparent) or to make a guess about the purpose of the child's misbehavior (e.g., "You seem angry" or "I'm guessing that you wanted to show me that I can't tell you what to do"). The third step is to engage the child in generating acceptable alternative behaviors. The counselor starts this process by saying to the child, "I bet that you can figure out something that you can do that isn't against the playroom rules." During the negotiation that follows, the counselor guides the child into an agreement that concretely specifies acceptable behavior. Most of the time, this is the final step in the limiting process. However, occasionally a child will decide not to abide by the agreement, in which case the therapist initiates an interaction by which they generate possible consequences for future transgressions.

With most children, the Adlerian play therapist may decide to use picking up the toys and straightening the room as a tool for reinforcing the idea that the play therapy relationship is a cooperative partnership (Kottman, 1995). If the counselor believes that he or she can use cleaning up the room as a way of strengthening the relationship with the child, 10 minutes before the end of each session, the counselor says, "In 5 more minutes, it will be time to clean up the room together." When there are 5 minutes left in the session, the counselor stands up and asks the child, "What do you want to put away, and what do you want me to put away?" The counselor and the child then work as a team to pick up the toys and put the room in order.

In the parent consultation sessions during the relationship-building phase of counseling, the counselor uses his or her therapeutic skills—such as reflecting feelings, paraphrasing, summarizing, clarifying, and self-disclosure—to establish rapport with the child's parent(s). It is important for the counselor to listen empathically to the parent(s)' "story"—their version of any struggles they have experienced in raising their child. Most parents who bring their child to play therapy are afraid that they have somehow failed in their parenting of their child and need to have someone listen to them in a caring way and to provide them with as much encouragement as possible. After the child and the parent(s) have begun to feel comfortable in the relationship with the counselor (the time this takes varies from half of a session to several months), the Adlerian play therapist can begin to shift the focus to the second phase of the play therapy, exploring the child's (and the parent's or parents') lifestyles.

Exploration of Lifestyle

In this phase of the Adlerian play therapy process, the counselor gathers information about the family atmosphere, the family constellation, the goals of the child's behavior, and the child's early recollections. Using these data, the counselor begins to formulate hypotheses about the child's lifestyle—basic convictions about self, others, and the world; the child's private logic; behavior and relationship patterns; and assets (Kottman, 1995).

Family atmosphere is the general affective tone of the family (Dewey, 1978; Kottman, 1995). It stems from the parent(s)' beliefs about discipline; their parenting techniques; their own lifestyles and basic beliefs about themselves, others, and the world; and their marital relationship. The child's beliefs about himself or herself and about others are affected by family atmosphere, which also has an impact on the child's behavior patterns and ways of gaining significance and gaining a sense of belonging (Dewey, 1978; Kottman, 1993).

The play therapist can gather information about the family atmosphere by (a) observing the child playing with the doll house, the puppets, and the kitchenware; (b) observing the interaction between the parent(s) and the children and between the parents in the waiting room and when the entire family comes to a session together; and/or (c) asking the child, the parent(s), or both questions about discipline and other relationship patterns within the family. The counselor can also ask the child to draw a

Kinetic Family Drawing (Knoff & Prout, 1985) and discuss the interactional patterns between the various members of the family (Kottman, 1993, 1995).

The Adlerian play therapist can use these same techniques to investigate the family constellation (Kottman, 1993, 1995). Because each birth-order position has certain characteristic liabilities and assets, it is helpful for the play therapist to learn how the child's thought processes and behaviors are typical of his or her psychological birth-order position. The primary purpose in Adlerian play therapy for gathering information about the child's birth-order position is to help the child optimize his or her strengths and appropriately compensate for his or her potential weaknesses.

Another important aspect of exploring the child's lifestyle is identifying the child's primary goal of misbehavior (Kottman, 1993, 1995). Adlerians believe that most children who struggle in their relationships and who manifest self-defeating, destructive behavior are striving toward negative goals of behavior (Dreikurs & Soltz, 1964). These children are unable to attain the "crucial Cs," or positive goals of behavior (Lew & Bettner, 1995a, 1995b). According to Dreikurs and Soltz, children's goals of misbehavior are attention, power, revenge, and proving inadequacy.

Kottman (1995) has postulated that there are three subcategories of the goal of power, depending on the type of family background and family atmosphere. She has labeled these subcategories "children who have too much power," "children who have too little power," and "children who come from chaotic families." Kottman believes that if the play therapist understands into which of these three subcategories of power a child fits, he or she can tailor the play therapy interaction in a way that will help the child begin to let go of the need for power and control.

Lew and Bettner (1995a, 1995b) have suggested that children strive toward the crucial Cs—(a) connecting with others (the positive goal of cooperation), (b) feeling capable (the positive goal of self-reliance), (c) feeling as though they count (the positive goal of contribution), and (d) feeling that they have the courage necessary to deal with life's challenges (the positive goal of resiliency). They believe that if children are not successful in attaining the crucial Cs they will move toward negative goals of behavior.

By examining the child's feelings and behavior, the reactions and feelings of the adults who interact with the child, and the child's reaction to correction, the Adlerian play therapist can formulate hypotheses about the goals of the child's misbehavior (Dreikurs & Soltz, 1964; Kottman, 1995). By watching the child's interaction with others and listening for the child's beliefs about himself or herself and for his or her feelings, the play therapist can conceptualize the positive goals and crucial Cs the child is struggling to attain (Lew & Bettner, 1995a, 1995b). Again, observing the child in the playroom and in the waiting room; questioning the child and the parents about behaviors, feelings, and reactions; and monitoring his or her own reactions toward the child can all provide the Adlerian play therapist with clues about the child's goals of behavior.

With older children (usually over the age of 8 or 9), the play therapist may also choose to solicit early recollections in order to help his or her understanding of the child's lifestyle (Kottman, 1993, 1995). According to Adlerian theory, people selectively remember experiences that fit into, and consequently represent, their worldviews (Ansbacher & Ansbacher, 1956). By asking children to describe "something that happened when you were little" (Kottman, 1995) or to draw pictures of early experiences (Borden, 1982; A. Nelson, 1986), the play therapist may get clues about their private logic, convictions about life, and the goals of their behavior. The accumulation of six to eight early recollections over a period of three or four sessions may yield patterns and themes that will help the play therapist better understand a child's perceptions of self, others, and the world (Kottman, 1993, 1995).

Working with the parent(s) during the second phase of play therapy, the Adlerian play therapist will gather information about the parent(s)' perception of the child and his or her behavior, relationships, and attitudes (Kottman, 1993, 1995). By asking additional questions about the parent(s)' perception of the relationships in their own families of origin and how they were parented, the play therapist can begin to form ideas about how to enhance their parenting skills and about ways that their own personal issues may be interfering with their relationships with their children (Kottman, 1993, 1995).

Helping the Child Gain Insight

Integrating the information gathered from the child and the parent(s) during the second phase with his or her own clinical impression of the child and the family, the play therapist begins to develop working hypotheses about the child's lifestyle, including goals of behavior, private logic, and basic convictions (Kottman, 1993, 1995). The Adlerian play therapist starts to share these hypotheses during the third phase of play therapy in order to help the child gain insight into his or her lifestyle as a preface for any behavioral or attitudinal changes the child might decide to make during the fourth phase of play therapy. To help the child gain an understanding of his or her motivation, actions, relationships, perceptions, and attitudes, the play therapist uses tentative hypotheses (guesses), metacommunication, artwork, metaphors, bibliotherapy, "spitting in the soup," and connections between the child's actions in the playroom and the child's actions in other settings (Kottman, 1993, 1995).

In Adlerian play therapy, the counselor interprets both play and verbalization to children in terms of tentative hypotheses (Kottman, 1993, 1995). By making guesses about (a) the goals of children's behaviors; (b) their perceptions of how they gain significance; (c) their attitudes toward themselves, others, and the world; (d) the relationship between those attitudes and their behavior; and (e) their interactions with their parent(s), siblings, teachers, and other important people in their world; the play therapist hopes to help them grow in self-understanding. It is essential to make interpretations in a tentative manner so that children can correct the counselor if an interpretation does not fit for them or if they are not ready to accept the implications of an interpretation yet. Children frequently do not respond verbally to interpretations, but they almost always respond either nonverbally (with some type of recognition reflex) or through the play (either with a play disruption or with a metaphoric response to the interpretation; Kottman, 1995).

One of the most important tools for helping children gain insight is metacommunication, which is communication by the therapist about the child's communication (Kottman, 1995). The Adlerian play therapist metacommunicates by (a) commenting on the child's reaction to interpretations or questions (e.g., "You didn't seem to like it when I asked you if you were sad about your sister being sick"), (b) noticing the patterns in the child's communication with the therapist (e.g., "Sometimes it seems like you like to tell me what to do"), and (c) making guesses about the meaning of the child's nonverbal communication (e.g., "You turned your back on me when I said that you like to be the boss. I am guessing that you were kind of mad when I said that"). Again, metacommunication should always be made in tentative form so that the child has a chance to give the counselor feedback about his or her understanding of what is going on with the child.

Many times, the therapist uses art to help the child gain insight (Kottman, 1995; Muro & Kottman, 1995). Sometimes this happens when the therapist watches as the child spontaneously produces artwork and asks questions about the process and product. Other times it happens when the therapist asks the child to participate in specific art exercises, such as body outline drawings, family drawings, school drawings, drawings about dreams, and so forth.

In addition to using art to communicate about their lives, many times children use play metaphors to communicate. Their situations at home, at school, or in other settings may be too painful or too "dangerous" to talk about directly, play directly, or draw, so they will use a "pretend" story to act out what is happening to them. For example, a little girl whose father is an out-of-control alcoholic may use the farm animals to tell a story about a father pig who "gets wild" and hits the mother pig and screams at the baby pigs. When this happens, the Adlerian play therapist must respect the child's need to use the metaphor to communicate and respond to the child indirectly through the metaphor. In the case of the example, the therapist might ask questions about what the mother pig does to protect herself and the children from the father pig; or he or she might make some guesses about how the baby pigs felt about the father pig and their situation.

The play therapist can also invent a therapeutic metaphor or use bibliotherapy to help the child gain a different perspective on a situation or to help the child better understand his or her motivations or a relationship (Kottman, 1995; Lankton & Lankton, 1989; Mills & Crowley, 1986). By making up a story about the animals, puppets, dolls, or "another little girl I know" or reading a book about a character who has parallels to the child and/or the child's situation, the therapist can express feelings, suggest solutions to problems, or cast new light on relationships. While the counselor is telling the story or reading the book, he or she must watch for nonverbal clues about the child's reaction to the metaphor. Sometimes it is helpful to the child to metacommunicate about his or her reaction to the metaphor, and sometimes it is more helpful to simply let the metaphor stand on its own without interpretation.

A uniquely Adlerian intervention in this phase is "spitting in the client's soup." This technique consists of gently pointing out situations in which the child is sabotaging himself or herself. For example, a child knows that he will have a detention for talking without raising his hand in class, but wants attention (even negative attention) so badly that he does it anyway. When he tells her the story of yet another detention, the Adlerian play therapist might point out to him that he must think the attention he gets from calling out his answers is worth the price of the detention. When the counselor uses this technique with children, it is essential to avoid a sarcastic or critical tone of voice. The child must feel that the play therapist is supportive for this strategy to evoke any insight on the part of the child. Otherwise, if the child feels criticized or ridiculed, he or she may become defensive or resistant, which would be counterproductive.

As a segue to the fourth phase of Adlerian play therapy, the counselor begins to make connections between the child's behavior, perceptions, attitudes, and goals in the playroom and his or her behavior, perceptions, attitudes, and goals in other settings and other relationships. By commenting on parallels between how the child acts, thinks, and feels in the play therapy process and how he or she acts, thinks, and feels at home, school, and other places, the play therapist hopes to help the child generalize the insights he or she has gained in the play therapy relationship to other relationships and other situations. This also helps the child begin to make decisions about potential changes he or she wants to make in relationships and situations, which leads into the fourth phase, reeducation–reorientation.

During the third phase, the Adlerian play therapist uses consultations with parents to (a) assist parents to gain insight into their child's lifestyle, (b) assist parents to gain insight into their own lifestyles and the ways that their child's lifestyle and their own might interact, and (c) teach Adlerian parenting skills, such as recognizing goals of behavior, setting up logical consequences, helping children attain the crucial Cs, and encouraging (Kottman, 1995; Lew & Bettner, 1995a, 1995b). The counselor monitors the parents' feelings and progress and provides encouragement to the parents for looking at their own issues and for making changes in their parenting strategies.

Reeducation–Reorientation

In the fourth phase of Adlerian play therapy, the focus is on helping both the child and the parent(s) to consolidate any changes they have made in attitudes and perceptions by helping them to transform their new cognitive and affective understandings into behavioral changes. The goal of this phase is for the child and the parent(s) to learn new skills and to transfer those skills to situations and relationships outside the counselor's office. The play therapist may engage the child in brainstorming and other problem-solving strategies, teach new behaviors to the child, help the child practice new behaviors, and encourage the child for progress and effort (Kottman, 1995).

Many children already have the skills and knowledge they need to be successful in their interactions, but they simply do not apply them in the appropriate situations. To capitalize on the child's store of information, the play therapist may wish to use brainstorming and problem-solving techniques to help the child generate alternate behaviors for situations in which he or she has previously demonstrated negative behaviors. By involving the child in determining appropriate alternatives for given situations, the play therapist can elicit more of a commitment from the child to a plan of action.

There are children who are not able to generate their own solutions to problems, even with guidance from the play therapist. Other children may lack specific skills or information that could help them solve particular problems they encounter. In these cases, the Adlerian play therapist may choose to teach skills or share information (Kottman, 1993, 1995). Most of the time, the teaching provided in Adlerian play therapy is related to social skills, negotiation skills, or problem-solving strategies. The teaching can also involve information about topics such as divorce laws, court procedures, or effects of adoption.

When the Adlerian play therapist decides to teach a skill to a child, he or she may choose to use the direct approach or the indirect approach. The direct approach involves explaining how the child would go about doing something. The indirect approach involves using role-plays, characters from stories or books, puppets, dolls, or toys to illustrate the desired behavior. The same thing is true for times when the play therapist decides to impart information.

This is also the case when the therapist wishes to help a child practice newly generated or acquired attitudes or behaviors. The child and the play therapist may simply practice, using real situations from the child's life or situations that occur naturally in the play therapy process. With a more resistant or defensive child, the therapist can choose to practice using the dolls, puppets, animal families, or other play media to act out various situations without mentioning the possibility that the child might want to use these skills in his or her life.

Finally, the Adlerian play therapist liberally uses encouragement in the reorientation–reeducation phase (Kottman, 1993, 1995). By acknowledging the progress the child has made, highlighting the child's assets, and focusing on the efforts the child is making, the counselor can help the child consolidate changes in attitude, motivation, cognitions, perceptions, and behavior.

The counselor will use this same set of skills with the parents in the reorientation–reeducation phase (Kottman, 1993, 1995). He or she will help parents generate alternative behaviors, teach them skills, and provide opportunities to practice new skills to transfer to other situations outside the parent consultation setting. Encouragement is also essential in the parent consultation component of this phase. By pointing out the parents' efforts in changing their parenting strategies and working on their own personal issues, by giving positive feedback on progress they have made in these areas, and by emphasizing their personal and parenting strengths, the Adlerian play therapist can support parents in helping make cognitive, affective, and behavioral shifts in their families.

To illustrate the process of Adlerian play therapy and conjoint parent consultation, the following case study includes a description of all four phases of play therapy with Stephanie Wills, "the big brat."[1]

☐ Case Study

Stephanie was a 6-year-old girl enrolled in first grade. Her mother called me in the middle of October, reporting that Stephanie had recently begun to indulge in long temper tantrums at both home and school. Before that school year, she had always been behaviorally compliant at home. However, since the first of the school year, her interactions with her parents and siblings had deteriorated. Ms. Wills described Stephanie as "impossible to live with. She always wants her own way, and when she doesn't get it, she screams the house down." Ms. Wills reported that Stephanie's teacher also had concerns about Stephanie's behavior at school, where she was disrespectful to the teacher and rude and intolerant to the other children. Although Stephanie's teacher acknowledged that her schoolwork was excellent, well above the performance of the other children in her class, her behavior at school was "out of control and getting worse."

I always schedule the first session of play therapy with the parent or parents without the child, so that I can explain the play therapy process, start building rapport with the parent(s), and begin gathering information about the family and the child. Mr. and Ms. Wills were both eager to talk about their family and the changes they perceived in their youngest child, Stephanie. Mr. Wills was the manager of a local grocery store. He described his job as "being the guy who has to keep everybody happy—the customers, the employees, and the owners." Ms. Wills had recently started working in a department store, making alterations. She reported that her job was much more stressful than she had anticipated because it "seems like nobody is ever satisfied. I try so hard, but there are always complaints." They were both 45 years old and had four daughters, Gerry (26), Melissa (20), Mary (19), and Stephanie (6). The Wills reported that they had not anticipated Stephanie's arrival because Ms. Wills experienced a series of miscar-

---

[1]The name and other identifying information have been changed to preserve the confidentiality of the clients in the case study.

riages after the birth of their third child. The entire family had been "ecstatic" when Stephanie was born. All three of her older sisters had "taken part in raising her—giving her all the love and attention that she could possibly want."

When I asked about any recent changes in the family, Mr. Wills explained that Gerry, the oldest daughter, had recently had a son (the first grandchild), Melissa had gotten married and moved out of state, and Mary had started attending a college about 200 miles away. Neither parent considered these changes to be negative for Stephanie, but they noted that Stephanie had not been as excited about the arrival of her new nephew as they had anticipated. They were concerned about the fact that Ms. Wills's new job necessitated Stephanie's staying in an after-school day care program. Stephanie had expressed a great deal of negative feeling about the fact that her mother had started working and "didn't have enough time for me" and that she no longer had her sisters to babysit. She had begged Mary to come home so that she could "take care of me after school and I wouldn't have to go to that yucky place where I have to share with all those other kids and everybody tells me what to do."

I gathered more information by asking about their family routine and the consequences for transgressions of rules. Mr. and Ms. Wills reported that they had a relatively predictable routine, but that they had difficulty following through with consequences for negative behavior, especially with Stephanie. They said that they "just hated it when the girls were upset"—particularly Stephanie, "who had always pouted and whined when she did not get her way." The recent temper tantrums and disrespectful behavior were extremely distressing to Mr. and Ms. Wills. They both seemed tearful as they described Stephanie's current behavior and stated that they "just don't know what to do."

As we talked, I formed a tentative hypothesis that Stephanie's goal of behavior was power and that she was a child who, until very recently, had had too much power. I believed that she had not had the opportunity thus far in her life of attaining the crucial C of feeling capable and the goal of self-reliance. These conclusions were based partially on her parents' description of her behavior and their reactions to her behavior. They were also based on my perception of her parents as wanting to please others and my guess that Stephanie had been pampered by her sisters and her parents, all of whom seemed ready to indulge her every whim but had not encouraged her to learn competence and self-control. I believed that the recent changes in the family had probably given her a sense of her life being out of control and of being unloved because the attention and pampering she was used to having had been significantly reduced. I also suspected that she felt "dethroned" by the birth of her nephew, who was now the center of attention in the family. To my way of thinking, these changes had probably triggered her current escalation of controlling and negative behavior.

I was not locked into these hypotheses. I continuously monitor the conclusions I am making about the child and his or her parents, checking my hypotheses against the behavior of the client and the other members of his or her family. However, it was important to begin to make some guesses about the dynamics of the family and how they affected Stephanie. With children whose goal is power, I adapt my style of interacting with the child and my suggestions to the parent(s) based on my beliefs about which of the three subcategories of power the child fits (Kottman, 1995). Especially with children who have been pampered, I tend to establish from the very beginning of the relationship that the child will have to share power with me in the playroom. I believe that sharing power in the playroom with a safe and nurturing adult helps the child to learn to relinquish some of his or her need for control in other situations outside the counseling setting.

Because children who have been pampered do not usually have to do anything to take care of themselves, they frequently do not learn that they can rely on their own skill and competency. By refusing to "take care" of Stephanie from the start of the relationship and encouraging her to take responsibility for taking care of herself in age-appropriate ways, I intended to enhance her feeling of being capable.

Building the Relationship

In the first several sessions of play therapy with Stephanie, she demonstrated none of the negative behaviors described by her parents and teacher. Stephanie usually chose to play with the animal families, the doll families in the doll house, and the puppets, acting out various scenes of family life. I tracked her behavior and restated the content of many of her comments. Stephanie frequently asked me to make decisions for her and to do things for her (such as tying her shoes). I reflected her feelings but did not make choices for her or do things for her that I believed that she could do for herself. As she played with the animal families and the doll families, there was a theme of the littlest member of each family being taken care of by the other family members. The "littlest member" of each family (who was always the largest available female animal, doll, or puppet) frequently talked "baby talk" and waited for the other members of the family to do things for her.

To establish from the beginning of the relationship that we would share power in the playroom, during each session I asked her to do something that she had not chosen for herself. For example, in the second session, I asked her to build a tower with the blocks. She had difficulty getting them to stand by themselves and repeatedly asked me to help her, getting progressively more frustrated with my refusal to assist her, whining and saying "I can't do it. You need to help me." I reflected her feelings of frustration with this process and with my refusal to take care of her, and (jumping to a fourth-phase intervention) I also metacommunicated about her wanting me to take care of her like her parents and her sisters usually did. Although she did not verbally respond to this interpretation, she did nod her head several times without looking at me. I used encouragement to focus on her efforts and persistence. When she succeeded, I pointed out the progress that she had made in understanding how to get what she wanted by herself.

By the third session, Stephanie began telling me that she "wouldn't always" do what I asked her to do. However, she continued to comply with my requests. In the fourth session, I asked her to draw a Kinetic Family Drawing. Her drawing showed herself in the middle of the family, with all three of her sisters and her parents surrounding her. The figure that represented her was slightly bigger than all of the other figures. She explained that Gerry was making hot chocolate for her, Melissa was tying her shoes, Mary was reading to her, their mother was making supper, and their father was mowing the lawn. Asked what she was doing, she replied, "Nothing."

In the sixth session, when I asked her to draw a Kinetic School Drawing, she refused, telling me, "That's a stupid idea. You always want me to do dumb things, and you can't make me do them." Although I did not insist, she refused to look at me or talk to me for the rest of the session. The next week, I decided to avoid future power struggles by giving her a choice of activities when I asked her to do things. She seemed to really like this method of sharing power, telling me, "It was a good thing you started letting me decide what I was going to do."

Stephanie dragged her heels when it was time to clean up the playroom. She would frequently start playing with a new toy right after I announced that it was time to clean up, and she consistently told me that she could not decide what I should pick up and what she should pick up. To give her a little more structure and to again establish the idea that we could share power, when she said this I would make a suggestion for what each of us could put away. This seemed to help facilitate the cleaning up, but she was still obviously reluctant to take care of herself in this way.

After about the fifth session, however, this changed. She began to order me to pick up everything in the playroom but refused to pick up anything herself. To avoid a power struggle with her, I challenged her to a game—I divided the playroom down the middle and suggested that we have a race to see who could pick up her half of the room faster. She responded by starting to pick up the toys in "her" half of the room. We continued to do this during the entire time she came to play therapy. When she "won" the race, she was very excited, and I used those opportunities to encourage her sense of competence and self-reliance. During the first several months of our relationship, when she lost the race, she tended to be sullen and pouty. However, as she began to feel more confident about her own abilities, she actually "let" me win several times in an attempt to build my self-efficacy.

Stephanie asked very few questions about me or my life, so I did not get to make many guesses about the purpose of her questions. I did ask her questions about herself and her life. She was willing to discuss her sisters and her parents and their life together, but she refused to talk about her new nephew, saying, "He is just a baby." She was reluctant to answer questions or guesses about her feelings, and she refused to talk about the temper tantrums and her relationship with her teacher. Because Stephanie was willing to answer most questions about her family directly, I did not have to resort to the indirect approach with my questions about the family aspects of her lifestyle. However, I did use the indirect approach to reflect feelings—especially feelings of being helpless and scared about taking care of herself—and to ask about her interactions with and attitudes toward her nephew and her teacher. I did this by making guesses about the feelings experienced by the animals, dolls, and puppets she chose to express herself. Sometimes I would ask her how the littlest member of the family felt about various circumstances. Sometimes I would introduce another character into the play— an even littler member of the family—and probe into how the various members of the family felt about this arrival. I used the same kind of tactics with her situation at school, asking what happened when the littlest member of the family went to school and had to deal with her teacher. Stephanie was quite willing to respond to interpretations and questions couched in this indirect manner, even about those topics that were "off limits" in our direct conversations.

It did not take much effort to build a relationship with Mr. and Ms. Wills. They were eager to like me and for me to like them. I encouraged them for the positive aspects of their parenting. In response to repeated questions from them, I reassured them that they had not "screwed up" their daughter. Because they were both pleasers, they were worried about alienating the teacher, Stephanie, their other daughters, and me. During this phase of parent consultation, my primary job with them was reassurance and support for their ability to take appropriate control of the family. I assured them that it would be much more helpful to Stephanie in the long run to be consistent and provide firm consequences for her inappropriate behavior, but I did not yet give them any homework assignments that involved changing their behavior during this phase.

Exploration of Lifestyle

Because this family was open about their family circumstances and responsive to questioning strategies, I began the exploration of Stephanie's lifestyle during my first interaction with her parents and continued to investigate her goals of behavior, family atmosphere, and family constellation for the next nine sessions with her and her parents. As I have described in the section on building the relationship, her Kinetic Family Drawing yielded some interesting perspectives on how she saw herself, others, and the world. So did the answers to the lifestyle questions I asked her. During the seventh, eighth, and ninth sessions, I included a request to "tell me something that happened when you were little" in the choices I offered for "my" activities. She never chose this option, so I gave up trying to elicit early recollections. I was not sure that I would get any new information or a vehicle for helping her gain clarity about her lifestyle through early recollections, so I decided not to pursue this avenue.

In my parent consultation, I asked many questions about Mr. and Ms. Wills' perceptions of the dynamics of both their current family and their families of origin. I discovered that both of them had grown up with an alcoholic parent and that they were both oldest children who had helped the sober parent "keep the family together." They had learned early that pleasing was the safest way to interact with others, and they had adapted their parenting style accordingly. This style had actually worked with their three oldest children, who were relatively compliant and responsible. However, it contributed to a problem with Stephanie.

By the 10th session, I had several hypotheses about Stephanie's lifestyle. I made the following list of her basic convictions about herself, others, and the world:

I am . . . not very competent.

I need . . . others to take care of me.

I must . . . grab power from others or I will be powerless.

I am . . . able to get what I want by whining, pouting, or having temper tantrums.

Others are . . . bigger, more powerful, and more competent than I am. (Seemed to apply to adults.)

Others are . . . always taking what is mine. (Seemed to apply to children.)

Others should . . . take care of me.

Others must . . . do what I want or I will figure out a way to make them.

Others are . . . afraid of me when I throw temper tantrums.

The world is . . . kind of a scary, overwhelming place if I don't get what I want.

The world is . . . too hard for me.

The world is . . . where I need to get others to take care of me or I won't get what I want.

On the basis of these convictions, Stephanie's behavior made sense. She was trying to make sure that she got what she wanted in order to be safe and feel competent. Whenever she did not feel powerful or in control, she tried to manipulate her way into being in control. She did not trust herself to take care of her own needs, but she did not trust others to take care of her, either. Stephanie seemed to feel betrayed by the changes in her family circumstances. Since her birth, her parents and sisters had catered to her desires. The shifts in their attention had created a rift in her world, and she was trying to cope with this rift by forcing the members of her family and the rest of the world to return to taking care of her in the manner to which she was accustomed.

Helping the Child Gain Insight

As I have suggested, the four phases of Adlerian play therapy frequently overlap. Even as early as the first or second session with Stephanie, I had begun to make tentative hypotheses about her goals of behavior and metacommunicate about the patterns in her communication and her nonverbals. During the seventh session, I read her *Alexander and the No Good, Horrible, Very Bad Day*, a book that contains the gentle suggestion that things will not always go the way we want them to go and that threats do not particularly help the situation.

At about the ninth session, I started using her metaphor of the littlest member of the family and making some interpretations about her feelings and need for control by talking about the feelings and need for control of the littlest member. I also pointed out that even though the littlest member was called "the littlest member of the family," she really was the tallest member of the family and that she was pretty strong and capable even when she was not always getting her way.

During the parent consultations, I began to teach Stephanie's parents Adlerian parenting strategies. I taught them about goals of behavior, the crucial Cs, logical consequences, and problem ownership. To help their learning, I asked them to read *A Parent's Guide to Motivating Children* (Lew & Bettner, 1995a). I also made some guesses that their need to please others was getting in the way of their ability to optimally parent Stephanie. They were very responsive to these interventions but were not sure about how to make changes in their parenting. As they were extremely compliant with all of my suggestions and seemed to understand the parenting skills, I began to give them very concrete homework assignments so that they could practice setting up logical consequences for disrespectful behavior and temper tantrums.

In a session with the entire family, I asked everyone to avoid taking care of Stephanie in circumstances where she was capable of caring for herself. So that she did not feel neglected with this shift, I suggested that the family members increase the amount of fun time they spent together, making sure that Stephanie had a big part in planning activities and that she got a great deal of encouragement for her demonstrations of competence. As Mr. and Ms. Wills struggled to make changes in their interactions, I used encouragement to support them in being consistent with consequences and tried to empower them so that they felt capable and competent in their ability to successfully carry out their assignments.

By the 14th session, Stephanie was demonstrating shifts in her perception of herself, others, and the world by making comments like "I know how to do things for myself" and not asking me to do things for her. She had also started to express enjoyment in her day care experience, even though she continued to complain about not getting to spend as much time with her sisters and her mother as she wanted. Stephanie was also trying more activities and materials in the playroom. She had started initiating art projects herself and frequently used the weapons to protect herself from "monsters" and "scary things that I don't like." Stephanie herself was pointing out parallels in her behavior and attitudes in the playroom and the rest of the world—making comments like "I know how to tie my shoes in here, and I can do it at home too. Nobody needs to help me with that kind of stuff."

Her teacher had reported improvement in her classroom behavior, but Stephanie was still resorting to temper tantrums when she did not get her own way. I had spit in her soup about this and made guesses about the goal of her behavior, but these interventions had not had a significant impact. I decided that changing this behavior might take a more direct approach, so I moved into the fourth phase of play therapy.

Reorientation–Reeducation

Stephanie was such a bright child and she had made such progress that there was little to do in the reorientation–reeducation phase. She needed quite a bit of encouragement, especially in the area of feeling capable and self-reliant but by the 17th session, she and her parents were doing the bulk of this intervention.

Stephanie had expressed interest in reducing the number of times she had temper tantrums. This seemed to be based on feedback she had started getting from the other children in her class, who sometimes called her "the big brat." I worked with her on anger management strategies, teaching her to count to 10, take deep breaths, and so forth when she got mad. We practiced these tactics in the playroom with the dolls and role playing until she informed me that she thought she could "do this stuff and not be a brat at school anymore." I consulted with Stephanie's parents and her teacher so that they would be able to support her in the use of the tactics she had learned in the playroom. They were enthusiastic about trying to help her learn to control her own anger. Although it took several attempts, she began to use the anger management techniques when she got into conflicts at school and at home. She was not perfect in her application of these strategies, but she was no longer "the big brat."

☐ Conclusion

Adlerian play therapy is a counseling intervention approach designed to help children and their parents. By using toys and play, the Adlerian play therapist can communicate with a child in his or her own natural "language" in order to build a relationship; explore the child's lifestyle, help the child gain insight into his or her lifestyle; and make changes in his or her attitudes, perceptions, and behavior. In consulting with the child's parents, the play therapist can help them gain insight into their child and themselves and learn new strategies for parenting. The case study of Stephanie Wills ("the big brat") was meant to illustrate the process of Adlerian play therapy, but it is not possible to fully demonstrate this approach with just one case study. Because each child is special and unique and each parent is special and unique, the process of Adlerian play therapy is always individual.

☐ References

Adler, A. (1963). *The problem child*. New York: Putnam Capricorn. (Original work published 1930)

Albert, L. (1989). *A teacher's guide to cooperative discipline: How to manage your classroom and promote self-esteem*. Circle Pines, MN: American Guidance Service.

Ansbacher, H., & Ansbacher, R. (Eds.) (1956). *The individual psychology of Alfred Adler: A systematic presentation in selections from his writings*. San Francisco: Harper & Row.

Bettelheim, B. (1987, March). The importance of play. *The Atlantic Monthly*, 35–46.

Bettner, B. L., & Lew, A. (1989). *Raising kids who can: Using family meetings to nurture responsible, capable, caring, and happy children*. Boston: Connexions Press.

Borden, B. (1982). Early recollections as a diagnostic technique with primary age children. *Individual Psychology, 38*, 207–212.

Christensen, O. (Ed.). (1993). *Adlerian family counseling* (rev. ed.). Minneapolis, MN: Educational Media.

Dewey, E. (1978). *Basic applications of Adlerian psychology for self-understanding and human relationships*. Coral Spring, FL: CMI Press.

Dinkmeyer, D., & Dinkmeyer, D. (1977). Concise counseling assessment: The children's life-style guide. *Elementary School Counseling and Guidance, 12*, 117–124.

Dinkmeyer, D., & Dinkmeyer, D. (1983). Adlerian approaches. In H. T. Prout & D. Brown (Eds.), *Counseling and psychotherapy with children and adolescents* (pp. 289–327). Tampa, FL: Mariner.

Dinkmeyer, D., Dinkmeyer, D., & Sperry, L. (1987). *Adlerian counseling and psychotherapy* (2nd ed.). Columbus, OH: Merrill.

Dinkmeyer, D., & McKay, G. (1989). *The parent's handbook: Systematic training for effective parenting (STEP)* (3rd ed.). Circle Pines, MN: American Guidance Service.

Dreikurs, R., & Grey, L. (1970). *A parent guide to child discipline*. New York: Hawthorne.

Dreikurs, R., & Soltz, V. (1964). *Children: The challenge*. New York: Hawthorne/Dutton.

Glenn, H., & Nelson, J. (1988). *Raising self-reliant children in a self-indulgent world*. Rocklin, CA: Prima.

Knoff, H., & Prout, H. (1985). *Kinetic drawing system for family and school: Scoring booklet*. Los Angeles: Western Psychological Services.

Kottman, T. (1992). Billy, the teddy bear boy. In L. Golden & M. Norwich (Eds.), *Case studies in child counseling* (pp. 75–88). New York: Macmillan.

Kottman, T. (1993). The king of rock and roll. In T. Kottman & C. Schaefer (Eds.), *Play therapy in action: A casebook for practitioners* (pp. 133–167). Northvale, NJ: Jason Aronson.

Kottman, T. (1994). Adlerian play therapy. In K. O'Connor & C. Schaefer (Eds.), *Handbook of play therapy, vol. 2* (pp. 3–26). New York: Wiley.

Kottman, T. (1995). *Partners in play: An Adlerian approach to play therapy*. Alexandria, VA: American Counseling Association.

Kottman, T., & Johnson, V. (1993). Adlerian play therapy: A tool for school counselors. *Elementary School Guidance and Counseling, 28*, 42–51.

Kottman, T., & Stiles, K. (1990). The mutual storytelling technique: An Adlerian application in child therapy. *Journal of Individual Psychology, 46*, 148–156.

Kottman, T., & Warlick, J. (1989). Adlerian play therapy: Practical considerations. *Journal of Individual Psychology, 45*, 433–446.

Kottman, T., & Warlick, J. (1990). Adlerian play therapy. *Journal of Humanistic Education and Development, 28*, 69–83.

Landreth, G. (1991). *Play therapy: The art of the relationship*. Muncie, IN: Accelerated Development.

Lankton, C., & Lankton, S. (1989). *Tales of enchantment: Goal-oriented metaphors for adults and children in therapy*. New York: Brunner/Mazel.

Lew, A., & Bettner, B. L. (1995a). *A parent's guide to motivating children*. Newton Center, MA: Connexions Press.

Lew, A., & Bettner, B. L. (1995b). *Responsibility in the classroom*. Newton Center, MA: Connexions Press.

Lord, B. (1982). On the clinical use of children's early recollections. *Individual Psychology, 38*, 198–206.

Mills, J., & Crowley, R. (1986). *Therapeutic metaphors for children and the child within*. New York: Brunner/Mazel.

Muro, J., & Kottman, T. (1995). *Guidance and counseling in elementary and middle schools: A practical approach*. Dubuque, IA: Brown & Benchmark.

Nelson, A. (1986). The use of early recollection drawings in children's group therapy. *Individual Psychology, 42*, 288–291.

Nelson, J. (1987). *Positive discipline*. New York: Ballantine.

Nystul, M. (1980). Nystulian play therapy: Applications of Adlerian psychology. *Elementary School Guidance and Counseling, 15*, 22–29.

O'Connor, K. (1991). *The play therapy primer*. New York: Wiley.

Piaget, J. (1962). *Play, dreams and imitation in childhood*. New York: Routledge.

Popkin, M. (1982). *Active parenting*. Atlanta, GA: Active Parenting.

Popkin, M. (1993). *Active teaching*. Atlanta, GA: Active Parenting.

Yura, M., & Galassi, M. (1974). Adlerian usage of children's play. *Journal of Individual Psychology, 30*, 194–201.

CHAPTER

Amy Lew

Parenting Education: Selected Programs and Current and Future Needs

Parenting education is as old as the first kinship group, as old as the first instruction a new parent received from grandparents and other elders of the prior and more experienced generation. From such simple beginnings in primitive society and through millennia of trial and error and accumulation of experience, societies varyingly have codified, ritualized, and standardized what was expected of parents, what was expected of children, and what parental actions would foster the socially necessary, socially desired outcomes. These old approaches to intergenerational teaching served the extended families of slowly changing agrarian societies more or less well until there was sudden, and disruptive, change as industrialization came upon the Western world and altered it irrevocably.

Psychology was born of the industrial age. In the late 19th and early 20th centuries, in the pre- and post-World War I intellectual ferment of Vienna and within the Vienna Psychoanalytic Society, known informally as Freud's circle, Sigmund Freud was developing a theory of psychology of a profoundly individual and interior nature. Alfred Adler, invited by Freud to join in forming the discussion circle in 1902, had entered into it in the belief that he came as an equal to explore new ideas about the newly posited human unconscious. Adler was soon to learn that the circle had room for only one leader and additional places only for disciples. Participants with their own ideas, notably Adler and Carl Jung, were driven out to form their own bodies of theory and schools of practice.

Adler's views of human beings were as profoundly relational as Freud's were individual and interior. Thus, although there is an apparent irony in the naming of Adler's school of thought as *Individual Psychology* (as opposed to his intended meaning

I would like to thank my colleagues, Betty Lou Bettner, Ph.D., and Carole Samworth for their invaluable help in the development of this chapter.

of emphasizing the indivisibility and unity of the person), it is not surprising that formal parenting education as we know it in postindustrial society sprang from the theoretical and clinical work of Adler rather than from that of the Freudians.

Adler's goal was to make psychology accessible to everyone. He carried this idea to such an extreme that, to the dismay of many of his colleagues, when his Society for Free Analytic Research met in Vienna's coffee houses, he refused to limit the meetings to professionals and opened them to all who were interested. The egalitarian and democratic orientation of Adlerian psychology was established from the start. Beginning in 1919, Adler founded the first of many child guidance centers in which he met with teachers, parents, children, and other interested community members in order to promote this universal accessibility—that is, to put directly into people's hands the means to help themselves.

By the time Adler immigrated to the United States, his parent–teacher education and child guidance movement had taken root in several European countries. Adler's warm and encouraging style made him a popular speaker in America, and the vitality and practicality of his teachings encouraged wide acceptance of them here. His first books for the trade market in the United States (Adler, 1929, 1930, 1992a, 1992b) are credited with initiating the self-help movement.

Following Adler's sudden death in 1937, Individual Psychology and the parent–teacher education and child guidance movement lost its chief and most talented proponent. The Freudians were swift to move into the vacuum to eclipse the work of their competitor and to promote emphasis on individual psychoanalysis. The psychoanalytic movement in the United States bitterly competed not only with Adler's school of thought, but with all other schools of psychology and their theorists and practitioners, as well.

Arriving in the United States in 1937, Rudolf Dreikurs, an Austrian who had studied with Adler in Vienna, discovered that Adlerian concepts had by then been marginalized and discredited by the Freudians and that the environment had become hostile to Adlerian concepts. Dreikurs resolved to carry forward Adler's parent–teacher education and child guidance movement and to do it openly, against the advice of many professionals who had suffered adverse consequences in the United States from their identification with Adler's work.

Adler could not have wished for a more courageous, articulate, and energetic disseminator and developer of his ideas than Rudolf Dreikurs. Had it been possible for Adler and Dreikurs to work together to advance the Adlerian movement in the United States, parent education might be more fully established today, and many of the social problems currently confronting us might have been avoided.

By 1938, Dreikurs had started an experimental clinic in a high school near Chicago. The initial 4-week program was such a success that the school's parent–teacher association (PTA) sponsored a 12-week continuation of the guidance clinic, which met one afternoon and one evening each week. The forum was open to students, teachers, and parents. Although the initial program revolved around teacher-referred students, the continuation involved all voluntary participants and the program grew from 19 to 100 participants. In 1939, Dreikurs opened a child guidance clinic at the Abraham Lincoln Center in a settlement house in a poor, racially mixed neighborhood in Chicago. In this community fraught with all the problems associated with extreme poverty and racial tension, the practical, encouraging, and democratic approach he taught was well received and well used.

As more centers were founded around Chicago, their hours were extended to Saturday mornings so that working mothers and fathers could attend. Committed to

the primary goal of educating all interested parents, in the 1930s Dreikurs began informal study groups for mothers and in 1947 he began training discussion leaders for
parent study groups in all of the centers. Dreikurs's (1948) book, *The Challenge of Parenthood*, served as a basis for discussion. In it, he introduced the constructs of the four
goals of misbehavior, relating to the Adlerian idea that all behavior has a purpose;
techniques for encouragement; the use of natural and logical consequences instead of
punishment; and the family meeting. In 1964, Dreikurs joined Vicki Soltz in coauthor-
ing *Children: The Challenge*, an example-filled primer still used today by discussion groups
throughout North America, Latin America, Europe, and Israel. Soltz formalized a structure for parent groups and wrote the first *Study-Group Leader's Guide* in 1967.

Soltz's 10-week format was the model for most Adlerian parenting groups until
1976, when Dreikurs's students Don Dinkmeyer and Gary McKay developed a new
program, *Systematic Training for Effective Parenting* (STEP). This well-packaged, profes-
sional-looking program added two important components to the parent study group:
the communication techniques of Thomas Gordon (1975) and audiotapes with actors
presenting typical parent–child problem situations. These tapes helped to stimulate
and structure direct discussion. The program made it easy for people who were not
previously trained or even familiar with Adlerian ideas to begin effective parenting
programs. School counselors, therapists, concerned parents, and clergy began groups
all over the United States and around the world.

The next major contribution to formalized Adlerian parent education came in
1983 when Michael Popkin, who had studied with Dreikurs's student Oscar Christensen,
decided to use the then-new technology of videotapes and created the *Active Parenting
Program*. A picture was indeed worth a thousand words, and many subtle concepts
(such as the demonstration of various ways parents might block communication) were
much more easily conveyed. Shortly thereafter, STEP's authors added video to their
programs, and both STEP and Active Parenting developed programs for teachers and
for parents of teens.

Both of these programs made teaching Adlerian parenting more accessible to
non-Adlerian leaders, but the well-packaged video had some drawbacks. First, this
technology brought with it high price tags, and many leaders who were not affiliated
with a school or other organization could not afford them. Second, the original videos
tended to represent White, middle-class families and examples. Many leaders working
with diverse socioeconomic and multicultural populations found that the parents in
their groups complained that because the people and the situations did not look like
them, and the approach was not applicable to them either. This apparent class bias was
especially unfortunate as much of Dreikurs's practical constructs had been developed
working with poor, minority populations.

Michael Popkin addressed this problem by revising his program in 1993. The
new videotapes of *Active Parenting Today* employ actors of different races and cultures,
use more generic scenery, and show single-parent families. Also added were auxiliary
parent guides that are written at simpler reading levels. In 1996, Popkin, Gard, and
Montgomery released a new program, *1 2 3 4 Parents!*, developed in part with funding
from the Georgia Indigent Children's Help Fund, which was specifically designed to
be used with parents of younger children who come from lower socioeconomic groups
and who are considered to be "at risk." According to the leader's guide, this fit is achieved
by limiting the course to three 90-minute sessions, focusing more on the "how to" of
parenting rather than on the "why," keeping the *Parent's Guide* simple to read, and
depicting families representing multicultural and lower and middle-class socioeconomic lifestyles. At the time of this writing, the STEP program was also being rede-

signed to address these concerns, but it was not available for review in time for inclusion in this chapter.

Adlerian parenting books number in the dozens, each one contributing its own particular variation of Adler's and Dreikurs's principles. This chapter, however, is limited to discussion of full-scale parent study-group programs. Today the leading programs are STEP, Active Parenting, Positive Discipline, Practical Parenting, and Raising Kids Who Can.

☐ Commonalities

Each of these five programs covers in discussion, examples, and exercises the following key concepts.

- democratic parenting as an alternative to autocratic or permissive parenting styles

- encouragement as a way to develop resiliency and build self-esteem and the dangers of using rewards and evaluative praise

- the underlying purpose and goals of misbehavior as described by Rudolf Dreikurs (seeking undue attention, seeking power, seeking revenge, avoidance of discouraging situations through displayed inadequacy). With the exception of Practical Parenting, all of the programs address the difference between misbehavior resulting from mistakes due to age or developmental level and behavior that has a misguided goal.

- discipline, including the use of logical and natural consequences instead of punishment and the importance of structure and limits

- communication techniques such as active listening and problem-solving dialogues

- Adlerian family meetings

☐ Other Program Attributes

1. *Systematic Training for Effective Parenting* (STEP) contains a parent's guide, a leader's guide, videotaped examples, posters, promotional tips, and materials to interest parents in attending. STEP also has programs targeted for early childhood parenting and parenting of teens, a program for teens, and a program that applies these principles to classroom teaching. The original parent program is available in Spanish. There is also a supplementary guide connecting the program to Christian family life.

   The STEP programs of Dinkmeyer and McKay and other contributing authors (see the Reference list) are available through American Guidance Service, Circle Pines, Minnesota.

2. *Active Parenting* programs (Popkin, 1993) also include a parent's guide, a leader's guide, videotaped examples, posters, promotional tips, and materials to interest parents in attending. As previously noted, there are different programs targeted for parents of teenage, school-aged, and young children and a program for teachers. Additionally, Active Parenting has video and audio programs for parents who are not able to attend a group. Most recently, the authors have released a program specifically designed to teach parents how to encourage and help their children in school. This three-session course includes tips for preparing children to succeed in school, ways to encourage positive behavior, and suggestions for reinforcing academic skills. The actual course does not cover all the material in the parent's guide. Parents who prefer classes to books will find simply attending the course valuable. Those parents who want to deepen their knowledge and skill will find much useful information in the accompanying parent's guide.

One particularly useful aspect of the Active Parenting videos is that they first present an example of the ineffective approach—one most parents will recognize—followed, after time for discussion, with a more effective example of how to achieve the parent's goal.

There are many similarities between the STEP and Active Parenting programs. Some experienced leaders use both and sometimes combine them. Although the choice of one program or the other is usually a matter of personal taste or familiarity, some leaders believe that the simpler format of the original STEP program may be useful for less sophisticated parents. A facilitator might choose one or the other program depending on the parent population to be addressed. However, as described above, Active Parenting has developed programs specifically designed for poor readers or nonreaders.

3. *Teaching Parenting the Positive Discipline Way*, by Lynn Lott and Jane Nelsen (1995), is a program that can be used with a book or on its own. It focuses mainly on providing the facilitator with numerous experiential activities and other resources that can be used in conjunction with any of the Adlerian parenting books and to enhance the various parenting programs. Included are outlines for 7-week study-group courses for 10 different parenting books. There are also facilitator's guides available for programs developed for single parents, parents in recovery, and parents of preschoolers. Each one of these is used with a book written by Jane Nelsen and coauthors for the targeted population (see the Reference list). The Positive Discipline programs are relatively low cost and are available through Empowering People, Provo, Utah.

4. *The Practical Parenting Programs* was designed by Stanley Shapiro (Shapiro, Skinulis, & Skinulis, 1996) in order to provide widespread, low-cost parenting education in the tradition of Dreikurs's model. His nonprofit organization, The Ontario Parenting Education Centre, has developed a model for two study groups, an 8-week basic parenting class and a 6-week advanced course. Volunteers who are given a free 2-day training program lead the programs. This community-based program is not dependent on outside funding and once started by a host organization (such as a school, church, or business) is self-perpetuating and inexpensive to run. The primary cost is for participants' materials. Practical Parenting has developed a text-

book and two study guides (one for the initial course and one for the advanced). Although these guides cover the same material as the other Adlerian parenting books, they are designed to be used with their own courses. The program's host group is asked to identify a coordinator, provide the site, and advertise the program to prospective participants.

Easily accessed facilitator training is a key to this program. The 2-day trainings are offered in many configurations, three evenings, one weekend, two weekdays, or two consecutive Saturdays. This variety enables people in all types of situations to participate. The centre estimates that for every 10,000 people who are informed about the program, 50 volunteers register for the training. Facilitators are parents and other concerned community members; they come from all economic and educational backgrounds. The only requirements are that they be willing to attend the program and acquire the materials (which can be subsidized). Although participants are not required to go on to lead a group, almost all of them do. The Ontario Parenting Education Centre provides the initial training for facilitators, but they strongly encourage that the subsequent training be done by community members.

Shapiro's goal is to have parent education available in every school system in Canada. He is available to help other communities organize similar programs. More information is available through the Ontario Parenting Education Centre, York University, Downsview, Ontario.

5. The *Raising Kids Who Can* parenting education program is designed around the Adlerian family meeting. The authors, Betty Lou Bettner and Amy Lew (1996), show how the family meeting enables parents to affect all the perceptions, qualities, and skills that are necessary to raise children who are resilient, capable, responsible, and cooperative and who grow into successful, contributing citizens. The program encourages parents to think about the qualities that they want to foster in their children and how their approach to parenting facilitates or interferes with their stated goals. This focus on what individual parents want and the effectiveness of their discipline techniques creates a culturally sensitive, nonjudgmental, and nonconfrontational program.

    The theory is presented in a commonsense, easy-to-understand format and drawn from the parents' own experiences. The foundation of personality development is presented as the need for the "crucial Cs":

    *   connection: the basic need to belong, first to family and then to the community, for physical survival and psychological security
    *   capability: the desire and need to grow and improve and become capable of taking care of oneself
    *   counting: the need to feel significant
    *   courage: the belief that one is able to face life's challenges

    Misbehavior (including Dreikurs's four goals) is presented as a coping strategy developed by children who are discouraged about their ability to achieve the crucial Cs through constructive means. Experiential exercises help parents see how even they "misbehave" when they are discouraged. Over the course of the program, parents begin to focus less on how to "make" their children behave and more on how to encourage them to develop the self-image, skills, and abilities necessary for constructive fulfillment of the crucial Cs.

The program can be given in five to eight sessions. The initial meeting can be given as a talk for a PTA or other community group in order to introduce the ideas and to encourage registration. Each session builds on the previous one, introducing each of the key concepts covered in all of the Adlerian programs but in the context of the family meeting. This developmental approach allows parents to introduce the meeting gradually: Each step is role played and practiced in the group, then the parents try it at home. The following week begins with a discussion of their experience with their families and suggestions for correcting any difficulties that they may have encountered. By the end of the course, most families have instituted a regular family meeting that enables them to encourage their children, develop a cooperative and supportive family atmosphere, teach and model problem-solving and communication skills, foster responsibility and self-discipline, and have fun together, all with an investment of only 30 to 60 minutes a week.

As the family meeting is introduced in all of the previously mentioned programs, this course is compatible with all of them. It can be used on its own, as an initial program followed by one of the others, or as a follow up to serve as a review and help parents to initiate the meeting in their own homes

The *Raising Kids Who Can* program consists of a low-cost *Leader's Guide*, a *Parent's Guide* covering the key concepts and tips for achieving them, and an example-filled book, *Raising Kids Who Can*, discussing the rationale and implementation of the family meeting. There is also a guide for teachers, *Responsibility in the Classroom*, that covers the same concepts and discusses the classroom meeting. The books are available through Connexions Press, Newton Centre, Massachusetts.

☐ Rationale for Parenting Groups

It is no longer enough or even safe to teach children to do as they are told and follow directions. Kids today must be able to make wise decisions and decide what is safe, what is dangerous, and who to trust; they must be able to choose between ever-expanding options and demands; and they must be resilient, able to cope with and adjust to a rapidly changing environment (in the past, most people expected to keep the same job for most of their lives, but today's young people can expect to have to retool or change occupations numerous times throughout their work lives.)

Parents need information, direction, and support. Educational parenting groups provide this necessary help in a nonthreatening, easily accessible atmosphere. Because the groups are educational in nature, parents can bring up problems, learn new ideas, and get feedback without feeling stigmatized by their participation. Sharing concerns with other people who are grappling with similar problems breaks down feelings of isolation, normalizes problem situations, and allays feelings of guilt and shame. Because parents are learning together, sharing their own experiences, and giving feedback to other parents, they feel more capable and connected and their own self-esteem is enhanced as they are able to help others as well as receive help.

Parenting programs are a low-cost, easily implemented approach to prevention of more serious problems. They allow concerned people, both mental health professionals and nonprofessionals, to have an impact on developing and protecting our most important resource, our children. They also take some of the pressure off the mental health system, leaving more time and resources for people in critical situations.

☐ Current and Future Needs

Changing family structures, greater mobility, and concurrent diminished contact with the extended family and stable community left parents isolated and often ill prepared for the job of raising children in the new atmosphere of industrial society. Today, in our evolving postindustrial society, we are seeing even more changes in family structure and in cultural diversity. We experience the greater stresses of heightened competition and the fracturing of community as the restructuring of socioeconomic classes widens the gulf between the wealthy and the poor and diminishes the middle class. We see a tense interface between new technologies and the society they confront, with a trend toward the substitution of technological contact for personal contact and, thus, even greater human isolation and alienation. We can expect social conflict and violence to increase and parenting to become even more difficult under these conditions—we may even see our democratic rights compromised or abridged as a remedy for this chaos— unless positive programs compatible with democratic principles are undertaken at once to effectively address these problems and inequities.

These conditions and demands can seal the demise of the American and other democratic experiments, or they can call forth our best and most creative ideas to achieve greater realization of democracy than human beings have yet known. The quality of life in each era is dependent on its leadership and citizenship; in turn, the quality of each generation's leadership and citizenship is dependent on the beliefs and values developed in early life in the family. Professionals who are committed to democratic principles and who believe that they are best fostered in early childhood can play a vital role in preventing and addressing our society's problems by providing this essential parent education.

☐ References

Adler, A. (1929). *The science of living* (B. Ginzburg, Ed.). New York: Greenburg.

Adler, A. (1930). *The education of children* (E. Jensen & F. Jensen, Trans.). New York: Greenburg.

Adler, A. (1992a). *Understanding human nature* (C. Brett, Trans.). Oxford, England: Oneworld. (Original work published 1927)

Adler, A. (1992b). *What life could mean to you* (C. Brett, Trans.). Oxford, England: Oneworld. (Original work published 1931)

Bettner, B. L., & Lew, A. (1996). *Raising kids who can: Using family meetings to nurture responsible, cooperative, caring, and happy children.* Newton Centre, MA: Connexions Press.

Dinkmeyer, D., Sr., & McKay, G. (1976). *Systematic training for effective parenting (STEP)*. Circle Pines, MN: American Guidance Service.

Dreikurs, R. (1948). *The challenge of parenthood*. New York: Hawthorn.

Dreikurs, R., & Soltz, V. (1964). *Children: The challenge*. New York: Hawthorn.

Gordon, T. (1975). *Parent effectiveness training*. New York: P. H. Wyden.

Hoffman, E. (1994). *The drive for self: Alfred Adler and the founding of individual psychology*. Reading, MA: Addison-Wesley.

Lott, L., & Nelsen, J. (1995). *Teaching parenting the positive discipline way*. Fair Oaks, CA: Sunrise Press.

Popkin, M. (1983). *Active parenting*. Atlanta, GA: Active Parenting.

Popkin, M. (1993). *Active parenting today*. Atlanta, GA: Active Parenting.

Popkin, M., Gard, B., & Montgomery, M. (1996). *1 2 3 4 parents!: Parenting children ages 1 to 4*. Atlanta, GA: Active Parenting.

Shapiro, S., Skinulis, K., & Skinulis, R. (1996). *Practical parenting: A common sense guide to raising cooperative, self-reliant, and loving children*. Toronto: Parent Education.

Soltz, V. (1967). *Study group leader's manual: To be used with children: The challenge*. Chicago: Alfred Adler Institute of Chicago.

☐ Parent Education Programs: A Bibliography

Active Parenting Programs

Popkin, M. (1990). *Active parenting of teens*. Atlanta, GA: Active Parenting.

Popkin, M. (1993a). *Active parenting today*. Atlanta, GA: Active Parenting.

Popkin, M. (1993b). *Active parenting today: The basics*. Atlanta, GA: Active Parenting.

Popkin, M. (1994). *Active parenting audiocassette program*. Atlanta, GA: Active Parenting.

Popkin, M., Gard, B., & Montgomery, M. (1996). *1 2 3 4 parents! Parenting children ages 1 to 4*. Atlanta, GA: Active Parenting.

Popkin, M., Young, B. B., & Healy, J. M. (1995). *Parents on board: Building academic success through parent involvement*. Atlanta, GA: Active Parenting.

Positive Discipline Programs

Lott, L., & Intner, R. (1995). *The family that works together*. Rocklin, CA: Prima.

Lott, L., & Nelsen, J. (1995). *Teaching parenting the positive discipline way*. Fair Oaks, CA: Sunrise Press.

Nelsen, J. (1987). *Positive discipline*. New York: Ballantine.

Nelsen, J., & Erwin, C. (1994). *Positive discipline for single parents—facilitator's guide*. Fair Oaks, CA: Sunrise Press.

Nelsen, J., Erwin, C., & Delzer, C. (1993). *Positive discipline for single parents*. Rocklin, CA: Prima.

Nelsen, J., Erwin, C., & Duffy, R. (1995). *Positive discipline for preschoolers*. Rocklin, CA: Prima.

Nelsen, J., Intner, R., & Lott, L. (1995). *Positive discipline for parenting in recovery*. Rocklin, CA: Prima.

Nelsen, J., & Lott, L. (1994). *Positive discipline for teenagers*. Rocklin, CA: Prima.

Practical Parenting Programs

Shapiro, S., Shapiro, S., Skinulis, K., & Skinulis, R. (1996a). *Advanced practical parenting study guide.* Toronto: Parent Education.

Shapiro, S., Shapiro, S., Skinulis, K., & Skinulis, R. (1996b). *Practical parenting study guide.* Toronto: Parent Education.

Shapiro, S., Skinulis, K., & Skinulis, R. (1996). *Practical parenting: A common sense guide to raising cooperative, self-reliant, and loving children.* Toronto: Parent Education.

Raising Kids Who Can Parenting Education Program

Bettner, B. L., & Lew, A. (1996a). *Raising kids who can: Leader's guide.* Newton Centre, MA: Connexions Press.

Bettner, B. L., & Lew, A. (1996b). *Raising kids who can: Using family meetings to nurture responsible, cooperative, caring, and happy children.* Newton Centre, MA: Connexions Press.

Lew, A., & Bettner, B. L. (1995). *Responsibility in the classroom: A teacher's guide to understanding and motivating students.* Newton Centre, MA: Connexions Press.

Lew, A., & Bettner, B. L. (1996). *A parent's guide to understanding and motivating children.* Newton Centre, MA: Connexions Press.

Systematic Training in Effective Parenting Program

Dinkmeyer, D., Sr., & McKay, G. (1978). *Padres eficaces con entrenamiento sistematico (PECES).* Circle Pines, MN: American Guidance Service.

Dinkmeyer, D., Sr., & McKay, G. (1989a). *Systematic training for effective parenting (STEP)* (3rd ed.; STEP Kit). Circle Pines, MN: American Guidance Service.

Dinkmeyer, D., Sr., & McKay, G. (1989b). *Systematic training for effective parenting for teens.* Circle Pines, MN: American Guidance Service.

Dinkmeyer, D., Sr., McKay, G., & Dinkmeyer, J. (1989). *Early childhood STEP.* Circle Pines, MN: American Guidance Service.

Dinkmeyer, D., Sr., McKay, G., Dinkmeyer, D., Jr., Dinkmeyer, J., & McKay, J. (1987). *The effective parent.* Circle Pines, MN: American Guidance Service.

Selected Adlerian Parenting Books

Albert, L. (1984). *Coping with kids.* New York: Ballantine.

Albert, L., & Einstein, E. (1986). *Strengthening your stepfamily.* Circle Pines, MN: American Guidance Service.

Bettner, B. L. (Ed.). (1989). *An Adlerian resource book.* Chicago: North American Society of Adlerian Psychology.

Corsini, R. J., & Painter, G. (1984). *The practical parent.* New York: Simon & Schuster.

Dinkmeyer, D., Sr., & McKay, G. (1996). *Raising a responsible child* (rev. ed.). New York: Fireside.

Glenn, H. S., & Nelsen, J. (1988). *Raising self-reliant children in a self-indulgent world.* Rocklin, CA: Prima.

Main, F. (1986). *Perfect parenting and other myths.* Minneapolis, MN: CompCare.

Nelson, J., & Glenn, H. S. (1991). *Time out: Abuses and effective uses.* Fair Oaks, CA: Sunrise Press.

Platt, J. (1989). *Life in the family zoo*. Sacramento, CA: Dynamic Training and Seminars.

Walton, F. (1980). *Winning teenagers over*. Columbia, SC: Adlerian Child Care Books.

Weinhaus, E., & Friedman, K. (1988). *Stop struggling with your teen*. New York: Viking Penguin.

Len Sperry

The Integration of *DSM-IV* Diagnoses and Adlerian Psychotherapy

Adlerian psychotherapy is a broad-based approach integrating psychodynamic, cognitive, behavioral, existential, and systems perspectives. The founder of this approach, Alfred Adler, did not consider diagnostic classifications to be essential in the assessment and treatment of individuals. Furthermore, most dynamically oriented as well as many systems-oriented clinicians have varying degrees of reservation about the theoretical tenability and clinical value of diagnoses and formal diagnostic classification systems. Nonetheless, contemporary norms for clinical practice require formal diagnoses and favor case formulations (Sperry, Gudeman, Blackwell, & Faulkner, 1991). This chapter addresses the issue of the theoretical tenability and clinical value and utility of diagnoses and case formulations (Sperry, 1996), particularly the diagnostic formulation system that is called the *Diagnostic and Statistical Manual of Mental Disorders* (fourth edition, or *DSM–IV*; American Psychiatric Association, 1994). The chapter describes this system and illustrates its compatibility with Adlerian psychotherapy, a contemporary, integrative dynamic systems approach.

☐ Diagnosis in Clinical Practice

Clinical assessment has always been an integral and familiar part of psychotherapy practice. Yet, formal diagnosis—one aspect of assessment—has never really been a familiar or an integral aspect of psychotherapy. That seems to have changed lately, particularly as a diagnosis is required for third-party reimbursement of individual psychotherapy and marital and family therapy. Nevertheless, for many clinicians there are varying degrees of ambivalence and uncertainty about the use and value of diagnosis in psychotherapy. This is largely due to the association of diagnosis with the medical model, which seems so foreign to the developmental model and systems theory model on which many therapy systems are based. Many clinicians have expressed the concern that they will be losing some of their heart or possibly selling their soul by incorporating diagnosis into their practice. Fortunately, diagnosis and *DSM–IV* can be very useful in the practice of psychotherapy.

After reflecting the concerns that many dynamically oriented clinicians share, Goldberg (1989) noted that the merits of diagnosis may outweigh these concerns. He believes diagnosis is particularly helpful in the recognition and assessment of a family member's potential for suicide, homicide, or other self-destructive behavior. Individuals with a major depression, borderline personality disorder, or alcohol and substance dependence are at a particularly high risk for these. Similarly, individuals in a manic state need to be promptly and accurately identified as they can do considerable damage to themselves, their partners, or family with inappropriate, uncontrolled behavior such as wild spending or promiscuity.

Hof and Treat (1989) believed that clinicians who practice marital and family therapy should have a thorough knowledge of individual psychopathology and its diagnosis. They contended that individual pathology has a great impact on couple and family functioning. With a working knowledge of *DSM–IV* criteria, clinicians can easily assess the nature and severity of individual issues: chronic anxiety, mood disorders, thought disorders, and personality disorders, as well as the influence of personality traits on marriage and family functioning. Such knowledge of diagnosis also increases the likelihood that clinicians will work within the limits of their training and experience and will facilitate decisions about appropriate referral when necessary.

Finally, Seligman (1986) suggested additional reasons why clinicians need competence in diagnosis. First, diagnosis provides a diagnosis for clients with insurance coverage; second, it aids in informing clients if their psychotherapy will be covered by medical insurance; third, it facilitates accountability and record keeping; fourth, it can facilitate communication with other helping professionals, such as counselors, physicians, and psychiatrists; and fifth, it can be useful in planning treatment.

In short, there are compelling reasons to conclude that diagnoses and classification systems, particularly *DSM–IV*, can be of considerable value to clinicians who treat individuals, couples, and families.

☐ Some Basic Tenets of Adlerian Psychotherapy

Adler believed that the hallmark of the healthy, nonpathological person was the capacity to move through life meeting the various life tasks with courage and common sense. Adler called this hallmark *social interest* (Adler, 1964a). He described the "neurotic disposition" as predisposing conditions that can result in psychopathology. The neurotic disposition stems from childhood experiences that are characterized either by overprotection or neglect or by a confused admixture of both. From these experiences, the young child develops a set of psychological convictions—about self, the world, and life goal, which becomes the lifestyle—of his or her inability to develop mastery or cope with the tasks of life (Adler, 1956). These convictions are confounded and reinforced by the child's perception of a hostile, punishing, or depriving environment at home or school, or one that is subtly demanding or frustrating. Rather than providing encouragement to engage in other efforts involving mastery and achievement, these experiences leave the youngster feeling discouraged and fearful. Rather than experiencing trusting and loving relationships, the young child grows to become distrustful and manipulative. To compensate for these exaggerated feelings of insecurity and anxiety, the child becomes self-centered and uncooperative.

For Adler, psychopathology could best be understood in terms of lifestyle (Adler, 1964a). A pathological lifestyle is an inflexible one. Problem-solving is based on a self-protective "private sense" rather than a more task-oriented and socially useful "common sense." Once this set of faulty psychological convictions has coalesced and self-protective patterns of coping are established, the individual has difficulty in viewing and responding to life in other terms. The end result is that the dysfunctional individual cannot productively cope with the tasks of life or enjoy the rewards of his or her labors, much less his or her relationships with others. In contrast, a set of psychological convictions and coping patterns that are shaped positively by the child's healthy experiences of mastery, creativity, and loving and pleasurable relationships will result in a flexible lifestyle.

Adler proposed a unitary theory of psychopathology wherein the individual "arranges" symptoms uniquely to serve as excuses for not meeting the tasks of life or to safeguard self-esteem either by aggression or distancing from others (Adler, 1964a). He discriminated pathological behavior along the dimensions of social interest and degree of activity. For instance, neurotics respond to the life tasks with "yes—but." With the *yes*, the individual acknowledges social responsibilities, and with the *but* symptoms are presented that excuse responsibility. Mosak (1984) described two types of "yes—but" responses: "yes—but I'm sick," which is the classic response of the psychoneurotic, and, "yes—but I defy it," the acting-out response of the character neurosis or personality disorder. On the other hand, psychotics respond to life tasks with *no* and cut themselves off from the common world. As to activity level, Adler noted a low degree is found in neurotic conditions such as depression and obsessive-compulsion, with a higher degree in anxiety neurosis, schizophrenia, and alcoholism. The highest levels were in mania and sociopathology (Adler, 1964b).

More specifically, Adler characterized four personality types: the ruling, getting, avoiding, and healthy, socially useful persons (Adler, 1964a). The first three types describe individuals who are discouraged and low in social interest and so would be considered dysfunctional. Mosak (1968, 1971) has briefly described several other personality types and has provided an in-depth analysis of the getting and controlling types.

Finally, it should be noted that at the outset of his career, Adler believed that psychopathology stemmed from various organ inferiorities. This was a rather biological and reductionistic position. Later, his view changed to a more intrapsychic view in which dysfunctional behavior was seen as a conflict between inferiority and superiority feelings. He described the neurotic disposition as the predisposing factor in the development of neurosis. The term *pampered lifestyle* eventually replaced this term. Still later, Adler developed a more psychosocial view in which psychopathology represented movement toward self-importance at the expense of the common good. In many respects, this last version of Adler's theory represented one of the first attempts at developing a integrative view of psychopathology (Adler, 1964a). In short, Adler's view is essentially a biopsychosocial view, and although it does not feature a detailed diagnostic and classification system, it nevertheless proposes a limited one.

☐ The *DSM–IV* and Adlerian Theory

The *DSM–IV* (American Psychiatric Association, 1994) provides clinicians a multiaxial system of diagnostic classification. Through the use of a five-axis system, clients can be assessed across a wide range of areas. The multiaxial system represent a biopsychosocial view of the individual.

The following is a brief description of the five axes and the clinical relevance of each axis to both individual psychotherapy as well as couples and family therapy. Also noted is the correspondence of each axis with the tenets of Adlerian psychotherapy.

Axis I: Clinical Disorders

Axis I is for clinical disorders and for other conditions that might be a focus of clinical attention, such as V codes. Axis I would entail listing, according to the criteria found in the manual, the major symptoms that are interfering with clients' functioning. Anxiety, schizophrenia, substance abuse, and other such disorders would be listed here. In addition, the V codes would be listed, those codes that are not attributable to a mental disorder but are still the focus of attention. Marital problem, parent–child problem, and occupational problem are three of the V codes listed.

Beavers (1985; Beavers & Hampson, 1990) indicated that unrecognized and undiagnosed Axis I conditions can wreak havoc in marital and family therapy. From a systems perspective, he believed that anxiety, mood, and thought disorders greatly influence couple and family functioning and that couples and families influence the expression of these disorders. In his research on levels of family functioning and family styles, he has shown how certain family styles generate diagnosable disorders. For instance, families functioning in the normal range typically "generate" adjustment disorders, and families functioning in the borderline centripetal range tend to "generate" individuals with obsessive–compulsive disorder. Families in the midrange are most likely to "generate" behavior or anxiety disorders. Not surprisingly, families in the severely dysfunctional range tend to harbor individuals with psychotic or antisocial disorders.

From an Adlerian perspective, the Axis I diagnoses would be the presenting problems. These would be determined by examining what Dreikurs (1954) referred to as the *subjective condition*. The client is prompted to talk about his or her circumstances, symptoms, discomfort, and dysfunctions. Accordingly, the clinician is able to better understand the client's concerns and expectations for therapy. The steps from understanding the presenting problem (the subjective condition) to the *DSM–IV* diagnosis is a relatively direct one: The list of complaints are matched up to the diagnostic criteria.

Axis II: Personality Disorders

Axis II is for descriptions of personality features. It is here that the presenting problems are linked to the personality pattern, such as paranoid, schizoid, passive–aggressive, antisocial, and so forth. A general rule of thumb for Axis II conditions is that if the client's complaints are about things happening to him or her (i.e., fears, bizarre thoughts, sleeplessness, etc.), the probable diagnosis is an Axis I condition. If the client complains primarily about his or her inability to function because of others (i.e., blaming spouses, jobs, etc.), the more probable diagnosis involves Axis II. A brief example is the client who complains about an inability to stop washing his hands. He reports that he cannot control what is happening, therefore the probable diagnosis would be an obsessive–compulsive disorder on Axis I. If, however, he reports that his wife is not organized enough, his children are too wild, and he has trouble being spontaneous, the Axis II diagnosis of obsessive–compulsive personality disorder might more appropriately be made.

Information about personality styles and disorders can be very useful in understanding specifically how an individual functions in relationships, as well as how effectively he or she will respond to treatment. For instance, the complementarity of a narcissistic exploitive style with the dependent submissive style or of the avoidant reticent style with the histrionic attention-seeking style must be considered in family interactions. This information not only helps to explain the dynamics but also helps to specify treatment goals and interventions. Dependent clients need to learn assertiveness and independence skills. Histrionic clients need to learn control and how to specify issues. Avoidant clients need to learn how to connect more effectively within the family unit. Although information about personality style cannot be used, in and of itself, to predict behavior, it does provide clinicians important information to aid in more accurately understanding family and couple dynamics.

From an Adlerian perspective, Axis II diagnoses provides a glimpse of the lifestyle. Given a certain set of beliefs, the clients will present with a particular style.

Axis III: General Medical Conditions

The third axis is for medical conditions or disorders that may be potentially relevant to the understanding or management of the case. Diabetes, heart conditions, chronic lower back problems, hypothyroidism, and such would be listed here. These conditions require a medical diagnosis, and without consultation, clinicians who are not medically trained should list conditions on this axis only from history or under the direction of a physician. Its use is optional.

Because marital and family therapy is usually associated with the social and psychological sciences, the idea of assessing biological factors in couples and families may at first appear odd. However, as the population is getting older, health problems are becoming more prominent in the lives of couples and families and do affect their functioning. To adequately understand their concerns and effectively treat them, clinicians will need to consider biological as well as psychological and social factors (Sperry & Carlson, 1989). Clinicians need to possess some understanding of health status, medication side effects, nutritional status, psychosomatic illness, and common medical and surgical conditions. The relationship among health, psychological well-being, and marital and family functioning and dysfunctioning is complex. Axis III prompts the clinician to consider how concurrent medical conditions have an impact on or trigger family and marital dynamics.

In Adlerian psychotherapy, Axis III would provide information about organ inferiorities, medical conditions, or other potential handicapping conditions that individuals might subjectively perceive as overburdening situations (Adler, 1956).

Axis IV: Psychosocial and Environmental Problems

The degree of social stress is very useful information for the clinician. Families with less stress may be more reluctant to continue treatment. However, families with too much stress may need to have the stress resolved before any insight or underlying dynamics are addressed. This information is helpful in terms of prioritizing treatment issues.

The fourth axis assesses the psychosocial and environmental stressors that can influence the diagnosis, treatment, and prognosis of Axis I and Axis II disorders. Such stressors deemed relevant to the client's current functioning are listed here. These can include social support problems, difficulties with personal resources, housing and financial problems, or work problems. When multiple stressors are noted, the clinician lists as many as are judged to be relevant during the year preceding the current evaluation. This information is helpful in understanding clients as well as the social context in which they live.

Adlerian psychotherapy has long emphasized understanding persons in their social context. Adler (1956) referred to this as understanding the "exogenous factor." In fact, he listed 10 typical occasions for the onset of a psychopathology that are similar to those noted in Axis IV.

Axis V: Global Assessment of Functioning

The last axis used in *DSM–IV* refers to the assessment of clients' overall functioning in life. The Global Assessment of Functioning (GAF) Scale assigns a numerical value to the level of functioning, with numbers ranging from 1 to 100. Scores of 81–90 would indicate virtually symptom-free functioning; scores of 1–10 would indicate a serious threat of harm to self or others. Axis V is optional as well.

The corresponding component in Adlerian psychology for the GAF Scale would be an assessment of the life tasks. Whereas Axis I examines the subjective condition, this axis assesses what Dreikurs (1954) referred to as the "objective situation." This specifies the client's life circumstances, the condition under which he or she lives, and how he or she actually functions. Adler provided a framework for such examination by pointing to the three life tasks: love, work, and friendship.

Understanding Axis V has another benefit; it assists clinicians in minimizing resistance. Adler (1956) and Dreikurs (1954) described the basis of resistance as a misalignment of goals between the therapist and client. GAF Scale scores can be assessed for both the current level of functioning and the highest level of functioning in the past year. If the discrepancy between the current level and highest level in the past year is too great, clinicians need to be sensitive to the pacing and goal setting in therapy; this is also true for scores that are relatively identical but low. In either case, resistance may be an issue for clinicians who do not closely attend to the meaning of the scores. For example, a woman whose current and highest past year GAF score is 41 may not have the same goals in therapy as a woman whose scores are 55 currently and 85 in the past year. Clinicians who determine treatment goals without examining GAF scores and collaboration from clients may experience undue resistance.

The assessment of levels of functioning of different family members can help to determine degrees of mutuality and dependency, as well as to determine whether or not insight or other approaches requiring higher intellectual capacity are even possible.

From this information specific tailoring can occur, with high-functioning families probably needing less direction and support and lower functioning families needing more direction and support.

Putting the above into a unified case formulation involves practice and supervision, but once learned it can prove to be quite beneficial. Briefly summarized, it would be something like this:

A client with this particular lifestyle (Axis II) has encountered a situation for which he or she is not adequately prepared (Axis IV). To safeguard, the client selects a particular group or cluster of symptoms to use to sidestep the demands and create distance (Axis I). What symptoms are chosen may in part be due to an organ inferiority or an overburdening situation such as a handicap (Axis III).

How adequately the client meets the tasks of life can be assessed. What degree of involvement he or she may be expecting to return to can be assessed in order to gain a quick estimate of the amount of social interest present and to help align treatment goals (Axis V).

In such a formulation, the principles of Adlerian psychotherapy are preserved, although dynamically oriented clinicians can have their ideas and conceptualizations framed in a common language of their peers.

☐ *DSM–IV* and Adlerian Psychotherapy: Some Additional Comparisons

Although the Adlerian approach has a unitary theory of psychopathology with a limited classification system, *DSM–IV* describes 18 distinct major classifications and diagnostic criteria for more than 200 mental disorders. Each *DSM* disorder has a unique set of descriptive—rather than dynamic—diagnostic criteria. A *DSM–IV* diagnosis is made by matching data from an individual's history and clinical presentation with the diagnostic criteria for a particular mental disorder.

Essentially, the *DSM–IV* system is based on a pathological model and a psychology of possession, whereas the Adlerian approach is based on a growth model and a psychology of use. Consequently, the Adlerian clinician might not be as concerned about making a *DSM–IV* type of descriptive diagnosis as about understanding the individual's dynamics, that is, movement and lifestyle themes.

Similar to the Adlerian emphasis on life-task functioning, *DSM–IV* views pathology in terms of maladaptive functioning in one or more of three areas: social relations, occupation, and leisure. Finally, as Adlerian psychotherapy strives toward a biopsychosocial understanding of the individual, *DSM–IV* allows for a multiaxial classification so that interrelated biopsychosocial facets of a person's life may be considered.

Unlike other psychotherapy systems that are based on a pathology or disease model, Adlerian psychotherapy is based on a growth model. It emphasizes the dynamics of discouragement rather than pathological symptoms (Mosak, 1984). Similarly, because it is a psychology of use rather than of possession, Adlerian theory does not emphasize the diagnostic classification of symptoms. Instead, Adlerians emphasize the meaning, purpose, and use of dysfunctional thinking, behavior, and symptoms. Because the Adlerian approach emphasizes the psychological reasons or mechanisms that are considered to be important in explaining behavior and symptoms, it has a psychodynamic focus. Because it also emphasizes attitudes and beliefs about self and the world, it has a cognitive focus. Finally, because it emphasizes family constellation, social interactions, and psychological movement it has a systems focus. In short, a clinical formulation for an Adlerian integrates psychodynamic, cognitive, and systems features. But because observations about the individual's movement and descriptions about the uniqueness of the individual are considered more useful than diagnostic categories, nosologies and personality typologies have limited utility in clinical practice among Adlerian clinicians. Nevertheless, the *DSM* diagnostic system complements the Adlerian system and is remarkably compatible with it.

☐ Case Formulations in Clinical Practice

A case formulation is a way of summarizing diverse information about a client in a brief, coherent manner for the purpose of better understanding and treating the individual. Basically, case formulations consist of three aspects: diagnostic formulations, clinical formulations, and treatment formulations (Sperry et al., 1991). A *diagnostic formulation* is a descriptive statement about the nature and severity of the individual's psychiatric presentation. The diagnostic formulation aids the clinician in reaching three sets of diagnostic conclusions: whether the patient's presentation is primarily psychotic, characterological, or neurotic; whether the patient's presentation is primarily organic or psychogenic in etiology; and whether the patient's presentation is so acute and severe that it requires immediate intervention. In short, diagnostic formulations are descriptive, phenomenological, and cross-sectional in nature. They answer the "what happened?" question. For all practical purposes, the diagnostic formulation lends itself to being specified with *DSM–IV* criteria and nosology. A *clinical formulation*, on the other hand, is more explanatory and longitudinal in nature and attempts to offer a rationale for the development and maintenance of symptoms and dysfunctional life patterns. Just as various theories of human behavior exist, so do various types of clinical formulations: psychoanalytic, Adlerian, cognitive, behavioral, biological, family systems, and biopsychosocial. Clinical formulations answer the "why did it happen?" question.

A *treatment formulation* follows from a diagnostic and clinical formulation and serves as an explicit blueprint governing treatment interventions. Rather than answering the "what happened?" or "why did it happen?" question, the treatment formulation addresses the "what can be done about it, and how?" question. In short, a complete case formulation consists of three components: diagnostic (i.e., *DSM–IV*), clinical (i.e., Adlerian, Freudian, family systems, etc.), and treatment. Case formulations and diagnoses need not be as reductionistic and limited in scope as they were in the past (Sperry, 1989).

☐ Clinical Illustrations

Two case examples are provided to illustrate how case material can be formulated in terms of both *DSM* criteria and dynamic and systems perspectives. The first case illustrates a *DSM–IV* diagnostic formulation along with a clinical formulation from an Adlerian perspective, and the second case illustrates a treatment formulation based on a diagnostic and clinical formulation.

Case 1

Glenda presented for treatment shortly after her 35th birthday because of increasing marital dissatisfaction and increased periods of sadness and tearfulness. She had been married to her second husband for 16 years, had three children—including one with her first husband—and had worked outside the home for only a few weeks (shortly after her marriage to her current husband).

She was the oldest of four children from an alcoholic family, and she reported that her father drank excessively and could be very abusive. In response to the question about childhood fears on the Life Style Inventory (Mosak & Shulman, 1988), she stated "My father threatened to kill us with a shotgun." A premarital pregnancy allowed her to escape the dysfunctional family system. She managed to complete her high school education, divorced her first husband, and remarried and bore two additional children soon thereafter.

Her presenting complaints were of long-standing dysphoria, tearfulness, a worsening of her long-standing lower back problems, and increasing dissatisfaction with her husband's emotional distance and domineering ways. Surprisingly, she demanded her husband leave their house but claimed that she was really "weak, rather inept." She stopped socializing, believed herself to be incapable of work—"because of my bad back"—and was growing increasingly depressed.

The five-axis *DSM–IV* diagnoses is

Axis I: 300.40 dysthymic disorder, late onset; 316.00 psychological factor affecting medical condition; V61.10 marital problem

Axis II: 301.90 personality disorder NOS (dependent personality disorder and self-defeating personality disorder)

Axis III: Chronic lower back pain [from history]

Axis IV: Psychosocial and environmental problems: marital problems and youngest child starting school

Axis V: Current GAF: 51

Highest GAF past year: 65

Glenda was the oldest born who attempted to take control of her family of origin. The harder she tried, the more dysfunctional she became. As she assumed more responsibility, her mother buried herself in a full-time job and her father increased his drinking. She "escaped" into two marriages to cold, occasionally abusive men who allowed her to "take charge" while they developed active lives outside of the families. She had little opportunity to work outside of the home and to develop outside contacts. Her lower back problem originated when she was very young. She described it as being a "family curse" that afflicted women in her family.

Glenda's lifestyle was a combination of victim–inadequate–pleaser types (Mosak, 1971). In spite of being criticized and abused, she continually attempted but was unable to please others. She believed she was "dumb," uneducated, and had no future. She admitted to "picking losers" and feeling guilty when things went right for her, including situations not involving her husband. Such a lifestyle matches the *DSM–IV* dependent personality disorder with self-defeating or masochistic features.

Given these underlying convictions, her "choice" of symptoms on Axis I becomes more understandable. She had chosen a man who, like her father, she could not please—marital problem. She used her organ inferiority to escape the responsibility of the work task and therefore reinforced her conviction of having to stay with her husband—psychological factors affecting a medical condition. Under stress, tension became focused on her weakest organ (Adler, 1956). Consequently, she appeared hopeless and depressed and fought back passively—dysthymic disorder.

The exogenous factor for the current crisis was the 5th birthday of her son. He was going to school and leaving her without much to do during her days. In addition, she had reached the same age as when her mother first went out to work and left Glenda at home to care for the others. Mother "left" when the youngest child started school. These internal timetables gave Glenda the sense it was time for her to make a similar move, but she felt inferior and incapable of following through. Though she mustered the courage to evict her husband, she lacked the confidence to take the next step.

Finally, she had considerable difficulty with the life tasks. She had avoided work, limited her social contacts, and was in a dysfunctional marriage. Even though she had been able to maintain some measure of stability in the previous year, she remained unhappy. With the onset of her birthday and her son's school year, the situation deteriorated.

Case 2

The most famous of Adler's cases was that of Mrs. A. (Adler, 1969). Following is a contemporary rendering of the case along with diagnostic, clinical, and treatment formulations. It should be noted that Adler did not treat Mrs. A; in fact, he never met her. He was asked to comment on the written case report of a fellow clinician. Although he did not personally interview Mrs. A, Adler was able to deduce Mrs. A's lifestyle themes from a few pages of the case report.

Mrs. A is a 31-year-old married housewife with two children who presents with a dysphoric mood, a cleaning compulsion, a knife phobia, and a fear of seriously harming her younger son. The client dates these progressively worsening symptoms of 18 months to a terrifying dream in which angels surrounded a coffin. But it appears the symptoms span the 8 years of her marriage, probably beginning with her immense disappointment that her first child was a boy rather than a girl. In time, she became jealous of her husband's popularity and friends, had difficulty relating to her neighbors, and, as their marital discord increased, threatened to kill herself and her son if things did not change. Her vanity was severely wounded when a second son was born about 3 years later. Soon thereafter, a drunken neighbor threatened to kill her with a knife. She soon moved out of her home and took her two children and moved in with her parents. During her absence, her husband had a "nervous breakdown" and begged her to return to care for him. After she returned, her obsessive thoughts and compulsions incapacitated her to the point that she sought psychotherapy.

Following her suicidal threats, her husband took her for an evaluation at which time she was diagnosed with a "nervous stomach," a functional or psychosomatic condition. Psychotherapy was neither recommended nor requested. This was approximately 4 years ago. The client denied any family history of psychiatric illness but noted alcoholism on her father's side of the family. Father was described as a construction worker who was impulsive, physically abusive, and a binge drinker. Her mother was described as hardworking but nonassertive. Relational conflict between her parents was precipitated by her father's drinking and loud threats to "cut everyone's throat." The client was the third of eight children, four girls followed by four boys. She described herself as a child as being cheerful, fun loving and well liked by everyone, except her oldest brother whom she described as selfish and inconsiderate. She described her older sister as selfish because she was silent and reserved and was severely disciplined for small matters.

She reports being in excellent health as a child, doing well in school and having many friends. She left high school before graduation—which was not uncommon among her female friends—and had a number of unskilled jobs before marrying. While she lived at home and worked, she did well. But when jobs necessitated, she lived away from home, and she developed numerous somatic symptoms including a severe skin condition and an enlarged thyroid gland. After her physician insisted that she return to live at home, her symptoms subsided. Thereafter she was able to return to work, choosing male-oriented jobs. She explained she did not want to work around things like fine glassware or china since she dreaded breaking such items. One day her father threatened to kill her with a shovel because her return home had become a financial drain on the family. She ran from the house and hid at a nearby church, vowing she would never return to live at home again. At the age of 21, she broke off an engagement of 3 years to a rather passive and clinging man. Soon thereafter, she met her husband while he was recuperating from wounds sustained in the military. He was all she had dreamed of in a mate: tall, handsome, and a nondrinker. Like their marriage, their courtship was conflicted. He left her, and she pursued him when she learned that she was pregnant with their child. A shotgun wedding followed.

A list of acute problems or symptoms exhibited by Mrs. A includes a cleaning compulsion and obsession involving aggressive behavior and fear of knives, indication of an obsessive–compulsive disorder; dysphoric mood of sufficient duration to warrant the diagnosis of dysthymia; and concerns about the safety of her children given her impulsive style, leading to the V-code diagnosis of parent–child problems. Longer term problems or issues include chronic marital problems (V code) and characterological issues of impulsivity, affective instability, and other symptoms characterized by the Axis II diagnoses.

The five axes *DSM–IV* diagnoses would be

Axis I: Obsessive–compulsive disorder (300.30) Dysthymic disorder (300.40) Partner relational problem (V61.20)

Axis II: Borderline personality disorder (301.83) with histrionic, narcissistic, compulsive, and dependent traits

Axis III: Somatic complaints: thyroid goiter [by history]

Axis IV: Chronic marital–family issues; homicidal ideation

Axis V: GAF = 46 (current); GAF = 58 (highest level past year)

On the basis of Adler's analysis and Shulman's (Adler, 1969) accompanying commentary on the case, the following lifestyle themes and convictions are noted. Mrs. A. viewed life as hostile, unfair, and overcontrolling. She saw herself as a victim who expected to be humiliated, but also believed she was entitled to be treated differently. Therefore, she demanded that others take care of her, and she used obsessions, compulsions, and threats of harming herself and her child to ensure that her husband and family continued in their caretaking roles. Mrs. A. also used interpersonal relationships as a means of gaining dominance and resisting submission, and so she would likely construe cooperation as conquest. Therefore, a clinician might anticipate that the development of cooperative therapeutic relationships would take some time and that the negotiation phase of therapy would be very important and could not be downplayed. Also, because Mrs. A showed relatively little insight and psychological mindedness and was rather ambivalent, the initial phase of treatment should not focus primarily on insight and interpretation. In short, a clinician would endeavor to gain Mrs. A's cooperation from the very onset by attending to her expectations of treatment and by encouraging her involvement, while being aware of her ambivalent, controlling, and entitled lifestyle.

☐ Treatment Formulation

The initial focus of treatment would be to elicit Mrs. A's expectations for treatment, for the therapist's role, and for her role in treatment. A mutually agreed-on treatment plan would then be negotiated. Presumably, the treatment plan would involve symptom reduction at first, followed by stabilization of marriage and family relations, and, in the later stages, would focus more on characterological or Axis II issues. A short course of treatment with a trial of an antidepressant, antiobsessive–compulsive medication (i.e., Prozac or Anafranil), and/or focused behavior therapy aimed at symptom reduction is indicated. In addition, whatever measures might be needed to ensure that Mrs. A did not harm her children or herself, such as consultation with a child protective services agency, would be advised. Then, because of the chronic severity of her condition and psychosocial stressors, as well as her histrionic, narcissistic, and borderline personality features, a course of individual supportive therapy, with adjunctive sessions involving her husband and/or children, as well as a consideration of group therapy, would be indicated. One-half-hour sessions would probably be scheduled twice weekly until sufficient symptom reduction was achieved and a stable therapeutic relationship had developed.

In the second phase of treatment, sessions might be weekly and focus on longer term problem issues such as parent–child, marital relations, and Mrs. A's characterological features and faulty lifestyle convictions about entitlement and overcontrol, as well as her need to somatize and threats of acting out, masculine protest, and so on. Because of these characterological features, it is likely that Mrs. A might prove to be a difficult patient. However, she would merit a fair to good prognosis, assuming she would continue in her commitment to treatment.

☐ Conclusion

Unlike other psychodynamic approaches, Adlerian psychotherapy appears to be remarkably compatible with *DSM–IV*. Because it is both a dynamic and a systems approach, Adlerian psychotherapy is comprehensive enough to appreciate the five axes and the biopsychosocial perspective of *DSM–IV*. On the other hand, a basic tenet of Adlerian psychotherapy is that it is a psychology of use. Accordingly, Adlerian psychotherapy is not as interested in diagnostic criteria and diagnostic labels as much as how data are used. If used wisely, *DSM–IV* diagnostic formulations can enrich the practice of Adlerian psychotherapy and provide a basis for greater communication with other professionals.

☐ References

Adler, A. (1956). *The individual psychology of Alfred Adler.* H. H. Ansbacher & R. R. Ansbacher (Eds.). New York: Harper & Row.

Adler, A. (1964a). *Problems of neurosis: A book of case histories.* New York: Harper & Row.

Adler, A. (1964b). *Superiority and social interest.* H. H. Ansbacher & R. R. Ansbacher (Eds.). New York: Norton.

Adler, A. (1969). *The case of Mrs. A: The diagnosis of a life style* (2nd ed.). Chicago: Alfred Adler Institute.

American Psychiatric Association. (1994). *Diagnostic and statistical manual of mental disorders* (4th ed.). Washington, DC: Author.

Beavers, W. R. (1985). *Successful marriages: A family systems approach couples therapy.* New York: Norton.

Beavers, W. R., & Hampson, R. B. (1990). *Successful families: Assessment and treatment.* New York: Norton.

Dreikurs, R. (1954). The psychological interview in medicine. In *Psychodynamics, psychotherapy and psychotherapy* (pp. 75–102). Chicago: Alfred Adler Institute.

Goldberg, M. (1989). Individual psychopathology from the systems perspective. In G. R. Weeks (Ed.), *Treating couples: The intersystem model of the marriage council of Philadelphia* (pp. 70–84). New York: Brunner/Mazel.

Hof, L., & Treat, S. (1989). Marital assessment: Providing a framework for dyadic therapy. In G. R. Weeks (Ed.), *Treating couples: The intersystem model of the marriage council of Philadelphia* (pp. 3–21). New York: Brunner/Mazel.

Mosak, H. H. (1968). The interrelatedness of the neuroses through central themes. *Journal of Individual Psychology, 24*(1), 67–70.

Mosak, H. H. (1971). Lifestyle. In A. Nikelly (Ed.), *Techniques for behavior changes: Applications of Adlerian theory* (pp. 77–84). Springfield, IL: Charles C Thomas.

Mosak, H. H. (1984). Adlerian psychology. In R. Corsini & B. Ozaki (Eds.), *Encyclopedia of psychology* (pp. 16–19). New York: Wiley-Interscience.

Mosak, H. H., & Shulman, B. H. (1988). *Life style inventory.* Muncie, IN: Accelerated Development.

Seligman, L. (1986). *Diagnosis and treatment planning in psychotherapy.* San Francisco: Jossey-Bass.

Sperry, L. (1989). Integrative case formulations: What they are and how to write them. *Individual Psychology, 45,* 500–508.

Sperry, L. (1996). Psychopathology and the diagnostic and treatment process. In L. Sperry & J. Carlson (Eds.), *Psychopathology and psychotherapy: From DSM-IV diagnosis to treatment* (2nd ed.; pp. 3–17). Washington, DC: Accelerated Development/Taylor & Francis.

Sperry, L., & Carlson, J. (1989). *Marital therapy: Integrating theory and technique.* Denver, CO: Love.
Sperry, L., Gudeman, J., Blackwell, B., & Faulkner, L. (1991). *Psychiatric case formulations.* Washington, DC: American Psychiatric Press.

CHAPTER 12

C. Edward Watkins, Jr.
Charles A. Guarnaccia

The Scientific Study of Adlerian Theory

In this chapter, we would like to address four issues:

1. On what topics do Adlerian-oriented investigations typically get conducted?

2. What have previous reviews about Adlerian-oriented research had to say?

3. Since those reviews, what have more recent Adlerian-oriented research studies had to say?

4. Considering all that, in what directions does Adlerian-oriented research need to move if the scientific study of Adler's theory is to most viably advance?

Quasi-experimental quantitative and qualitative investigations are necessary for testing any theory's propositions and constructs and, ultimately, determining its verifiability (see Patterson & Watkins, 1996). Without such investigation, the theory's hypotheses and foundations will forever be open to question and its advancement and possible need for revision and refinement will forever be stymied. In our view, scientific study is critical if a theory is to evolve; remain vital, vibrant, and current; and move forward. Moreover, without quantitative and qualitative research the validity of theoretical constructs cannot be judged.

What Has Been Studied

1970–1981. In an earlier paper, Watkins (1983) examined all research studies appearing in the *Journal of Individual Psychology* (*JIP*) for the years 1970 through 1981 and categorized them according to their primary focus. On the basis of that analysis, the topics and number of studies conducted on them were as follows: birth order, 24 studies; social interest, 19 studies; early recollections, 6 studies; lifestyle, 4 studies; and other (a miscellaneous grouping; e.g., parenting education), 22 studies.

1982–1990. In a more recent paper, Watkins (1992c) examined all research studies appearing in the theory–research issues of *Individual Psychology* (*IP*; formerly *JIP*) for the years 1982–1990 and again categorized them according to their primary focus. On the basis of that analysis, the topics and number of studies conducted on them were as follows: birth order, 25 studies; early recollections, 23 studies; social interest, 21 studies; lifestyle, 7 studies; and other, 27 studies.

1991–1996. To update the preceding papers, we examined all research articles appearing in the theory–research issues of *IP* for the years 1991–1996 and categorized them according to their primary focus. On the basis of that analysis, the topics and number of studies conducted on them were as follows: social interest, 10 studies; lifestyle, 9 studies; early recollections, 9 studies; birth order, 9 studies; and other, 9 studies.

So what? Birth order has always been a much researched subject, both within Adlerian ranks as well as outside them (Forer, 1977; Miley, 1969; Stewart & Stewart, 1995; Vockell, Felker, & Miley, 1973; Watkins, 1986). Social interest, because of the development of a few social interest measures in the 1970s (Crandall, 1975; Greever, Tsung & Friedland, 1973; Sulliman, 1973), has fared well, too, being a subject of fairly frequent study by Adlerians over the past 25 years. The biggest shifts we see relate to lifestyle and early recollections. Early recollections, because of the development of early recollection research scoring tools (e.g., Manaster-Perryman Manifest Content Early Recollection Scoring Manual; Manaster & Perryman, 1974), have become a subject of increasing study among Adlerians since the 1980s. Lifestyle, a central construct in Adler's theory, has always lagged far behind. Yet with the development of what appear to be some reliable, valid lifestyle measures, for example, the Life Style Personality Inventory (Wheeler, Kern, & Curlette, 1982) and Basic Adlerian Scales for Interpersonal Success—Adult form (BASIS-A; Wheeler, Kern, & Curlette, 1993), lifestyle has become a more researched topic in the past decade. That seems to bode well for the future of Adlerian research, with more balanced attention now able to be given to several key Adlerian constructs as opposed to only one or two.

Solid instrument development is necessary if solid scientific study of Adler's theory is to occur. Like any other area of psychosocial research, careful attention to the psychometric properties of an instrument is required if we are to understand what is being measured (Carmine & Zeller, 1979; DeVillis, 1991). Some instruments or measures of certain Adlerian concepts have been criticized (e.g., Crandall, 1981). But if nothing else, this brief summary of numbers of articles by topic clearly shows this: When an instrument to measure an Adlerian concept has been developed, research on that concept has substantially increased. The goal now may be to render those instruments as reliable and valid as possible through continued work and refinement, as was done, for example, with the BASIS-A—a product of 17 years of research work (Kern, Gfroerer, Summers, Curlette, & Matheny, 1996). Only through such effort can we ever hope to build a solid scientific base for Adler's theory. Such instrument development work should, at a minimum, include evaluation of factor structure as well as reliability and validity (DeVillis, 1991).

What Do Research Reviews and More Recent Research Studies Have to Say?

Birth-Order Research, 1981–1991.   In a past paper, Watkins (1992b) critically reviewed 25 birth-order studies that had appeared in *IP* from 1981 through mid-1991. Some selected results of that review were as follows: (a) "when providing age information, 14 studies provided only an age range, and eight studies did not specify any age at all"; (b) "most studies used only one assessment method in the data-gathering process"; (c) "10 studies used assessment methods developed by the article authors for these particular investigations"; (d) "in half the studies, subjects' race went unspecified"; (e) "four studies were cross-cultural in nature"; (f) "psychological position was examined in only five of the studies"; and (g) "subjects' sex and sibship size were controlled for in 19 and 11 studies, respectively, but siblings' sex, age spacing, and SES appeared to be controlled for in only one or two studies" (p. 365). Watkins ended the review by concluding

> that intervening variables [e.g., psychological position, subject sex, siblings' sex, sibship size, age spacing, and SES] in birth-order research have yet to be adequately dealt with. These variables must be confronted if birth-order research is to produce meaningful results and can best be handled by greater experimental manipulation and control. (p. 366)

So how has birth-order research fared since that review?

Birth-Order Research, 1991–1996.   It is difficult to compare these 9 studies, summarized in Table 12.1, with the earlier 25, but a few observations can be made: (a) Virtually all of the studies found some support for the birth-order concept, whatever it was being tested on (e.g., dominance, relationship-related cognitions); (b) 6 of the studies provided specific age information on their samples, 4 provided race information, most used college students as participants, and most used only one instrument for data-gathering purposes; and (c) most studies controlled for only one or none of the intervening variables that have been identified as so important to control for in birth-order research. Those studies, then, add further to our knowledge base about birth order and offer further support for the concept. Still, if the scientific study of this concept is to most fruitfully advance, then more efforts must be made to control for the intervening variables previously noted. If that is not done, then "we will have to remain highly tentative over what significant findings do emerge, and the promise of birth-order research . . . will continue to be only minimally realized" (Watkins, 1992b, p. 366).

Social Interest Research, 1981–1991.   In a relatively recent paper, Watkins (1994) critically reviewed 45 social interest studies that had appeared in various journals (e.g., *IP, Journal of Research in Personality*) from 1981 through the latter part of 1991. Some selected results of that review were as follows: (a) Most studies drew on undergraduate and graduate students as subjects, and in only 7 of 45 studies were clinical patient samples used; (b) age was not specified in 13 studies, and race was not specified in 40; (c) the Social Interest Index (SII) was used exclusively in 13 studies, the Social Interest Scale (SIS) was used exclusively in 17 studies, the Sulliman Scale of Social Inter-

Text continues on page 212.

TABLE 12.1
Summary Characteristics of Adlerian Birth Order Studies, 1991-1996

Authors	Sample Characteristics	Assessment Age (years)	Methods Used
Campbell, Stewart, & White (1991)	390 female & 171 male undergraduate and graduate students	Male M = 23.82 Female M = 28.70	White-Campbell Birth Order Inventory
Chalfant (1994)	28 male & 32 female college students; 32 male and 32 female students and warehouse workers	Range = 18 to 24; 25 and older	24-item questionnaire
Harris & Morrow (1992)	82 males & 145 female undergraduates	M = 21	Demographic sheet & CPI scales
Hester, Osborne, & Nguyen (1992)	336 female & 358 male high school & university students	M = 20.7 form	Self-made survey
Nelson & Harris (1995)	201 female undergraduates	NS	Demographic items and selected questions from 16PF and EPPS
Phillips & Phillips (1994)	110 upper-level undergraduates (67% male)	M = 22.8	Demographic items Attribution questionnaire
Simpson, Bloom, Newlon, & Arminio (1994)	National Census Bureau survey data from June 1980, 1985, & 1990		434-item questionnaire
Sullivan & Schwebel (1996)	47 female & 46 male undergraduates	M = 20	Relationship Belief Inventory
Todd, Friedman, & Steele (1993)	145 female & 110 male community residents	M = 28.8	Demographic form and 16-item Self-Rating Scale

Note: M = mean; CPI = California Psychological Inventory; SES = socioeconomic status; 16PF = 16 Personality Factor Questionnaire; EPPS = Edward Personal Preference Schedule.

Variables Controlled For	Primary Results	Comments
Age, sibling gender, spacing, psychological position	Significant relationship found for actual birth order and psychological birth order across four birth order positions	No race information provided
	Relationship found between birth order and perception of favoritism	No race information
Gender found to have interactive effect on perceived dominance	Birth order and gender	94% Caucasian
Sibship size	Number of sibling cohabitants affected gender expectations for self/child	Ethnically diverse sample
Sex	First born not significantly more group-oriented or affiliative	No race information
	First borns made stronger internal attributions than later borns	No race information
	Provided national percentages of Adlerian and ordinal birth-order proportions	
Sex	Relationship-related cognitions linked to birth order	84% Caucasian
SES, sibling gender	Gender and ethnicity created a structural context that affected being later born and being dethroned	Ethnically diverse sample

est [SSSI] was used exclusively in one study, and a combination of scales was used to assess social interest in 14 studies; (d) in general, social interest has been found to relate positively to certain characteristics (e.g., empathy, altruism) as Adler's theory would suggest and to relate negatively to characteristics (e.g., hostility, depression) that Adler's theory would suggest; and (e) "the SII, SIS, and SSSI [the primary means of measuring social interest to date] may all have a place in the future of SI [social interest] assessment, but refinements, revisions, or extensions are now needed in each of them" (Watkins, 1994, p. 92). So how has social interest research fared since that review?

Social Interest Research, 1991–1996. We examined all social interest studies appearing in *IP* from the latter part of 1991 through 1996; those are summarized in Table 12.2. These comments or observations seem merited: (a) In most studies, negative relationships were found between social interest and negative characteristics and positive relationships were found between social interest and positive characteristics, thus being consistent with Adler's conceptualization of the term; (b) most studies relied on the SIS, SII, SSSI, or SISII (the linear combination of standardized SIS and SII scores) for measuring social interest; (c) a good variety of subjects were sampled, ranging from social service agency clients to classroom teachers to laundromat patrons (this is particularly important as it begins to test the robustness of relationships as subject samples vary); and (d) some good efforts were made to push the research of social interest into interesting, uncharted waters (e.g., Edwards & Kern, 1995; Hedberg & Huber, 1995). This handful of studies, then, lends further weight to the empirical foundation undergirding Adler's social interest construct. However, because most relied on the SII, SIS, SSSI, or SISII for measurement purposes; because it has been said that refinements, revisions, or extensions are needed in each of those measures; and because no such refinements, revisions, or extensions have as yet been made in those measures, that criticism needs to be borne in mind. Still, the weight of the evidence comes down solidly in support of Adler's construct.

Early Recollections Research, 1981–1990. In an earlier review, Watkins (1992a) critically reviewed 30 Adlerian-oriented early recollection studies that had appeared in various journals (e.g., *IP*, *Journal of Clinical Psychology*) from 1981 through 1990. Some selected results of that review were as follows: (a) "The studies' hypotheses or aspects of them were largely supported and, in turn, were considered to support the Adlerian view of EMs [early memories]"; (b) the Manaster-Perryman Early Recollection Scoring Manual was most frequently used to rate EMs; (c) samples tended to be varied in nature, but race typically went unspecified; (d) Mosak's (1958) criteria for defining EMs were most frequently used across studies; (e) the modal number of EMs elicited across studies was two; and (f) when reported, interrater reliability in the rating of EMs was very high (pp. 249–259).

Watkins (1992a) tried to emphasize in his review the importance of controlling for certain variables that can affect the outcome of EM studies. Specifically, each study was examined to see if gender, age, IQ, socioeconomic status, or ethnicity were controlled. Watkins found that "a number of competing variables . . . generally went uncontrolled for across studies or were not as tightly controlled for as was possible" (1992a, p. 260). Watkins concluded by saying that "as it now stands, the general lack of control for IQ, SES, gender, age, and ethnicity in these 30 studies certainly tempers the strength of my conclusions and renders them more suggestive than otherwise" (p. 260). To be able to draw the most solid conclusions from EM studies, then, those variables need to be better controlled. So how have we done with that in the past few years?

Early Recollections Research, 1991–1996. We examined all EM studies appearing in *IP* from 1991 through 1996; they are summarized in Table 12.3. These comments or observations seem merited: (a) The results of those studies tended to offer further support for Adler's conceptualization of ERs; (b) the Manaster-Perryman Scoring Manual was again often used, being used in over half these studies; (c) a healthy sampling of nonuniversity subjects is evident, though the sample size was sometimes limited (e.g., as low as 19 subjects for one study, 38 for another); (d) mean age was specified in five studies, gender was specified in virtually all of the studies, ethnicity was not specified in most of them; (e) two to three raters were used to rate ERs, with interrater reliability always being adequate to very good; (f) three ERs were solicited in the majority of studies; and (g) most studies, with Chaplin and Orlofsky (1991) and Elliott, Fakouri, and Hafner (1993) being the exceptions, failed to control for variables such as IQ, socioeconomic status (SES), gender, age, and ethnicity.

These studies, then, criticisms notwithstanding, further bolster the base of support for Adler's view of ERs. Although other views about ERs exist (Bruhn & Last, 1982), Adler's appears to be the most robust, having garnered far more research attention and research support than any other perspective. Still, in looking ahead, it seems important that we strive to control for as many of those previously identified competing variables (e.g., SES, IQ) in future research efforts. Though making the research endeavor more difficult, the extra effort in our view could be richly rewarded, allowing us to place more confidence in our research results, remove these rival competing variables as alternative explanations, allow us to regard our findings as "more suggestive than otherwise" (Watkins, 1992a, p. 260) and further provide Adler's view of ERs the solid, unshakable research foundation it so richly deserves.

Lifestyle Research, 1981–1990. For the sake of comparison, what can we say about lifestyle research in the 1980s? As Watkins pointed out, seven such studies were conducted from 1982 through 1990 (Watkins, 1992c). The characteristics of those studies are summarized in Table 12.4. Some primary conclusions or observations we could make include the following: (a) A mixture of qualitative and quantitative analyses were involved, with some studies working to develop and validate lifestyle measurement instruments and others relying on interpretation of interview data; (b) some progress was made in quantifying lifestyle; (c) most studies failed to provide any ethnicity and age information; (d) some studies failed to specify gender; and (e) lifestyle research, although still in its infancy, seems to provide some support for the concept of lifestyle and its personality implications.

Lifestyle Research, 1991–1996. Table 12.5 summarizes characteristics of lifestyle research appearing so far during this decade. From analysis of these studies, we can say the following: (a) These past few years have been a period of further instrument development and validation, with the BASIS-A clearly emerging as a major contribution to our measurement of lifestyle; (b) virtually all, if not all, of the BASIS-A data appear to have been gathered in the Southeast (limiting generalizability); (c) lifestyle

Text continues on page 216.

TABLE 12.2
Summary Characteristics of Adlerian Social Interest Research Studies, 1991-1996.

Authors	Sample Characteristics	Age (years)
Edwards & Kern (1995)	60 female and 2 male classroom teachers and 1,366 elementary school students	M = 30 for teachers
Hedberg & Huber (1995)	20 heterosexual males 20 homosexual males 21 heterosexual females 21 homosexual females	M = 38.2
LaFountain (1996)	177 elementary, middle school, and high school students (58% female)	NS
Leak (1992)	Study (S)1: 65 undergraduate students (75% female)	S1: M = 19.9
	Study 2: 121 male and female students (65% female)	S2: M = 20.9
Miranda & White (1993)	168 clients of a social service service agency (58% male)	M = 28.5
Murphy (1994)	108 females & 65 males (undergraduates & laundromat patrons)	M = 24.6

Measures Used	Primary Results	Comments
Behavior Rating Checklist Matthews Youth Test for Health Life Style Personality Inventory	Significant negative correlation found between teacher social interest and problematic teacher behaviors; significant positive correlation found between teacher social interest and constructive teacher behaviors	First study to examine social interest on teachers' classroom behavior
SSI Belonging-Social Interest Scale of BASIS empirical study	No support found for view that homosexuality is a result of deficient social interest	Authors say Adler's theory must accommodate to changes suggested by
Student specified goals	Appeared to be a relationship between goals with a social interest component and goal attainment	Ethnicity data not ; gathered; two master's level counselors provided all student goal assessments; reanalysis of earlier study.
S1: SISII Quest scale Several other religious measures or scales	S1: High social interest positively correlated with sincerity, devoutness, and commitment	Study done on Catholics
S2: SISII and various religious measures or scales	S2: High social interest positively correlated with frequency of church attendance and prayer and religious commitment	
Three-part questionnaire with one part being Life Style Personality Inventory	Positive correlation found between social interest and cultural loyalty	Hispanic sample, vast majority immigrants
SIS Activity Scale Bem Sex Role Inventory	Relationship found between social interest and stereotypically feminine characteristics and activity level and stereotypically masculine characteristics	

Table 12.2 continues on page 216.

TABLE 12.2. Continued

Authors	Sample Characteristics	Age (years)
Rodd (1994) SII	109 mothers	Range = 20 to 40+
Watkins & Blazina (1994)	80 university students (61 females & 19 males), 74% being undergraduates	M = 24.7
Watkins & St. John (1994)	87 male and 120 female university students	M = 20.7
Watts & Trusty (1995)	45 female and 9 male counselors in training	Range = 23-48

Note: M = mean; SISII = linear combination of standardized SIS and SII scores; SIS = Social Interest Scale; SII = Social Interest Index; SSSI = Sulliman Scale of Social Interest; BASIS-A = Basic Adlerian Scales for Interpersonal Success-Adult Form; NS = not specified.

research during this period offers further support for the concept of lifestyle and its personality implications; (d) ethnicity still went unspecified in most studies; and (e) age could have been better specified in several studies.

When we look at lifestyle research over the past 15 years, we see a promising beginning has been made in our quantifying and better understanding Adler's lifestyle concept. Although it would not hurt to better specify ethnicity and age information in future studies, and although it would help for others to take up the lifestyle mantle, using the BASIS-A in more places beyond the Southeast and with more diverse samples, all those issues are easily correctable. Lifestyle research has surely advanced, and we have no doubt that much more of the same can be expected in the future.

☐ Where to from Here?

With all the foregoing considered, in what directions does Adlerian research need to move if it is to most fruitfully advance? We think that question, in large part, has al-

Measures Used	Primary Results	Comments
Biographical questionnaire Parental Stress Index	Significant small to moderate correlations found between social interest and global measure of psychological well-being	All mothers had at least one child under five years age; majority Anglo Australian
SSSI	Moderate degree of support found for test-retest reliability of SSSI at three and five week intervals	85% Caucasians
SSSI Interpersonal Rectivity Index; Berkman Social Network Index; Narcissistic Personality Inventory; Happiness self-rating	Findings offered support for validity of SSSI and its viability as a social interest measure	78% Caucasian Mostly freshman or sophomores
SII Counselor Evaluation Rating Scale (CERS)	Correlation between SII and CERS scores not significant	

ready been answered in the preceding section. Let us recap the main needs as we see them and put forth a few additional ideas as well.

First, we need to identify sample characteristics as specifically as possible in future research. Such specification allows for easier replication and for cross-study comparisons to be made.

Second, we need to better control for intervening, rival hypothesis variables in ER and birth-order research. Besides simply measuring intervening variables of siblings' sex, age spacing, SES, psychological position, and sibship size, a more consistent effort needs to be made to learn how these interacting variables operate (McClelland & Judd, 1993). Such control allows us to place more confidence in our findings and more solidly add to the empirical foundation undergirding Adler's theory. Such more sophisticated, empirical tests will also allow the possible extension and focusing of existing theory to match observations better.

Third, we need to refine, revise, or extend some of the useful social interest measures that have been developed. We need to further work toward quantifying Adlerian concepts in as meaningful, quantifiable a manner as possible. A model example of this

Text continues on page 226.

TABLE 12.3
Summary Characteristics of Adlerian Early Recollection Research Studies, 1991-1996

Sample Authors	Assessment Characteristics	Age (years)	Methods Used
Allers, White,, & Hornbuckle (1992)	63 female & 37 male master's-level counseling students	M = 31	Manaster-Perryman Manifest Content; Early Recollection Scoring Manual; Beck Depression Inventory
Barker & Bitter (1992)	46 female and 26 male graduate students	M = 34.5	Early Recollections Questionnaire; Early Recollections Rating Scale
Buchanan, Kern, & Bell-Dumas (1991)	Pilot: 33 university students	NS	Manaster-Perryman Manifest Content; Early Recollection Scoring Manual
	Study: 10 psychiatric inpatients, 16 alcohol/drug outpatients, & 12 graduate students	NS	Manaster-Perryman Manifest Content; Early Recollection Scoring Manual
Carson (1994)	5 male physicists, 6 male mathematicians & 4 male & 4 female psychologists	4 in 20-29 age group, 6 in 30-39, 7 in 40-49, 2 in 60-69	Early recollection questionnaire
Chaplin & Orlofsky (1991)	45 white male veterans in alcoholism treatment vs. 45 white non-alcoholic males	M= 42.4 M= 41.4	Manaster-Perryman Manifest Content; Early Recollection Scoring Manual; Mayman's Scoring System; Short Michigan Alcoholism Screening Test; Social Interest Scale; Nowicki-Strickland Locus of Control Scale for Adults; Rosenberg Self-Esteem Scale; Early Recollections Survey

Variables Controlled For	Primary Results	Comments
	Expected relationships found between ERs and depression scores, being consistent with Adler's theory	Ethnicity NS: two raters used; three ERs rated
	Low relationship found between levels of social interest projected projected in subjects' created and actual ERs	Ethnicity NS; two raters used; three ERs solicited
	Consistency found between created and actual ERs greater than chance	Gender and ethnicity NS: only one rater used to rate ERs. Three ERs solicited
	Persistence of themes in created and actual ERs greater than chance	Gender and ethnicity NS; two judges used for ratings; three ERs solicited
	Qualitative analysis revealed relationship between scientific attitude and skepticism	Virtually all Caucasian; author did own inter-pretations; low response rate; three ERs solicited
Gender, age, ethnicity, education; groups means comparable on SES	ERs found to be useful projective techniques in revealing the personality traits of alcoholics	Nicely done study; three ERs solicited

Table 12.3 continues on page 220.

TABLE 12.3. Continued

Sample Authors	Assessment Characteristics	Age (years)	Methods Used
Elliott, Fakouri, & Hafner (1993)	26 black & 24 white male federal prisoners	M = 35.34	Manaster-Perryman Manifest Content; Early Recollection
	24 black & 24 white male non-prisoners	M = 32.83	Scoring Manual; Early Recollection Scoring Manual
Nichols & Feist (1994)	10 male & 26 female psychology students, the optimistic group	M = 23	Attributional Style Questionnaire; Early recollection
	vs. 14 male & 22 female psychology students, the pessimistic group	M = 23	questionnaire
Rule (1992)	118 university students; gender equally divided	NS	Survey of ERs
Statton & Wilborn (1991)	3 male & 6 female children in treatment group vs. 9 children in non-treatment group	Between 5 and 12	Manaster-Perryman Manifest Content; Early Recollection Scoring Manual
Watts, Trusty, Canada & Harvill (1995)	54 master's-level counseling students; 9 male & 45 female	Between 23 and 48	Counselor Evaluation Rating Scale; Perceived Early Childhood Family Influence Scale

Note: ERs = early recollections; NS = not specified; SES = socioeconomic status.

Variables Controlled For	Primary Results	Comments
Gender; efforts made to match control and non-control subjects on age, education, and ethnicity	Content of prisoners' ERs more negative overall, with results generally being in the expected direction	Two raters used, obtaining 91% agreement; two ERs solicited
	Optimists' ERs reflected more positive content; for example, showing more mastery	Ethnicity NS; two raters used; one ER solicited
Gender	Relationships found between different ER variables and subjects' attitudes toward personal problems and therapeutic intervention; findings consistent with Adler's theory	Ethnicity NS; two raters used; three ERs solicited
Subjects matched on age and sex variables	More changes in early memories found for treateament as opposed to control group	Three raters rated ERs, obtaining 90% level of inter-rater agreement; three group pre-counseling and three post counseling ERs collected from each subject
Age differences	Significant correlation between counselor effectiveness and perceptions of early childhood family influence	Results are consistent with the only two previous studies investigating somewhat similar variables

TABLE 12.4
Summary Characteristics of Adlerian Life Style Research, 1982-1990

Sample Authors	Assessment Characteristics	Age (years)
Bichekas & Newlon (1983)	6 home care nurses	NS interview
Chandler & Willingham (1986)	681 (193 males & 488 females) undergraduate students	NS
Emerson & Watson (1987)	9 home care nurses	NS
Jorgensen & Newlon (1988)	10 unmarried Anglo pregnant adolescents who had chosen to keep their babies after birth	Range = 15-18
Mullis, Kern, & Curlette (1987)	1,010 participants	NS
Newlon & Mansager (1986)	43 Catholic priests	Most over 55 years of age
Wheeler, Kern & Curlette (1986)	715 undergraduate and graduate students	NS

Note: NS = not specified

Methods Used	Primary Results	Comments
Structured life style	Life styles reflected internal inconsistency, fear, confusion or unpredictability, extremism	Three expert consultants met to analyze lifestyle themes; ethnicity NS; gender NS
Perceived Early Childhood Family Influence Scale (PECFIS) Life Style Analysis Social Interest Index	Instrument development effort, with PECFIS factors being related to life style type and social interest as would be expected	Ethnicity NS
Structured life style interview	Life style reflected discomfort with unpredictability and need to control; findings for most part did not replicate Bichekas & Newlon (1983)	Ethnicity NS; gender NS; interviews conducted by graduate students
30 minute tape recorded interview	Life styles reflected expectation of being afraid, unknowing, or confused, goal of excitement, and desire for close, idealized relationship with someone	Three expert Adlerian judges used to interpret data
Life Style Personality Inventory (LSPI)	Study provided support for LSPI as valid measure of life style	Ethnicity NS; however, efforts made to capture a sample representative of general population
Life Style Questionnaire Inventory Judge's Rating Form General Questionnaire	Judges able to agree on priests' life styles at better than chance level; priests' life styles were unevenly distributed but one was most prominent	From Diocese of Tucson; 3 judges used for judging life style types
Research Questionnaire	Four dimensions of questionnaire produced, similar to Dreikurs' four goals of misbehavior	Ethnicity NS; gender NS

TABLE 12.5
Summary Characteristics of Adlerian Life Style Research, 1991-1996

Sample Authors	Assessment Characteristics	Age (years)
Appleton & Stanwyck (1996)	115 graduate students (17% male)	NS
Axtell & Newlon (1993)	10 White bulimic females	Range = 21-42
Butler & Newlon (1992)	90 male adolescents previously identified as children of trauma	Between 13 to 16
Keene & Wheeler (1994) freshmen	64 female & 39 male college	Female M = 18.4 Male M = 18.8
Kern, Gfroerer, Summers, Curlette, & Matheny (1996)	173 female college students	M = 21
Logan, Kern, Curlette, & Trad (1993)	129 couples	Range = 21-78
Stiles & Wilborn (1992)	381 third, fourth, & fifth graders	8, 9, 10, & 11 year olds
Wheeler & Acheson (1993)	160 undergraduates (53% female)	Approximately 18

Methods Used	Primary Results	Comments
BASIS-A; Pupil Control Ideology Form; Leader Behavior Description Questionnaire	Research supported relationship between teacher personality, pupil-control ideology, and leadership style	Ethnicity NS; southeastern sample
Adlerian Life Style Questionnaire	Pervading themes included pleasing, perfectionism, high standards, hard work, fear, and loneliness	6 of 10 were self-diagnosed, not clinically diagnosed; limited sample size
Life Style Interview	Life styles reflected common themes; Expectation that bad things will happen, expectation of a world filled with trouble and conflict, and desires to be special and be noticed	Ethnicity NS; three judges used to interpret life styles; small sample size
Life Style Personality Inventory; Sensation Seeking Scale; McAndrew Alcoholism Scale; Substance Use Survey	Exploiting themes present in life styles of substance abusers; pampered life style positively related to drug use	Ethnicity NS; few subjects reported frequent drug use; southeastern sample
BASIS-A; Coping Resources Inventory for Stress	Study empirically related personality variables to coping resources, providing "extensive construct validation for personality variables based on Adlerian theory" (p. 51)	155 of 173 Caucasian; southeastern sample
Life Style Personality Inventory Dyadic Adjustment Scale	Results support idea that those with similar life style themes are better adjusted as couples	Ethnicity NS
Child Life Style Scale (CLSS)	Instrument development effort, with CLSS being identified as useful for research and exploration purposes	10% of sample ethnic minorities but not specified which minorities were involved; gender NS
Life Style Personality Inventory Personality Research Form	Study provided additional validity support for LSPI	Ethnicity NS; southeastern sample

Table 12.5 continues on page 226.

TABLE 12.5. Continued

Sample Authors	Assessment Characteristics	Age (years)
Wheeler & White (1991)	61 female & 50 male undergraduates & 154 female & 27 male graduate students	NS

Note: NS = not specified; BASIS-A = Basic Adlerian Scales for Interpersonal Success-Adult Form.

can be found in the BASIS-A, a product of almost two decades of research work. By means of such clear, meaningful quantification and solid instrument development, we further bring Adler's theory under our experimental control and investigative scrutiny.

Fourth, we further need good Adlerian research that is theory driven, clearly grounded in rationale, and programmatic in nature. Some nice examples of that are readily evident in the literature (e.g., the series of studies by Leak, 1992, on social interest). But more such programmatic efforts are needed to push Adlerian research to a new level, where our empirical inquiry reflects the maturity and true potential of Adler's theory.

Fifth, we need studies of Adlerian counseling and psychotherapy. Where are they? They are few, far between, and hard to find. Perhaps a major reason that Adlerian therapy has not become a better part of the treatment scene is that we have not researched it. But what exactly is "it?" What exactly is Adlerian counseling or psychotherapy? I do not think we have defined "it" in any concrete, researchable way. So how can we research it? We cannot.

Adlerians have been described as unified in theory, eclectic in practice (Manaster & Corsini, 1982). However, if we are to investigate some of what some of us do in treatment, then we must concretize it so that empirical study can occur. Because we are eclectic in practice does not mean we will be unable to identify some specific interventions that some Adlerians use and practice. What we may arrive at may not reflect all Adlerians, but even a reflection of some Adlerians would be good in our opinion.

How could that be done? One way to begin would be to develop an Adlerian treatment manual, which could be used to train therapists and guide research. Manuals have been developed for other approaches, for example, cognitive, Gestalt, behavioral, and psychodynamic (Stein & Lambert, 1995), but not Adlerian. Lambert and Ogles (1997) indicated the purpose and value of treatment manuals:

> Psychotherapy treatment manuals have been developed primarily for training beginning therapists who participate in psychotherapy outcome studies. Researchers were the first to use manuals as a way of standardizing the administration of treatment across therapists. This trend in psychotherapy outcome research is now beginning to have a substantial impact on the training of psychotherapists generally, particularly as extended to specialized techniques. These manuals have been successfully used in outcome studies. (p. 429)

Methods Used	Primary Results	Comments
Adult Norwicki-Strickland Internal-External Locus of Control Scale Life Style Personality Inventory (LSPI)	Significant positive correlations found between external locus of control and Exploiting/Passive and Displaying Inadequacy life style themes	Ethnicity NS; LSPI identified as promising assessment tool; southeastern sample

Such manuals are not a panacea, and problems attendant to them must be borne in mind (Lambert & Ogles, 1988; Watkins, 1997a, 1997b). Yet they could be one viable means of allowing us to begin to research the Adlerian therapy process, its effects, its outcome. Until we begin to more aggressively investigate what we do as therapists, or some of what some of us do, Adlerian counseling and therapy will forever remain on the periphery of stardom—a promising player that never made the big time.

Sixth, in the vein of Carlson (1989), who called on Adlerians to go "beyond Adler," "to modify Adlerian ideas to today's tough issues, issues that did not exist in the 1920s" (p. 411), so too must Adlerian researchers. We must forever strive to be creative in our research endeavors, being flexible in our Adlerian thinking and integrating it most effectively with contemporary needs and presses. Perhaps, as Hartshorne (1991) might ask, "How can we distill the meaning of Adler's body of work and use it to spring us forward into the 21st century, going beyond Adler in our study and research of problems and issues now as opposed to then?" Such "creative flexibility" can only help, taking us in some potentially new and uncharted directions in our future research inquiries.

☐ Conclusion

Let us close by saying there is a base of support for some of Adler's most central concepts; that base has grown more solid over time. Yet efforts could be made to make that base more solid still. We have attempted to identify some of how that could be done.

Research can breathe new life into a school or system of thought, forcing revisions or extensions as needed. Research of Adler's system is vital. Where concepts have been defined and quantified, research has quickly followed (e.g., as with social interest). Let us continue to refine definitions and quantification measures where needed. Where concepts have been left undefined and unquantified, research has been minimal (e.g., the study of Adlerian counseling and therapy). Let us begin to define and quantify the undefined and unquantified. Adler's system is too valuable a theoretical and practical legacy not to be studied in all its facets.

☐ References

Allers, C. T., White, J., & Hornbuckle, D. (1992). Early recollections: Detecting depression in college students. *Individual Psychology, 48*, 324–329.

Appelton, B. A., & Stanwyck, D. (1996). Teacher personality, pupil control ideology, and leadership style. *Individual Psychology, 52*, 119–129.

Axtell, A., & Newlon, B. J. (1993). An analysis of Adlerian life themes of bulimic women. *Individual Psychology, 49*, 58–67.

Barker, S. B., & Bitter, J. R. (1992). Early recollections versus created memory: A comparison for projective qualities. *Individual Psychology, 48*, 86–95.

Bickekas, G., & Newlon, B. (1983). Life-style analysis of hospice home care nurses. *Individual Psychology, 39*, 66–70.

Bruhn, A. R., & Last, J. (1982). Earliest childhood memories: Four theoretical perspectives. *Journal of Personality Assessment, 46*, 119–127.

Buchanan, L. P., Kern, R., & Bell-Dumas, J. (1991). Comparison of content in created versus actual early recollections. *Individual Psychology, 47*, 348–355.

Butler, T. L., & Newlon, B. J. (1992). Children of trauma: Adlerian personality characteristics. *Individual Psychology, 48*, 313–318.

Campbell, L., Stewart, A., & White, J. (1991). The relationship of psychological birth order to actual birth order. *Individual Psychology, 47*, 380–391.

Carlson, J. (1989). On beyond Adler. *Individual Psychology, 45*, 411–413.

Carmine, E. G., & Zeller, R. A. (1979). *Reliability and validity assessment.* Newbury Park, CA: Sage.

Carson, A. D. (1994). Early memories of scientists: Loss of faith in God and Santa Claus. *Individual Psychology, 50*, 149–160.

Chalfant, D. (1994). Birth order, perceived parental favoritism, and feelings toward parents. *Individual Psychology, 50*, 52–57.

Chandler, C. K., & Willingham, W. K. (1986). The relationship between perceived early childhood family influence and the established life-style. *Individual Psychology, 42*, 388–394.

Chaplin, M. P., & Orlofsky, J. L. (1991). Personality characteristics of male alcoholics as revealed through their early recollections. *Individual Psychology, 47*, 356–371.

Crandall, J. E. (1975). A scale for social interest. *Journal of Individual Psychology, 31*, 187–195.

Crandall, J. E. (1981). *Theory and measurement of social interest: Empirical tests of Alfred Adler's concept.* New York: Columbia University Press.

DeVillis, R. F. (1991). *Scale development: Theory and application.* Newbury Park, CA: Sage.

Edwards, D., & Kern, R. (1995). The implications of teachers' social interest on classroom behavior. *Individual Psychology, 51*, 67–73.

Elliott, W. N., Fakouri, M. E., & Hafner, J. L. (1993). Early recollections of criminal offenders. *Individual Psychology, 49*, 68–75.

Emerson, S., & Watson, M. J. (1987). Another look at life-style analysis of hospice home care nurses. *Individual Psychology, 43*, 308–311.

Forer, L. K. (1977). Bibliography of birth order literature in the '70s. *Journal of Individual Psychology, 33*, 122–141.

Greever, K. B., Tsung, M. S., & Friedland, B. (1973). Development of the Social Interest Index. *Journal of Consulting and Clinical Psychology, 41*, 454–458.

Harris, K. A., & Morrow, K. B. (1992). Differential effects of birth order and gender on perceptions of responsibility and dominance. *Individual Psychology, 48*, 109–118.

Hartshorne, T. S (1991). The evolution of psychotherapy: Where are the Adlerians? *Individual Psychology, 47*, 321–325.

Hedberg, C., & Huber, R. J. (1995). Homosexuality, gender, communal involvement, and social interest. *Individual Psychology, 51*, 244–252.

Hester, C., Osborne, G. E., & Nguyen, T. (1992). The effects of birth order and number of sibling and parental cohabitants on academic achievement. *Individual Psychology, 48*, 330–348.

Jorgensen, J. A., & Newlon, B. J. (1987). Life-style themes of unwed, pregnant adolescents who chose to keep their babies. *Individual Psychology, 44,* 466–471.

Keene, K. K., Jr., & Wheeler, M. S. (1994). Substance use in college freshmen and Adlerian life-style themes. *Individual Psychology, 50,* 97–109.

Kern, R., Gfroerer, K., Summers, Y., Curlette, W., & Matheny, K. (1996). Life-style, personality, and stress coping. *Individual Psychology, 52,* 42–53

LaFountain, R. M. (1996). Social interest: A key to solutions. *Individual Psychology, 52,* 150–157.

Lambert, M. J., & Ogles, B. M. (1988). Treatment manuals: Problems and promise. *Journal of Integrative and Eclectic Psychotherapy, 7,* 187–204.

Lambert, M. J., & Ogles, B. M. (1997). The effectiveness of psychotherapy supervision. In C. E. Watkins, Jr. (Ed.), *Handbook of psychotherapy supervision* (pp. 421–446). New York: Wiley.

Leak, G. K. (1992). Religiousness and social interest: An empirical assessment. *Individual Psychology, 48,* 288–301.

Logan, E., Kern, R., Curlette, W., & Trad, A. (1993). Couples adjustment, life-style similarity, and social interest. *Individual Psychology, 49,* 456–467.

Manaster, G. J., & Corsini, R. J. (1982). *Individual psychology: Theory and practice.* Itasca, IL: F. E. Peacock.

Manaster, G. J., & Perryman, T. B. (1974). Early recollections and occupational choice. *Journal of Individual Psychology, 30,* 232–237.

McClelland, G. H., & Judd, C. M. (1993). Statistical differences of detecting interactions and moderator effects. *Psychological Bulletin, 114,* 376–390.

Miley, C. H. (1969). Birth order research 1963-1967: Bibliography and index. *Journal of Individual Psychology, 25,* 64–70.

Miranda, A. O., & White, P. E. (1993). The relationship between acculturation level and social interest among Hispanic adults. *Individual Psychology, 49,* 76–85.

Mosak, H. H. (1958). Early recollections as a projective technique. *Journal of Projective Techniques and Personality Assessment, 22,* 302–311.

Mullis, F. Y., Kern, R. M., & Curlette, W. L. (1987). Life-style themes and social interest: A further factor analytic study. *Individual Psychology, 43,* 339–352.

Murphy, P. L. (1994). Social interest and psychological androgyny: Conceptualized and tested. *Individual Psychology, 50,* 18–30.

Nelson, E. S., & Harris, M. A. (1995). The relationships between birth order and need affiliation and group orientation. *Individual Psychology, 51,* 282–292.

Newlon, B. J., & Mansager, E. (1986). Adlerian life-styles among Catholic priests. *Individual Psychology, 42,* 367–374.

Nichols, C. C., & Feist, J. (1994). Explanatory style as a predictor of earliest recollections. *Individual Psychology, 50,* 31–39.

Patterson, C. H., & Watkins, C. E., Jr. (1996). *Theories of psychotherapy* (5th ed.). New York: Harper Collins.

Phillips, A. S., & Phillips, C. R. (1994). Birth order and achievement attributions. *Individual Psychology, 50,* 119–124.

Rodd, J. (1994). Social interest, psychological well-being, and maternal stress. *Individual Psychology, 50,* 58–68.

Rule, W. R. (1992). Associations between personal problems and therapeutic intervention, early recollections, and gender. *Individual Psychology, 48,* 119–128.

Simpson, P. W., Bloom, J. W., Newlon, B. J., & Arminio, L. (1994). Birth order proportions of the general population in the United States. *Individual Psychology, 50,* 173–182.

Statton, J. E., & Wilborn, B. (1991). Adlerian counseling and the early recollections of children. *Individual Psychology, 47,* 338–347.

Stein, D. M., & Lambert, M. J. (1995). Graduate training in psychotherapy: Are therapy outcomes enhanced? *Journal of Consulting and Clinical Psychology, 63,* 182–196.

Stewart, A. E., & Stewart, E. A. (1995). Trends in birth-order research: 1976-1993. *Individual Psychology, 51,* 21–36.

Stiles, K., & Wilborn, B. (1992). A life-style instrument for children. *Individual Psychology, 48,* 96–106.

Sulliman, J. R. (1973). *The development of a scale for the measurement of social interest.* Unpublished doctoral dissertation, Florida State University, Tallahassee.

Sullivan, B. F., & Schwebel, A. I. (1996). Birth-order position, gender, and irrational relationship beliefs. *Individual Psychology, 52,* 54–64.

Todd, J., Friedman, A., & Steele, S. (1993). Birth order and sex of sibling effects on self ratings of interpersonal power: Gender and ethnic differences. *Individual Psychology, 49,* 86–93.

Vockell, E. L., Felker, D. W., & Miley, C. H. (1973). Birth order literature 1967-1971: Bibliography and index. *Journal of Individual Psychology, 29,* 39–53.

Watkins, C. E., Jr. (1983). Some characteristics of research on Adlerian psychological theory, 1970-1981. *Individual Psychology, 39,* 99–110.

Watkins, C. E., Jr. (1986). A research bibliography on Adlerian psychological theory. *Individual Psychology, 42,* 123–132.

Watkins, C. E., Jr. (1992a). Adlerian-oriented early memory research: What does it tell us? *Journal of Personality Assessment, 59*(2), 248–263.

Watkins, C. E., Jr. (1992b). Birth order research and Adler's theory: A critical review. *Individual Psychology, 48,* 357–368.

Watkins, C. E., Jr. (1992c). Research activity with Adler's theory. *Individual Psychology, 48,* 107–108.

Watkins, C. E., Jr. (1994). Measuring social interest. *Individual Psychology, 50,* 69–96.

Watkins, C. E., Jr. (1997a). Reflections on contemporary psychotherapy practice, research, and training. *Journal of Contemporary Psychology, 27,* 5–22.

Watkins, C. E., Jr. (1997b). Some concluding thoughts about psychotherapy supervision. In C. E. Watkins, Jr. (Ed.), *Handbook of psychotherapy supervision* (pp. 608–616). New York: Wiley.

Watkins, C. E., Jr., & Blazina, C. (1994). Reliability of the Sulliman Scale of Social Interest. *Individual Psychology, 50,* 164–165.

Watkins, C. E., Jr., & St. John, C. (1994). Validity of the Sulliman Scale of Social Interest. *Individual Psychology, 50,* 166–169.

Watts, R. E., & Trusty, J. (1995). Social interest and counselor effectiveness: An exploratory study. *Individual Psychology, 51,* 293–298.

Watts, R. E., Trusty, J., Canada, R., & Harvill, R. (1995). Perceived early childhood influence and counselor effectiveness: An exploratory study. *Counselor Education and Supervision, 35,* 104–110.

Wheeler, M. S., & Acheson, S. K. (1993). Criterion-related validity of the Life-Style Personality Inventory. *Individual Psychology, 49,* 51–57.

Wheeler, M. S., Kern, R. M., & Curlette, W. L. (1982). *Life style personality inventory.* Unpublished test.

Wheeler, M. S., Kern, R. M., & Curlette, W. L. (1986). Factor analytic scales designed to measure Adlerian life style themes. *Individual Psychology, 42,* 1–16.

Wheeler, M. S., Kern, R. M., & Curlette, W. L. (1993). *BASIS-A inventory.* Highlands, NC: TRT.

Index